ARISTOPHANIC COMEDY

1 Contemplation of this Greek countryman, and contemplation particularly of the expression on his face, may help us to imagine the people who constituted the greater part of Aristophanes' audience.

ARISTOPHANIC COMEDY

K. J. Dover

Professor of Greek
University of St. Andrews

University of California Press
Berkeley and Los Angeles
1972

First published 1972

© K. J. Dover 1972

Made and printed in Great Britain by
William Clowes & Sons, Limited
London, Beccles and Colchester
for The University of California Press
Berkeley and Los Angeles, Calif.

ISBN 0 520 01976 8 (cloth)
0 520 02211 4 (paper)

LCCC NO. 70 182681

Preface

This book is designed primarily for the reader who does not know Greek but is interested in Greek culture or in the history of comedy as an art-form. If I had been writing for professional scholars my argument would have been the same but my order of topics different; I would have referred more often, and more briefly, to individual passages of Aristophanes and would have devoted much more space to discussion of language, style and metre. I hope nevertheless that some of my observations may be of interest to scholars.

I have quite deliberately begun the book with an account of the transmission of the text of Aristophanes, believing that it is right to remind the reader of the evidence upon which the study of Greek literature rests. Any reader to whom textual criticism and related topics are abhorrent might prefer to read Chapters II–V before reading Chapter I.

The parade of references to learned journals and monographs in some footnotes is also deliberate, since I judge it important to remind the reader that our understanding of Greek literature is continuously augmented by the discovery of papyri and inscriptions and by fresh ideas.

The book began to take shape during a course of lectures which I gave at Berkeley in 1967 to a class which included scientists and social scientists as well as classicists. I am greatly indebted to Professor George Devereux for his helpful comments on nearly all the chapters in their penultimate version, and to university teachers and students in several countries for criticism and discussion of many detailed points.

St Andrews   K. J. DOVER

Contents

The Plates

The author and publisher wish to thank the following for permission to reproduce plates appearing in this book: the American School of Classical Studies,
Athens, for plates 6 and 7; Alison Frantz for plate 5; D. A. Harissiades, Athens,
for plates 1 and 9; the Istituto Papirologico G. Vitelli, Florence, for plate 2;
A. W. Sijthoff's Uitgeversmaatschappij N. V., Leiden, for plate 3 (from B. A.
van Groningen, *Short Manual of Greek Palaeography*, 1940, plate IV); Professor
T. B. L. Webster and the Town Clerk of Stockport for plate 4.

The author and publishers are also grateful to the following for help in ob-
taining illustrations or tracing owners of copyright: the Clarendon Press,
Oxford; the Institute of Classical Studies, London; Princeton University Press;
and the Society for the Promotion of Hellenic Studies, London.

Transliteration

The columns show:

(1) The letter-form generally used at Athens at the time of Aristophanes' first play.

(2) The letter-form generally used at Athens at the time of his last play, where different from (1).

(3) The letter-form used in the following generation, where different from (2).

(4) The medieval letter-form from which modern printed Greek is derived.

(5) The transliteration used in this book.

(6) The approximately correct pronunciation.

(7) The pronunciation generally used in English-speaking countries, where different from (6).

(1)	(2)	(3)	(4)	(5)	(6)	(7)
A			α	$\bar{a}$	*a* as in French *rare*	
AI			ᾳ	$\bar{a}i$	$\bar{a} + i$	$= \bar{a}$
AY			αυ	$\bar{a}u$	$\bar{a} + u$	$= au$
A			α	*a*	*a* as in French *bat*	*a* as in English *bat*
AI			αι	*ai*	*ie* as in *tie*	
AY			αυ	*au*	*ow* as in *howl*	
B			β	*b*	*b*	
Δ			δ	*d*	*d*	
E	H		η	$\bar{e}$	*è* as in French *père*	*ai* as in English *wait*
EI	HI		ῃ	$\bar{e}i$	$\bar{e} + i$	$= \bar{e}$
EY	HY		ηυ	$\bar{e}u$	$\bar{e} + u$	*eu* as in *feud*
E		EI	ει	$\bar{e}$	*eh* as in German *Ehre*	*ai* as in English *wait*
E			ε	*e*	*é* as in French *été*	*e* as in English *bet*
EI			ει	*ei*	*e + i*	$= \bar{e}$

(1)	(2)	(3)	(4)	(5)	(6)	(7)
EY			ευ	eu	e + u	eu as in *feud*
Λ	Γ		γ	g	g	
H	[nothing]		ʽ	h	h	
I			ι	ī	i as in *machine*	
I			ι	i	i as in French *vite*	i as in English *bit*
K			κ	k	c as in French *camp*	c as in English *camp*
X			χ	kh	ch as in Scots *loch*	
XΣ	Ξ		ξ	ks	x as in English *fox*	
ᴌ	Λ		λ	l	l as in French *lait*	l as in English *lay*
M			μ	m	m	
N			ν	n	n (but before g and k as in English *bank*)	
O	Ω		ω	ɔ̄	o as in French *fort*	o as in English *no*
OI	ΩI		ῳ	ɔ̄i	ɔ̄ + i	= ɔ̄
O		OY	ου	ō	o as in French *role*	oo as in English *boot*
O			ο	o	o as in French *dos*	{ o as in English *pot* / o as in English *November* }
OI			οι	oi	oi as in English *boil*	
OY			ου	ou	o + u	= ō
Π			π	p	p as in French *pain*	p as in English *pain*
Φ			φ	ph	p as in English *pain*	f as in English *faint*
ΦΣ	Ψ		ψ	ps	ps as in English *apse*	
P			ρ	r	r as in French *rare*	r as in English *rare*
Σ			σ, s	s	s as in English *case*	
Ⲍ	Z		ζ	sd	sd as in *Desdemona*	dz as in English *adze*
T			τ	t	t as in French *table*	t as in English *table*
Θ			θ	th	t as in English *table*	th as in English *thin*
Y			υ	ȳ	u as in French *mur*	eu as in English *feud*
Y			υ	y	u as in French *cru*	English *eu* shortened

The accent is tonic; the acute indicates a high tone, the circumflex a rising and falling tone. The acute is normally written as a grave, indicating that the tone is not raised, when a final syllable on which it falls is not the last of a clause. Since the circumflex can stand on a long vowel or diphthong, the sign of the long vowel is omitted when the circumflex is added.

I have not been entirely consistent in the transliteration of proper names; I find it goes too much against the grain to write, let alone say, 'Thoukydides' (*Thōkȳdídēs*) and therefore retain the Latinized form 'Thucydides'. Some other names, e.g. Plato, Apollo, are Latinized, and 'Aristotle' is Anglicized.

'Attic' and 'Athenian' may be treated as synonymous throughout.

A NOTE ON TRANSLATION

I have translated the verse of Aristophanic dialogue into English prose except where the language and metre of the original indicate tragic quotation or parody; in those cases I have translated into blank verse and nineteenth-century poetic diction. I have given simple metrical shape to translations of Aristophanes' lyric verse, but have not attempted to reproduce the metres of the original. In all the translations I have tried to say in English neither more nor less than Aristophanes says in Greek and to keep, as far as is practicable, to the 'register' of the original. Here and there I have invented or resurrected words to correspond to what may be inventions on the part of Aristophanes (e.g. p. 70, 'banqueteer') and have changed idioms which would sound strange in English if translated literally (e.g. p. 142, 'prepared to do what is just' rather than 'prepared to do something just'). I have commonly omitted those Greek particles which are best represented in English by intonation or cadence, and I have seldom translated literally the oaths and exclamations ('By Poseidon', 'by Demeter', 'O Zeus and gods!', etc.) with which Aristophanic dialogue is liberally seasoned.

I

The Evidence

THE SURVIVAL OF THE TEXT

Eleven plays have come down to us under the name of Aristophanes; the earliest of the eleven was produced in 425 B.C., the latest in 388 B.C. Since he wrote at least forty plays, we have to judge him on only a quarter of his output; and yet the passage of time has dealt more kindly with him than with almost any other Greek poet. Out of all the work of some fifty Athenian comic dramatists whose careers overlapped that of Aristophanes, not a single play has survived; as for tragedies, out of some five hundred which received their first production at Athens during his lifetime we possess only twenty-six. It is worth while to consider for a moment the process of survival, in order to understand why we have any Greek poetry at all, why we do not have more, and how we can interpret what we do have.[1]

The Roman Empire, which after the absorption of Egypt in 30 B.C. included the entire Mediterranean basin, was predominantly Greek-speaking eastwards of a line drawn from Albania to Tunisia, and the Greek literature of the preceding seven centuries was part of its cultural inheritance. During the reigns of (say) Nero or Hadrian it would not have been difficult, anywhere within reach of a substantial Mediterranean city, to acquire a copy of any play of Aristophanes. Cultural changes in the period from 250 to 550 A.D. created a quite different situation and diminished the prospect of survival for pagan Greek literature. In the western half of the Empire movements of population from central Europe interrupted and eventually destroyed both the cultural and the political continuity of the Greco-Roman world. In both halves the

---

1   See further L. D. Reynolds and N. G. Wilson, *Scribes and Scholars: a Guide to the Transmission of Greek and Latin Literature* (Oxford, 1968), especially chapters I and II.

spread of Christianity diverted intellectual energy from pagan literature to Christian theology and virtually extinguished that nostalgic
enthusiasm for 'classical' ideals which had characterized the literary
culture of the early Roman Empire. As pagan Greek poetry, no longer
the focus of culture, was demoted to propaedeutic or peripheral status,
much of it ceased to be read at all; therefore the multiplication of
copies slackened and lost or damaged copies were not replaced.

With the severance and disruption of the western Roman Empire,
the continuity of a culture now predominantly Christian was left to the
Greek-speaking eastern half, with its capital at Byzantium (Con-
stantinople). It was there that interest in the literature of pagan Greek
antiquity reawoke in the latter part of the ninth century of our era. It
was too late to rescue and perpetuate the hundreds of works which had
slowly and unobtrusively disappeared between six hundred and three
hundred years earlier; all that could be done was to locate and transcribe
such few manuscripts as had by good fortune survived the total neglect
of the last seven or eight generations. That was the time during which
the life of pagan Greek poetry had hung by a thread; the extant eleven
plays of Aristophanes are one body of work for which the thin thread
held, and we owe our enjoyment of them today to the enthusiasm of a
few Byzantine scholars and churchmen of the late ninth century.

Even their work had one more peril to surmount. By 1200 interest
in the literature of the pagan past was widely disseminated in Byzantine
society, and it would not have been difficult for a fairly prosperous man,
at any rate in Byzantium or Thessaloniki, to acquire a copy of Aristophanes. In 1204, however, the Crusaders sacked Byzantium, and in the
course of the disaster a great many manuscripts were burned. This was
the final blow to a small number of little-known works which had
survived the neglect of the seventh and eighth centuries, but not a
decisive setback to an author as widely read as Aristophanes. After the
reoccupation of Byzantium by a Greek emperor in 1261 interested
scholars again set about the task of picking up the threads and multiply-
ing copies of the surviving texts. When Byzantium at last fell to the
Turks in 1453 Italians had long been buying (or otherwise acquiring)
Greek manuscripts, which made the survival of Aristophanes and other
poets independent of anything that might happen to Byzantine culture
at Turkish hands. The first printed edition of nine of Aristophanes'
plays appeared at Venice in 1498, and the remaining two of the extant
eleven were first printed at Florence in 1515.

From the time of the poet himself down to the invention of printing the text could only be perpetuated by manual copying. Although it should be possible in theory for a copyist, checking and counter-checking, to produce an absolutely correct copy of his exemplar, in practice this degree of fidelity is rarely if ever achieved; equally, as we all know, not even the most scrupulous typesetting and proof-reading can guarantee the elimination of all misprints. No two manuscripts of Aristophanes, or of any other Greek author, ever exactly agree, and it would not take long to select two which would exhibit differences, on the average, of one syllable every three lines. It must not be imagined that the transmission of Aristophanes remained accurate and scrupulous down to the end of the ancient world and was then corrupted whole-sale by careless and ignorant Byzantines. From the fragments of ancient copies discovered during the last eighty years in Egypt (where the un-usual physical conditions have favoured the survival of pieces of papyrus and parchment under the ground) it is clear that an ancient copyist could be so hasty and reckless as to render a passage almost unintelligible, whereas a Byzantine scholar of the fourteenth century, giving his mind to what he was copying and weighing up the alterna-tives presented by two or more exemplars, could do a very impressive job. The process of corruption began from the moment at which the first text left the poet's own hands; and this is not a hypothesis which textual critics have invented in order to keep themselves occupied, but a fact of life accepted, however much regretted, by the ancients them-selves. If we stand back far enough and treat a century as the smallest unit of time concerned, we can see that a copy's distance in time from the original author tends to decrease the likelihood that it will actually represent what he wrote, but we ought not to speak in terms more precise than that. The earliest medieval manuscript sometimes makes sense in a passage where all later manuscripts do not, and an ancient fragment sometimes makes better sense than the whole medieval tradition (it can even offer confirmation of an emendation made in recent times), but factors which should modify a mechanical reliance on mere age are: the total number of stages of transmission between author and extant copy, which is not the same thing as the total distance in time; the absence of correlation between the scrupulousness of a given copyist and the time at which he lived; and the fact that some copyists had the opportunity, while others did not, to compare several exemplars and correct one from another.

In the manuscripts which have survived to our own day the eleven plays are unequally represented. The earliest manuscript of all, the

Ravennas (now in the library at Classe, near Ravenna), probably written about 1000 A.D., contains all eleven; one of these, *Women at the Thesmophoria*, occurs in no other manuscript except a copy made from the Ravennas itself in the fifteenth century. The only extant manuscript apart from the Ravennas to antedate the Crusaders' sack of Byzantium is the Venetus, written in the twelfth century and containing seven plays. All other manuscripts of Aristophanes date from the time of the Paleologan dynasty which reigned at Byzantium from 1261 down to the fall of the city to the Turks in 1453. In nearly all manuscripts which contain more than one play *Wealth* comes first, and most Paleologan manuscripts contain only the trio *Wealth, Clouds, Frogs*. It is an interesting indication of difference between medieval and modern taste that *Wealth*, generally regarded nowadays as the least attractive of the eleven plays, should survive in more than a hundred and fifty manuscripts while *Lysistrata* survives in only eight; for *Women at the Thesmophoria* we are dependent solely upon the Ravennas and on scraps of a few lines in a papyrus of the second century A.D.

Reference has been made above to passages in which one manuscript 'makes sense' and another does not, to 'corruption' which may affect all surviving texts of a given passage, and to the attempt by 'emendation' to restore what we believe the poet to have intended. To the reader unfamiliar with what really goes on in the criticism and edition of ancient texts, this may sound arrogant. It is important, however, to remember that Greek is not a 'dead' language in the sense in which, say, Hittite or Assyrian is dead—extinguished and replaced, even in the area where it was spoken, by other languages—but only in the sense that Chaucer's English is dead; that is to say, it is an early stage of a language which has never ceased to be spoken and written. If we possessed no Greek at all except the text of Aristophanes and the spoken dialects of modern peasants we could still, I think, given time and patience and sound philological method, produce a plausible edition of Aristophanes and work out more or less what it meant; but fortunately the situation is not so desperate. Aristophanes became an object of systematic study in little more than a century after his own death. Each of those who studied him was himself a Greek-speaker and had available to him all the Greek literature written up to his own time; and the works of these ancient commentators, explaining rare or archaic words and political and literary allusions, were transmitted in parallel with Aristophanes' own work. The process of studying and interpreting Aristophanes is thus a continuum from the third century B.C. to the present day—interrupted, of course, by the indifference of the seventh and eighth centuries, but no more interrupted than the transmission of the poetry which was the object of the study.

Ancient commentators on Aristophanes wrote books which were physically separate from copies of the plays, but towards the end of the Roman Empire it became increasingly common for readers to transfer material from commentaries on to the margins of the texts (particularly poetic texts), and there are signs of a growing tendency to produce copies of texts with big enough margins to facilitate this process. In medieval manuscripts the normal place for a commentary is the margins, and a high proportion of the Aristophanes manuscripts have their margins filled with explanatory notes ('scholia'). These scholia are the end-product, drastically abbreviated and sometimes vitiated by mis-understanding, of several centuries of ancient study. They record, on occasion, the different opinions of individuals, whether pioneering scholars of the earlier Hellenistic period or the secondary, 'parasitic' commentators of Roman times, e.g. 'Kallistratos says . . .; but Sym-makhos says . . .; and there are some who . . .'. On occasion a scholion may offer an interpretation of something other than what the text of the play says, and in these cases it may happen that the text presupposed by the scholion is actually preferable. For example, in *Clouds* 868f., the young man Pheidippides is anxiously presented by his father to Socrates as a prospective pupil. Socrates says, contemptuously:

Well, yes, he's still pretty much of a baby, and he has no experience of the ropes (*kremathrôn*) we have here.

The sense is satisfactory, because when the young man's father first entered the school Socrates was suspended on a rope in order to study astronomy from above ground level; but if it is what the poet wrote, it is metrically abnormal, because the position of the word *kremathrôn* in the line requires the scansion ⌣ — —, and in the dialogue of comedy the middle syllable of this word should be short, as in line 218. The scholion in the Venetus runs as follows:

On which the philosophers are suspended. Alternatively: of the astronomical and geometrical instruments; for these are hung in the school. It should be taken that way if the reading *kremastôn* is adopted.

This shows that the commentator from whose work the scholion is ultimately derived knew of an alternative reading *kremastôn*, which would be free of any metrical objection and would make the required allusion to Socrates' earlier suspension on a rope, but would make it more colourfully by suggesting ignorance of technicalities (cf. our expression 'know the ropes') for *kremastá* was a technical term for the rigging of a ship. Examples of this kind can be cited from the scholia on most of the plays. On the other hand, we sometimes have reason to believe that a corruption was universally established before the ancient commentators turned their attention to a passage. In *Birds* 1680f. the human hero of the play, negotiating with an embassy from the gods, has demanded the goddess Basileia as his wife. Of the three gods on the embassy, two (Poseidon and Herakles) are Greek and one is foreign, with a limited command of the Greek language. This foreign god, asked for his opinion, utters some gibberish which Herakles interprets: 'He says, hand her over'. Poseidon indignantly replies (I translate the manuscript text literally):

No, *he* doesn't say to hand her over, if not to walk as the swallows.

The scholion shows how the ancients wrestled with this text:

Symmakhos: the sense of this is not clear. The gait of swallows has no special significance—indeed they cannot even get along as other birds do, particularly the birds that do not fly. Didymos interprets thus: it would be appropriate if he said '*to* the swallows', meaning 'if he doesn't walk to the swallows'; that is why he will go on to say 'So he says to hand her over to the swallows', since he himself is walking to them, to Cloudcuckooland.

Richard Bentley at the beginning of the eighteenth century observed that it would make admirable sense if instead of *badísdēn*, 'to walk', Aristophanes actually wrote *babásdei g'*, 'he babbles, at any rate', since (*a*) the idiom translated literally 'he doesn't say . . . if not, at any rate, he babbles . . .' means 'he doesn't say . . .; on the contrary, he babbles . . .' (cf. *Knights* 185f.), and (*b*) the Greeks often compared the speaking of foreign languages to the twittering of swallows. Hence:

No, *he* doesn't say 'hand her over'; he's just twittering like the swallows.

IDENTIFICATION OF SPEAKERS

Anyone who looks at the text of an Aristophanic play as it actually appears in the Ravennas may be struck by the fact that whereas the

2 This scrap of papyrus, datable to the second century A.D. (*Papiri della Società Italiana*, no. 1194, fr. 3), contains part of lines 273–298 of *Women at the Thesmophoria*. The fifth line from the top is a stage direction (cf. p. 10), and the old man who is the principal character of the play is indicated simply as 'kinsman' (*sc.* of Euripides; cf. p. 165).

3 This is the first page of *Frogs* in the Codex Ravennas (cf. p. 4). The text is written in an even, confident hand characteristic of the late tenth century A.D., but the marginal scholia are written in a script of older type.

speakers are indicated most of the time by abbreviations ('sigla') of their names, e.g. 'Pheid' for 'Pheidippides', there are sometimes several pages running in which no indication of the speakers' names appears at all, but only a sign (a double point or a long dash) to show that the following words are not spoken by the same person as the previous words. In a passage of dialogue which involves only two characters, we can manage not too badly without the addition of the siglum to the sign for 'change of speaker', provided that the sense of what is said helps us along and we can trust the accuracy of the manuscript. But the sign is obviously liable to be accidentally omitted or confused with some other mark of punctuation, and deficiency or instability in the indication of speakers can land us in real trouble when a dialogue involves three or four persons. Ancient fragments of dramatic texts show that this kind of inadequacy in the Ravennas is not the fault of its copyist, nor does it reflect an indifference of the period at which he was working; it is quite clear that texts of plays in the ancient world imposed on the reader a much harder task of interpretation than do modern texts, in which every speaker is unambiguously indicated by name. Just how little was indicated in a written text of Aristophanes' own time must be a matter for speculation, since we have no fragments as early as that time, but it is apparent from the scholia that ancient commentators treated the assignation of the right words to the right speakers not as a matter of continuous tradition from the author's own pen but rather as a matter falling within their own province as interpreters of the transmitted text. Commentators who seem rarely or never to have considered emending the text itself evidently felt free to alter assignations, and this perhaps tells us more than anything about the nature of the copies which they inherited. For example, in *Frogs* 49–51 Dionysos, accompanied by his slave Xanthias, is boasting about the part he has played in a sea-battle on a ship commanded by Kleisthenes. The Ravennas has:

HER. And you fought a battle?: Yes, and we sank twelve or thirteen ships. You two? Why, yes, by Apollo! THE. And then I woke up!

(THE. here is an abbreviation for *therápōn*, 'slave', i.e. Xanthias). The scholion, a chaotic blend of different annotations, runs as follows:

'You two': Herakles says 'you two' in wonderment and disbelief. Some put a double point at 'Apollo' and at 'woke up'. He is making fun of Dionysos; 'And I', he says, 'woke from a dream', showing that he did all this in a dream. Some say that Dionysos speaks the words 'And then I woke up', in the way in which people who tell tall stories add that, and in that way it is shown that what is described resembles a dream. Others assign this to Herakles.

Situations of this kind are quite common, and the modern editor, grateful as he may be for information in the scholia about ancient assignations, has to do the job afresh for himself in the same way as they did, considering what is theatrically most plausible and what contributes to producing the most coherent picture of Aristophanes' technique.

In one important respect the modern editor is a great deal more cautious than some of his ancient counterparts. Many characters in Aristophanes are not named in the actual words of the play, and this often confronts us with two problems: first, are we ever justified in attaching a name to a character who never speaks his name and is never addressed or referred to by name! And secondly, when two or more unnamed but similar characters appear at different points in a play, are we to think of them as the same person or as different persons? An example of the first difficulty occurs at *Frogs* 464, when Dionysos, disguised as Herakles, knocks on the door of the palace of Pluto in the underworld. It is opened by someone who, as soon as Dionysos declares himself to be Herakles, rants in fearful tragic style, for one of the legendary labours of Herakles was to bring up the terrible dog Kerberos from the underworld, and this new character is grimly pleased to have caught the dog-thief. In the Ravennas the character is called 'Aiakos', a legendary hero who in Aristophanes' time was regarded as one of the judges in the underworld and in later times as 'holding the keys' of the underworld or as its 'doorkeeper'. The Venetus, on the other hand, abbreviates his name THERA., i.e. *therápōn*, 'slave', the scholia refer to him as 'one of those in the underworld', and one scholion introduces a peculiar complication by recording that when he asks 'Who's this?' and receives the answer (from Dionysos, one would have thought), 'The mighty Herakles', one school of thought held that this answer is given by Aiakos,—'which', adds the scholion, 'is unlikely'. An example of the second type of difficulty is provided later in the play at line 605, where someone arrives with policemen to arrest the putative Herakles. Is this 'Aiakos', whom we last saw at 477, threatening that he was going to fetch Gorgons who would tear 'Herakles' to pieces, or is it someone else? The Ravennas and the Venetus both give his name as 'Aiakos', but the scholia offer without comment two alternative theories: one, that the speaker is Pluto himself, the god of the underworld; and the other, that the part is to be divided between Pluto and a slave of Pluto. We are still not out of the wood. After everything has been amicably settled, there is a scene (738–813) in which Dionysos's slave Xanthias chats with a slave of Pluto. This character too is called 'Aiakos' in the Ravennas, despite the fact that he is obviously a slave, whereas the Aiakos of legend had been a notable king. The scholia do not suggest anyone but a slave.[2]

It seems that the commentators, accustomed as they were (from the late fourth century onwards) to comedies in which all the characters had names, were perhaps over-anxious to give us 'information' which Aristophanes himself did not think it necessary to give in those copies of his plays which were circulated in writing. This kind of officiousness has made its mark on the sigla and even, at times, on the text. In *Clouds* 21–31 Strepsiades, reading aloud from his account-book, speaks of owing twelve minae to 'Pasias' for a horse of the breed called *koppatīās* and three minae, for a racing-chariot body and a pair of wheels, to 'Ameinias'. Twelve hundred lines later he has to deal with two creditors who come to claim, respectively, twelve minae needed for the purchase of a 'starling-coloured' horse (1224f.) and an unspecified sum borrowed for an unspecified purpose (1267–1270). He drives away both creditors, the first by insults alone and the second by attacking him with a racing-goad. As the second creditor retreats, Strepsiades cries out, according to the Ravennas and Venetus, 'Get a move on, Pasias!', but according to the other manuscripts, 'Get a move on, samphoras!' Now *samphórās* is a word for a particular breed of horse, and the actual cry 'Get a move on, samphoras!' encouraging a horse, occurs at *Knights* 603. Someone in antiquity, however, seems to have thought that the creditor thus driven away is the 'Pasias' mentioned at the beginning of the play. This is hardly possible, since if either of the creditors is meant to have a name Pasias should be the first one, who has lent twelve minae; but the idea, having once been suggested, was taken so far as to give rise to a theory that what appears to be two creditors is in fact only one, who after his first repulse comes back in a new guise (the second creditor, unlike the first, laments an accident in racing) without Strepsiades' making any remark on his reappearance. This interpretation, which in many ways

2   Similarly, a scholion in the Ravennas gives the name 'Kephisophon' to the slave of Euripides who opens the door at *Ach*. 395, since in *Frogs* 1452f. Kephisophon is referred to as a collaborator in the writing of Euripides' plays; but *Ach*. 401 makes it plain that the man who opens the door is a slave.

is at odds with Aristophanes' dramatic technique, all arises from an insistence on naming and identifying speakers whose identity Aristophanes himself was content to leave open.

STAGE DIRECTIONS

Since the reader was left to work out for himself how many characters there were in a play, which of them were present in a given scene, and who actually spoke a given line, it is not surprising that he was also left to construct from the text, as best he could, the movements, gestures and tones which in a modern dramatic text are prescribed in stage directions. It is arguable that a very small number of stage directions in tragedy and comedy—much less than one per play—go back to the author's own day. These are all indications of the playing of a musical instrument (e.g. *Frogs* 1263, 'a tune is played on a pipe') or the uttering of a song or cry; the most convincing is in tragedy, Aiskhylos, *Eumenides* 129, where 'a high-pitched whine, twice' is ascribed to the sleeping Furies, and although it is easy to see how their whining could be deduced from the text there is nothing from which 'high-pitched' or 'twice' could have been deduced. Ancient commentators made good the deficiencies of the transmitted texts by suggesting stage directions in accordance with their own visualization of the action. For example, at *Clouds* 11 Strepsiades, exasperated at the sight of his son sleeping while he himself lies awake worrying, exclaims:

Oh, all right! Let's cover ourselves up and snore away!

The scholion in the Venetus says:

Stage direction. He screws up his face (*lit.*, '*makes it ugly*') and imitates the position of the young man; as the young man was asleep, he turns over and tries to sleep himself, drawing the blankets over his head.

It is a pity that commentator from whom this scholion is ultimately derived forgot that Aristophanic actors wore masks, so that however Strepsiades changed his expression we could not see him do so; but that is a useful reminder that ancient stage directions of this kind cannot absolve us from constructing our own on the basis of our study of the text. In the case of plays preserved only in manuscripts whose scholia are sparse and drastically abridged, we are deprived even of such suggestions as our ancient colleagues can offer.

A case of this kind occurs at the beginning of the last scene of *Lysistrata*, and the bare text is so bewildering that we may wonder

whether any ancient commentator ever reconstructed the scene to his
own satisfaction. The male citizens of Athens and Sparta, brought to
their knees by the sex-strike of their womenfolk, have agreed to make
peace. To celebrate their agreement the two groups of negotiators have
gone into the Akropolis for a party. The Chorus sings a humorous
song, and then comes 1216ff.; I translate the manuscript text as we
have it, and I indicate by ^{s} and ^{p} whether a second person pronoun or
verb is singular or plural:

> SLAVE: Open^s the door. Don't you^s want to get out of the way?
> You^p, what are you^p sitting here for? Do you^p really want me to
> set fire to you^p with my torch? It's a vulgar place. I won't do it. But
> if I've *got* to do it, we'll take the trouble to do you^p a favour.
> CHORUS: Yes, and we'll join you^s in taking trouble. Go^p away!
> You^p'll be sorry for your hair. Go^p away, so that the Spartans, now
> that they've had a good dinner, can come out and go off in peace.
> ATHENIAN: I've never in my life seen a party like it! They were very
> nice, those Spartans; and we're pretty bright at a party, when there's
> plenty to drink.

The first line is metrically faulty in Greek, and has to be emended, most
easily in a manner which would give the sense, 'You^s ought to have got
out of the way'. The words which I have translated 'it's a vulgar place'
admit of other interpretations, e.g. 'it's a commonplace motif', and the
word for 'I've seen', *ópōpa*, suits a Spartan speaker rather than an
Athenian, from whom we would expect to hear *heórāka*. But these are
marginal difficulties compared with the problem of understanding, un-
aided by stage directions, who is sitting outside the door, why a threat
to set fire to anyone is made, and what is the point of 'I won't do it',
'take trouble' and 'favour'. Probably the humour of the scene, unlikely to be appreciated (and not deserving appreciation) by the modern
reader or spectator lies entirely in the bullying and threatening of slaves
by tipsy citizens and in the exaggerated manifestations of fear on the
part of the slaves, thus:

> (*Slaves have gathered outside the door, ready to escort their masters home.
> The door begins to open.*)
> FIRST ATHENIAN: (*Shouting from inside to a doorkeeper who is also inside*)
> Open the door! (*The doorkeeper opens it fully and the First Athenian
> pushes him so that he falls head over heels*) You ought to have got out
> of the way!

(*A group of Athenians and Spartans, all carrying torches, comes out*) (*To the waiting slaves*) What are you sitting here for? Shall I set fire to you with my torch? (*He leaps at them, brandishing his torch. They shriek and gibber and tumble in all directions*) This place is a slum! (*Quietening down, conciliatory and reassuring*) I won't do it. (*They cautiously reassemble*) (*With ferocious sarcasm*) But if I've *got* to do it— I don't mind doing you the *favour*—we'll take the *trouble*!

SECOND ATHENIAN: (*Heartily*) Yes, and we'll join you in taking that trouble!

FIRST ATHENIAN: (*Again threatening the slaves with his torch*) Get away! You'll be sorry for your hair! (*More frantic clowning by the slaves*) Get away, so that the Spartans can come out and go home in peace after their dinner.

SPARTAN: I've never seen such a party in my life!

FIRST (or SECOND) ATHENIAN: They were very nice, those Spartans; and we're pretty bright at a party, when there's plenty to drink.

CHRONOLOGY

In Aristophanes' time plays were performed at two great festivals in honour of the god Dionysos, the Lenaia (commonly corresponding to late January) and the City Dionysia (commonly late March); we know that in the fourth century there were other festivals at which plays could be put on, but so far as Aristophanes is concerned we hear of none but the Lenaia and Dionysia.[3] The performance of plays, like the performance of several types of non-dramatic chorus at these festivals, was competitive; a jury placed in order of merit the plays presented by the dramatists. During the Peloponnesian War (431–404) the number of comedies presented at each festival was three; before the war and after it the number was five. An official record of the order of merit was kept, and in the late fourth century this was put up on a large public inscription, of which we have some pieces. It was also put into circulation as a book, so that from that time onwards a scholar anywhere in the Greek world could simply look up in his copy of the book the date at which any given play of Aristophanes (or any other dramatist) was performed.

During the Hellenistic period a demand grew up for 'hypotheses' of

3   Recently discovered fragments of an ancient commentary on a comedy (*Oxyrhynchus Papyri* XXXV (1968), no. 2737) seem to suggest a belief (probable enough; see n. 4) that performance at the City Dionysia had higher prestige than performance at the Lenaia.

classical plays, i.e. brief summaries of the plot. These could be combined with information drawn from the record to make a sort of potted history of dramatic literature. It then became customary to add the hypothesis (including the chronological information) to every copy of the text of the play concerned, and hypotheses so added have survived in the medieval texts. Thus it is possible to arrange Aristophanes' extant plays in chronological order, and thanks to information drawn by the ancient commentators (and occasionally by other writers) from the record we can also fill in the dates of some of his lost plays. The following table sets out what is known about Aristophanes' life and works, and I have added some data which may be of use in relating Aristophanes to his background.

In or soon after 450: Aristophanes born. This date is an inference from *Clouds* 528–533, in which he implies that he was exceptionally young and diffident at the time of his first play, *Banqueters*.

431   Outbreak of the Peloponnesian War between Athens and Sparta.

430   The great plague at Athens.

429   Death of Perikles.

428/7 Birth of Plato.

427   *Banqueters* (lost).

426   *Babylonians* (lost). In consequence of this play Aristophanes was indicted by Kleon for ridiculing the elected magistrates of the city in front of an audience (at the City Dionysia) containing many foreign visitors.[4] The indictment does not seem to have been successful.

425   *Acharnians* (extant); Lenaia, first prize.

424   *Knights* (extant); Lenaia, first prize.

423   Original version (lost) of *Clouds*; City Dionysia, placed third out of three.

422   *Wasps* (extant); Lenaia, second prize.

421   Peace treaty suspending hostilities between Athens and Sparta. *Peace* (extant); City Dionysia, second prize.

c. 417 Partial revision (extant) of *Clouds*; not performed.

415   Athens despatches a great expedition to Sicily.

414   *Amphiaraos* (lost); Lenaia. *Birds* (extant); City Dionysia, second prize.

4   The Greeks were nervous of navigation during the winter months, and the City Dionysia was regarded as the end of the winter; delegations from the subject-allies brought their tribute to Athens in time for the festival.

413   Sparta resumes hostilities.
       The Athenian expedition to Sicily is destroyed.
411   *Lysistrata* (extant); Lenaia (on the dating see p. 169).
       Women at the Thesmophoria (extant); City Dionysia (see p. 169).
       Oligarchic revolution at Athens succeeds temporarily, but the
       democratic constitution is restored some months later.
408   *Wealth* (lost; not the later play of the same name).
406   Death of Euripides.
       Death of Sophokles.
405   *Frogs* (extant); Lenaia, first prize.
       Decisive defeat of Athens; naval blockade of Athens.
404   Sparta imposes peace; an oligarchic group (the 'thirty tyrants')
       is put in power.
403   Civil war and democratic restoration.
399   Indictment and execution of Socrates.
395   Renewal of war against Sparta, but with a different alignment of
       allies; first steps to reconstruction of Athenian naval power.
392   *Women in Assembly* (extant); the date depends mainly on internal
       evidence, and may be a year out.
388   *Wealth* (extant).
After 388: *Aiolosikon* (lost) and *Kokalos* (lost), produced by one of
Aristophanes' sons.

It seems from *Ach.* 652ff. that at the time of that play (425) Aristophanes lived on the island of Aigina, which the Athenians had colon-
ized, expelling the native inhabitants, in 431.[5] We know that his sons
were comic dramatists, but we know nothing about his father (Philippos
by name) or his social and economic status.[6]

5 Since *Acharnians* was produced by Kallistratos it is possible that all references
to 'producer' and 'poet' in the parabasis of the play are to him, not to Aristophanes. The statement in the anonymous *Life of Aristophanes* to the effect that
Aristophanes lived on Aigina cannot be treated as confirming the inference
drawn from *Acharnians*, but is itself based on such inference.
6 Although the poet drew some kind of pay about the time of the festival (cf.
p. 16), he could not make a living from his writing, since the Greeks had no
system of royalties and no law of copyright. Royal patrons might at times be
found abroad (e.g. Arkhelaos the king of Macedon or Dionysios the tyrant of
Syracuse), but patronage at home was not to be expected.

II

Theatrical Conditions

ORGANIZATION

Since the number of plays to be performed at each of the dramatic festivals was predetermined, it was necessary to make a selection from among the poets who had plays to offer. The responsibility for this selection was imposed on officials appointed annually by lot; they were unlikely to possess any special qualifications for judging plays, and they had a wide range of other duties, so that unless they consulted connoisseurs of drama among their acquaintances (taking upon themselves, of course, the responsibility for the final decision) it is probable that they played safe by giving the highest priority to the dramatists whose reputations were most firmly established. The officials entered on their year of duty soon after the middle of the summer, six to seven months before the Lenaia, and a dramatist who was not in a position by then to make a firm promise of a play, perhaps even to give a fairly detailed account of its content, must have been in danger of missing his chance. He had the opportunity to introduce topical allusions into the text up to the last minute (a few passages of this nature can be identified in Aristophanes), but there are practical limits to changing and augmenting a play once rehearsals have begun, and whenever we consider the relation between the subject of an Aristophanic play and the political situation at the time of its performance we must not forget that the situation at the time of composition was sometimes significantly different.

A dramatist was commonly, but not necessarily, his own producer (*didáskalos*, 'teacher'); Aristophanes in fact gave his first three plays, *Banqueters, Babylonians* and *Acharnians*, to a certain Kallistratos to produce, and some of his later plays to Philonides. Actors were allocated and paid by the state, but the maintenance, costuming and training of the chorus (a comic chorus had twenty-four members) was the responsibility of a *khorēgós*, a term which must originally have meant 'chorus-leader' but by Aristophanes' time corresponds rather to what we would call a 'manager'. The Athenian state did not tax income directly and did not even raise a capital levy except in unusual emergencies, so that the revenue needed for internal purposes was raised in part by indirect taxation and in part by allocating much of the responsibility for festivals, ceremonies and the maintenance of warships to individuals whose registered capital was sufficient to sustain it. It appears from *Frogs* 367,

> ... or anyone who nibbles at the poets' pay—and he a politician!

that a comic poet was paid, but we do not know how much or for how long a period before the performance of his play.

At the City Dionysia three tragic poets competed, each with three tragedies and a 'satyr-play', whereas only one play apiece was required of the comic poets. It seems that on each of the three days devoted to drama the three tragedies and one satyr-play presented by one tragic poet were followed by one comedy; that at least is a fair inference from *Birds* 786–789, where the Chorus of birds expatiates on the advantages of having wings:

> For example, if anyone among you spectators had wings, and were getting hungry and fed up with the tragic choruses, he could fly off home and have his lunch, and then fly back to *us* again when he was full.

We do not know for sure how things were arranged before the Peloponnesian War, when five comedies were put on at the City Dionysia, or after it, when the pre-war pattern was reinstated; nor do we know the arrangements at the Lenaia, where there were fewer tragedies.

The panel of judges who arranged the plays in order of merit at the end of the festival was drawn by lot at the last minute from lists submitted by each of the ten *phȳlai* into which the whole citizen-body was divided. There were ten judges, one from each *phȳlḗ*, and the final decision was based on a random drawing of five out of their ten individual verdicts. We do not know on what criteria the original ten lists were compiled.

When specific allusions are made to the audience in the text of a comedy they seem to presuppose an audience of men and boys, but two passages of Plato's *Laws* (658A–D and 817C) reflect an assumption that at least at the time of writing (the middle of the fourth century) women could be spectators of all kinds of drama.[1] There is no good reason to postulate a difference in this respect between Plato's time and Aristophanes'. It is natural that a comic poet should speak of his audience as male, since at Athens it was the taste and judgment of men which carried weight and determined the standing and reputation of the poet; positive reactions of approval or disapproval by women in the presence of men would not have been welcomed. We should not, I think, imagine that a woman, unless she was a priestess occupying a seat assigned to her office, could without impropriety seat herself while a man remained standing or stand with a good view of the action while a man was pushed back into a bad viewpoint, but rather that when the adult male citizens[2] had seated themselves women, children, foreigners and slaves saw as much of the plays as they could. Women of citizen status were expected to be decorous and easily embarrassed, and there may appear at first sight to be a certain contradiction between this social requirement and enjoyment of the unrestricted obscenity of Aristophanic comedy. But in a society which imposes great restraints on women in the presence of the opposite sex we sometimes find equally extravagant absence of restraint on the conversation of women among themselves, and if the women tended to congregate separately from their menfolk at the performance of comedies or at phallic processions and the like there is no reason why they should not have enjoyed themselves. As for the boys, the Athenians took it for granted that they would enjoy obscene humour; at *Clouds* 538f. Aristophanes refers to a certain type of exaggerated phallic costume as designed 'to make the little boys laugh'.

THE THEATRE

When we stand below the Akropolis today and look at the theatre, almost everything that we see is of Hellenistic or Roman date. Excavation has made it possible for us to recover in some detail the theatre as it was after its major reconstruction in the late fourth century B.C., and

1   There are also some anecdotes about fifth-century tragedy which presuppose the presence of women in the theatre. Such anecdotes can never be dismissed offhand as later inventions, since the work of two gossipy writers of the fifth-century, Stesimbrotos and Ion, was still read during the Roman Empire.
2   Some delegates from other states might be given privileged seats, and this was normal for Athenian officials; *Birds* 794 refers to a section of the auditorium in which members of the Council were seated.

the evidence of theatres in other parts of the Greek world helps us to complete our general picture of the design of the Greek theatre at that period. Aristophanes, however, lies half a century and more further back in time, and only a fraction of the total complex of foundations uncovered in the area of the theatre at Athens can be assigned to so early a date.[3] In order to envisage the theatre in which his plays were performed[4] we need to combine these exiguous remains with inference from later theatres, a few items of information given by other writers, and the implications of some passages of his own plays.

The essential features of the Aristophanic theatre were a circular space (the 'orchestra'; *orkhêsthai* = 'dance'), some sixty-six feet in diameter; a rising auditorium, consisting of concentric rows encompassing rather more than the north-west half of the orchestra; and a building ('skene') lying south-east of the orchestra, at right angles to the axis bisecting auditorium and orchestra, and leaving substantial approaches right and left to the orchestra (*ésodoi*, later *párodoi*, roughly our 'wings'). A reference in Xenophon (*Cyropaedia* vi.1.54) to a tower which had 'timbers as thick as those of a tragic skene' indicates that the skene was wooden even in Xenophon's time, the first half of the fourth century; his word 'tragic' will include 'comic', since all types of play were performed in the same theatre and no word for 'dramatic' was in general use.

Examination of the remains of the theatre at Eretria, of fourth-century date, suggests that there the area immediately in front of the skene was slightly higher than the orchestra, and certain passages in Aristophanes seem to point to the same feature in the Athenian theatre. Some of these passages admit of other explanations, but one which cannot easily be explained away is *Wasps* 1341–1344, where the old man Philokleon has returned from a party with someone else's slave girl in tow. He says to her:

> Come up this way, my little golden beetle. Put your hand round this rope. Hold on to it, but be careful, because the rope's pretty old; all the same, it doesn't mind a bit of friction.

The 'rope' in question is obviously the large artificial penis which was

3 See W. B. Dinsmoor, 'The Athenian Theatre of the Fifth Century', *Studies Presented to David Moore Robinson* (Saint Louis, 1951), i 309–330.

4 There is a theory that at the Lenaia the theatre used was not what we regard as *the* theatre of Athens, situated below the south slope of the Akropolis, but a smaller and simpler structure west of the Akropolis. I am not satisfied with the evidence offered in support of this theory.

a normal part of the comic actor's costume, but the words are chosen as if the girl were going up a ladder or a steep staircase with a guide-rope at the side. If in fact Philokleon and the girl are moving in the direction of the skene on completely level ground, without even a single step to ascend, it is hard to see how this passage could be acted or why the idea should have occurred to Aristophanes at all. On the other hand, one or two steps would be adequate motivation for the joke. We should not imagine the actors on a really high stage separated from the chorus down in the orchestra; much action in comedy and tragedy alike, especially action in which a character seems to be attacked and surrounded by a chorus, presupposes freedom of movement between the orchestra and the front of the skene,[5] and the archaeological evidence suggests that the high stage was an innovation of the Hellenistic period.

Plays were performed in daylight and in the open air, and there was no way of creating an illusion of darkness. Accordingly, when the dramatist wishes to portray action in the dark (as at the beginning of *Clouds* and *Wasps* and throughout the first four hundred lines of *Women in Assembly*) he must make the situation clear to the audience through what the characters say, and the rest requires the co-operation of the audience's imagination.[6] Similarly, action which in real life would take place inside a building must be shown in the theatre as exterior action, and there are occasions on which a slight strain imposed by this condition makes itself apparent. In *Peace*, for example, when Trygaios arrives at the abode of the gods and knocks at their door, Hermes opens it and tells him that the gods have moved, leaving their old house to War. At 232f. Hermes says:

But I'll be off. I rather think he (*i.e. War*) is just going to come out; anyway, he's making a noise from inside.

So Hermes goes away, Trygaios hides to one side, and War comes out with his slave Tumult to pound up in a mortar ingredients which symbolize the various Greek cities. When the mixture is ready, he sends Tumult to get a pestle; but Tumult returns empty-handed, and War says eventually (287f.):

Take all this stuff away again. I'll go in and get a pestle made.

5 The scholion on *Frogs* 297, while seeming to take the use of a high stage for granted (in the commentator's time it was universal and long-established), envisages Dionysos and Xanthias as being at that moment in the orchestra.
6 We might compare the readiness of cinema audiences to accept the highlighting of figures in a scene which is meant to portray action in the dark.

Thus War, Tumult and their stage-properties return indoors; and if we ask why they ever came out, the answer is that Aristophanes had no other way of portraying what was going on. The Greeks lived in the open air more than we do, and were more familiar with work and leisure in the open, but even so they may have felt an element of theatricality in *Clouds* 631–633. Strepsiades has earlier been accepted into the school of Socrates as a pupil; now Socrates comes out of the house exasperated by his pupil's stupidity:

> But all the same, I'll call him out here into the daylight. Where's Strepsiades? Come on, pick up your bed and come out!

We have been given to understand previously (195–199) that Socrates' pupils grow pale and wan because they are compelled to stay indoors and forbidden the open air. That joke has to be dropped and forgotten when it becomes necessary to set before us examples of the difficulty Strepsiades has in understanding what Socrates tries to teach him.

It will be clear from what has been said so far that the Athenian audience cannot have made exacting demands for theatrical illusion; indeed, 'illusion' may be an inappropriate word to use of theatrical procedures which contributed so much less than the words of the text and the audience's co-operation to the construction of imaginary situations. Since there was no stage curtain, properties required for the opening scene must have been brought on in full view of the audience before the play began, and when the opening scene includes a character who is asleep (as in *Clouds* and *Wasps*) that character too must have walked on and taken up a sleeping position. This seems odd to us, because we are accustomed to indoor theatres and stage curtains, but it is questionable whether any theatrical procedure can seem absurd or clumsy or in any way objectionable to an audience which is not acquainted, either directly or by report, with a more refined procedure. Once a thing has been done well, people criticize its being done badly; but Aristophanes' audience, placed as they were close to the very beginnings of European drama, is likely to have ignored many theatrical problems for which our own culture has devised solutions.

At a certain point in *Peace*, after the goddess Peace has been hauled out of the deep cave in which War had imprisoned her, the chorus is encumbered with tools and ropes which will not be wanted again in the play. The chorus-leader says (729–733):

> (*To Trygaios*) Go on your way, and good luck go with you. (*To*

the Chorus) Meanwhile, let's hand over all this equipment to the attendants to keep safe. You often get an awful lot of thieves peering around the skenai, up to no good. (*To the attendants*) Now make a good job of it, and look after all this. (*To the Chorus*) As for us, let's tell the audience the way our argument goes and all that's in our mind.

There is an ambiguity in the words *tôis akolóuthois*, which I have translated 'the attendants', for they could very well mean 'our slaves', i.e. not a gang of slaves owned by the manager and suddenly coming on for the purpose of taking away the properties, but silent characters who have throughout played the part of slaves of the farmers' chorus. Possibly, however, the ambiguity is more than merely linguistic. If we were in a Greek household, talking to the master of the house, we should take no notice of the comings and goings of his slaves as they went about their business; why, then, should the audience concern itself with the identity and function of silent slaves who perform necessary work in the theatre?[7] In real life a group of farmers who had been using ropes and tools would naturally tell their slaves to take the stuff away; the actual incorporation of the orders in the text of the play may be in part due to the unusually large scale of the operation, which it would have seemed more artificial to pass over than to mention, but is probably due in the main to the poet's desire to make a wry joke about the theft of properties during performances. We can discern some other occasions on which a property must have been removed without explicit mention, e.g. the passage of *Clouds* (631–633) quoted above. The bed which Strepsiades is told to bring out with him in 633 was outside the school in 294; in 505 he is told by Socrates

Buck up and follow me, this way!

and he goes indoors after Socrates in 509. At some time between 509 and 627 someone must have carried in the bed, and a slave whom we can (if we wish) regard as a silent and nameless inmate of the school is the natural person to do this.

The movement of properties is a comparatively trivial matter. Much harder and more complicated is a pair of interrelated problems: how many doors were there in the skene, and what was the method of

---

7 Modern audiences do not seem to mind the removal of furniture in opera by scene-shifters dressed in a manner consonant with the period and place portrayed by the opera itself.

effecting a transition from an explicitly exterior scene to a scene which the poet wishes the audience to think of as indoors?[8]

In many passages the words of the text plainly refer to the door of a particular house; thus in *Acharnians* 393–395:

> DIKAIOPOLIS: Now it's time for me to pluck up my courage; I must go to Euripides. Hi, slave!
> SLAVE: Who's there?
> DIKAIOPOLIS: Is Euripides in?

In *Frogs* 35–39 Dionysos arrives at the house of Herakles:

> DIONYSOS: Now I've reached this door, here, which was the first place I had to call at. Slave! Hi, slave!
> HERAKLES: (*As it seems, opening the door himself*) Who beat on the door? He charged it like a centaur, whoever he was!

So too in *Lysistrata* 428–431 the Proboulos is preparing to force open the gates of the Propylaia when they are opened from the inside and Lysistrata comes out:

> You don't have to force it with crowbars. I'm coming out of my own accord. What's the need of crowbars?

There are other passages, however, in which it sounds as if a door in the skene serves simply as an indeterminate point of transition from out-of-doors to indoors, and we are not expected to identify it as the door of any particular building. Thus in *Thesm.* 930 the policeman is told to take the Old Man 'in' to fasten him in the portable stocks, and in 1007 the policeman disappears for a while to 'bring out', as he says, a mat to sleep on. At the beginning of the play there was certainly a door which represented Agathon's house; then (279) we had to regard the scene of the action as moving to the sanctuary of Demeter and Persephone; but there is no reference in the text to the sanctuary as having a door, and it would be quite inappropriate to wonder why the policeman expects to find a mat in a temple. In cases of this kind the door of the skene is simply a point of transition to an unspecified 'indoors' which is also the source of properties (ch. p. 143, on *Birds*).

It is natural enough that a door into the skene should be given an identity when the action so requires but allowed to resume an indeter-

8 I have discussed the problems more fully in 'The Skene in Aristophanes,' *Proceedings of the Cambridge Philological Society*, cxcii (1966), 2–17.

minate character when the need for identification has passed. It is equally natural that the same door should assume different identities in different parts of a play: for example, the house of Herakles in *Frogs* 35–165 and the house of Pluto from line 431 onwards, conventionally ignored by the audience during the journey of Dionysos (166–430) from the former house to the latter. But it is not quite so easy to believe that the same door represented two different houses within the same scene. Some modern interpreters of Greek comedy feel sure that it did, so that when in *Acharnians* 1069–1142 the text suggests that both the door of Dikaiopolis's house and the door of Lamakhos's house are in continuous and simultaneous use Aristophanes is actually exploiting the limitations of his theatre for humorous effect. This view can claim some support from the fact that no extant tragedy, with the possible exception of one scene in Aiskhylos's *Choephori*—a scene which admits of alternative methods of production—can be regarded as requiring more than one door. The importance of this fact is a little diminished by reflection on the great differences between tragedy and comedy in the type of story enacted, and it is not justifiable in any case to assume that the Athenians designed their theatre primarily with tragedy in mind and expected comedy somehow to manage with less than it really needed. Strictly speaking, drama does not *need* anything except people, as anyone who has taken part in charades will testify; everything *could* be mimed. If we knew for certain, on independent grounds, that Aristophanes had available to him only one door, and never more than one, then of course we could not say 'comedy needs more than one door'; we should have to reconstruct the production of every Aristophanic play—as indeed we *can*—to conform with our datum, allowing the single door any number of changes of role, no matter how rapid the alternation. As it is, our earliest incontrovertible evidence is provided by representations of the three-door skene in Hellenistic art, combined with the prologue of Menander's *Dyskolos* (316 B.C.), in which the three buildings which will be in use throughout the play are pointed out to us and identified. Our question thus becomes, 'Was the multiple-door skene, attested for the end of the fourth century, already in use in the time of Aristophanes?', and the relevant evidence is those passages of Aristophanes of which we can ask, '*If* Aristophanes had only one door available, would he have written this passage in quite this way?' The assumption which underlies this hypothetical question is that whereas a comic poet may well have extracted humour from theatrical limitations he is not likely to have written passages which would merely puzzle or confuse the audience when he could easily have written them otherwise.

A case in point is the first scene of *Clouds*. Strepsiades asks Pheidippides (92):

> Do you see that door and the little house?[9]

He goes on to explain that it is the school of Socrates, in which he wishes Pheidippides to enrol as a student. Pheidippides refuses, and after a short but stormy exchange breaks off by saying: (125):

> Well, I'll go in, and I shan't take any notice of you!

By 'in' he means 'into our own house', for when Strepsiades is thus left alone he decides that there is nothing for it but to enrol as a student himself, despite his advancing years and bad memory. So he says to himself (131):

> Why do I go on shilly-shallying like this, instead of knocking at the door? Slave, slave!

—whereupon the door of the school is opened to him by a student. If only *one* door was available to Aristophanes, why did he compose the scene in this confusing way, when he could have made Pheidippides say simply 'I'll be off' (like Hermes in *Peace*) [10] and go off into the wings? The high probability that two doors were in use throughout *Clouds* is strengthened by a passage near the end of the play (cf. p. 108), and it can similarly be argued that *Women in Assembly* also requires at least two (p. 198).

A tragic poet often requires to show us a character dead, dying, sick or insane, in such circumstances that in the imaginary situation portrayed by the play the chorus, or some other character, is regarded as entering a building to find the one who is dead or otherwise immobilized. What actually happened in the theatre was the extrusion of a trolley from the central door of the skene; the interior scene, in fact, is brought out into our presence, and it is left to our imagination to turn the spatial relationships, as it were, inside-out. This is no doubt why, in two Aristophanic scenes in which a tragic poet is visited at home

9 The words for 'door' and 'house' used here are diminutives, *thýrion* and *oikídion*, but 'little' is almost too ponderous in English; the word-forms represent little more than the speaker's affectionate and conciliatory attitude.

10 One very late manuscript of *Clouds* has *eîmi*, 'I'll go' instead of *éseimi*, 'I'll go in', but its chances of preserving an ancient reading are negligible, and if we adopt *eîmi* we have to emend the rest of the line to restore the metre.

(Euripides in *Ach.* 395–479 and Agathon in *Thesm.* 95–265) he is 'rolled out' and 'rolled in' instead of walking on his two feet like an ordinary being. Whether this theatrical trolley was used in comedy except to make fun of tragic practice or when it was for some reason unavoidable (cf. p. 135) is an open question. Its use has been suggested in *Clouds* for the revelation of the interior of the school, since only a few lines after Strepsiades had cried to the student (183) 'Open the door!' the students revealed by its opening are described as being 'in the open air' and are told to 'go in' (195–199). We should however observe that if the trolley was employed in this scene it must have carried at least two groups of at least two students (187–192), geometrical and astronomical instruments and a map (201–206) and the bed on which Strepsiades is shortly to be 'initiated' (254). We have to consider, as an alternative to the trolley, the possibility that the school is 'opened' by the removal of a screen—the door pointed out at line 92 will have been a door in this screen—and that the students told to 'go in' at line 195 enter a door in the permanent skene, which for the rest of the play represents the door of the school. The use of movable 'sets' in the fifth-century seems to be indicated by a statement of Aristotle (*Poetics* 1449^a 18) that Sophokles introduced *skēnographía*, 'scene-painting', into tragedy; this can hardly have been a permanent representational treatment of the skene itself, for successive tragedies on the same day, if they were to have a representational background at all, usually needed different backgrounds.[11] It is probable that the rocky ground covered with bushes in *Birds* (54, 92, 207f.) was visibly represented; the rocks in the 'mouth of the cave' in *Peace* (224f., 361) must have been objects constructed to look like rocks.

The skene had a flat roof (in *Wasps* 67f. Bdelykleon, sleeping on it, is pointed out to us) and two storeys, for in *Wasps* 364–402 Philokleon lowers himself from an upper window on a rope; it is also probable that in *Ass.* 877ff. two upper windows are in use (cf. p. 197). Tragedy sometimes uses a crane to bring deities and heroes flying through the air; the actor would in such a case be suspended on a rope and swung into our

11 There is the further point that if 'scene-painting' means a permanent decoration of the skene it is inappropriate to the context in Aristotle, which is concerned with the development of dramatic form, and it would more naturally be attributed to an artist or architect than to a poet. Aiskhylos had a fondness for presenting a set of three tragedies which dealt with the same legend and functioned rather as three successive acts of one great drama, but this practice was not compulsory and was not favoured by Sophokles or Euripides. Hence a background appropriate to any given play might be inappropriate to the immediately succeeding play.

view by the crane, which would be mounted on the top rear of the skene. In *Peace* Trygaios's flight to heaven on a giant beetle requires the crane, and the text puts this beyond doubt when Trygaios says (173–176), with a comic rupture of dramatic illusion:

> Oh dear, I'm scared—I'm not joking now! Crane-man, do pay attention to what you're doing with me! I'm beginning to get collywobbles, and if you're not careful I'll be giving the beetle a meal! [12]

Socrates is similarly suspended in the air at *Clouds* 218–237.

THE ACTORS

A tragic poet was normally required to design his play in such a way that the roles in it could be divided between three actors, though he was free to use any number of silent extras, and we occasionally find small parts for children in tragedy. Some of Aristophanes' plays cannot be acted by less than four people; there are too many passages of four-cornered dialogue, and even more in which there would be no time for a change of costume between the departure of one character and the arrival of another. In the first scene of *Lysistrata*, for example, it is easy to distinguish Lysistrata, two Athenian women, and Lampito, identifiable by her Spartan dialect; thus in 99–106 we have:

> LYSISTRATA: Don't you miss the fathers of your children, serving in the army? I know very well that every one of you has a husband away from home.
> KALONIKE: Well, my husband, anyway, has been away in Thrace for five months, keeping an eye on Eukrates.
> MARRHINE: Yes, and mine, too, seven months at Pylos.
> LAMPITO: Aye, and mine too, if he ever does come back from his regiment, he picks up his shield and he's off, flown away.

On the other hand, any number in excess of four seems to be ruled out in this scene; the Corinthian woman and Theban woman, whom we might have expected each to speak for her own countrywomen, remain silent and are spoken about but not addressed. In *Clouds* 886f. Socrates, telling Strepsiades and Pheidippides that Right and Wrong will appear before them in person, adds without further explanation, 'I shan't be here'; evidently the actor playing Socrates was required to play Right

12   It is a dung-beetle, and in comedy fear is often described or portrayed in terms of its effect on the bowels.

or Wrong. In *Thesm.* 929–946 the part of the Policeman is played by a silent extra, for the Prytanis, the Old Man and the Woman are all on stage and Euripides has departed only a moment before. Hence the Policeman is told to take the Old Man indoors in order to chain him to the portable stocks. When they come out again the Prytanis has been gone for fifty lines and the part of the Policeman can now be taken by the actor who played the Prytanis. Passages in which the medieval manuscripts present us with more than four characters at once turn out on investigation to be very easily reducible to four; sometimes, indeed, as in *Peace* 1191–1269, it emerges from the text that the apparent multiplicity of characters must have originated in careless interpretation by commentators of the Roman period. The only passage which resists re-interpretation is the first scene of *Acharnians*—where, however, the fifth role is that of a Persian who speaks only one line of garbled Persian and one of garbled Greek.

When we perform the exercise of distributing the parts of a play between four actors, we can either give as much as possible to three, treating the fourth as very little more than an 'extra,' or divide the work between all four as fairly as possible. There is something to be said for the former procedure, in so far as ancient commentators seem to have regarded three as the standard number and the presence of four in one scene as deserving remark; also, the Hellenistic theatrical troupes do not seem to have contained more than three comic actors. If, however, we do distribute the roles in this way, minimizing the fourth actor's share, it is important to remember that it is we who have done it, and not to treat our own manipulations as evidence for what actually happened. We have no information on the distribution of roles, and at least in *Clouds* we cannot cut down the responsibilities of the fourth actor below a certain level, for both Right and Wrong are substantial roles. We also have to remember that the Hellenistic troupes are of limited relevance, since they did not perform Aristophanes.

Male and female roles were both played by men, as in tragedy; the children who have small parts in *Wasps* 254–315 and *Peace* 114–149 and 1265–1304 were presumably speaking and singing extras. There are many silent parts for beautiful young women, some of them personified abstractions and others slave-girls. In one passage, *Wasps* 1342–1387, the words of the text imply that the part of a slave-girl is taken either by a live girl who is naked or by somebody (male or female) wearing tights on which pubic hair is depicted. The end of *Women in Assembly* seems to introduce some girls whose sole function is to contribute an element of spectacle to the festive dancing with which the play closes (cf. p. 193); were they absent, nothing dramatic would be lost, and it is open to question whether dressed-up men would have been regarded as funny enough *per se* to contribute more to the theatrical effect than real dancing girls.

The presence of silent extras playing the parts of attendant slaves is sometimes indicated by the text at points where the modern reader has not been expecting it. In *Thesm.* 279ff., for instance, the old man has been dressed up as a woman and sent off to the Thesmophoreion; it does not occur to us that he has also been provided with a female slave, but his words when he arrives are addressed to such a slave. Occasionally the sole purpose of silent extras is to provide the material for a single joke; thus in *Ach.* 860–869 the Boeotian who comes to Dikaiopolis's market is accompanied by a pair of Boeotian pipers, whose music Dikaiopolis mistakes for the buzzing of wasps, but once this stock joke has been made the pipers are needed no further.

Actors (again, as in tragedy) wore masks, and this naturally affected the techniques of production and acting. An actor could not show us any change in his facial expression, and any modern interpretation of an Aristophanic passage which depends solely on expression must for that reason be wrong. We should probably be right to imagine that the trunk and the arms played a greater part in expressing emotion than they do in modern acting, and it is observable that characters in Greek plays often say 'I weep' or 'I laugh' (or words to that effect) in circumstances in which a modern dramatist would confine himself to a stage-direction. It is to be regretted, though it cannot be helped, that the Greeks have not bequeathed to us any information about preferred styles of acting.

A mask had to have an unnaturally large aperture for the mouth, and some sculptural representations of masks (not as early in date as we would have wished) suggest that the apertures for the eyes were also abnormally large. These considerations must have created some difficulty in the making of what was often desirable in Aristophanic comedy, a portrait-mask of a living contemporary. The use of such portrait-masks is implied by *Knights* 230–233, where one of the slaves of 'Demos' (a personification of the Athenian people) warns the Sausage-seller about the 'Paphlagonian' (who represents Kleon):

And don't be afraid; he's not portrayed to the life, because the property-makers were so afraid that not one of them was willing to make a likeness of him. All the same, he'll be recognized; the audience is smart.

Aristophanes may well have taken this line because Kleon's face was unremarkable and not one of which a portrait could be recognized once the practical requirements of a comic mask had been met; by not making a likeness, he was free to express his attitude to Kleon by presenting the Paphlagonian as hideous in the extreme, in conformity with his picture of Kleon (*Wasps* 1031-1035, *Peace* 753-757) as a supernatural monster.[13] In a society in which no one shaved the face or smoked or wore glasses portraiture cannot always have been easy, as we may realize by considering the predicament of a political cartoonist in similar circumstances.[14]

The characteristic costume of an actor playing a male role included an artificial penis of abnormal size. *Wasps* 1341-1344, quoted above in connection with the steps in front of the skene, is a scene in which this article must have been brought into play, and there are a few other passages which could be acted more easily with it than without it; but it is obviously not likely to have been worn by actors playing female roles, and in the case of most male roles the text does not help us to decide whether it was worn or not.

13 This, I think, is the humorous point of *Knights* 230-233: Aristophanes means that the real Kleon looked so horrible that a property-maker would have quailed before the sight of the mask taking shape in his hands, and so the mask of the Paphlagonian, horrible though it may be, falls far short of the reality.
14 For a fuller discussion of this question see my article 'Portrait-Masks in Aristophanes', *Komoidotragemata* [Studies in honour of W. J. W. Koster] (Amsterdam, 1967), 16-28.

III

Fantasy

THE PLOT OF BIRDS

Birds is the longest extant comedy, to modern taste one of the most imaginative and stylish, and on any reckoning one of the most spectacular. In it an Athenian citizen, Peisetairos, in whom the energy, ambition and fluent ingenuity of his countrymen are highly developed, persuades the birds to build a great fortified city in the sky between the gods and mankind. The gods, thus blockaded, are forced to come to terms, and Peisetairos demands and receives as the price of peace the sovereign power of Zeus, 'father of gods and men'. He takes in marriage Basileia ('Queen'), the divine housekeeper who has charge of the thunderbolts, the traditional weapon and deterrent of Zeus, and so becomes ruler of the universe.

This fantasy exhibits in an extreme form two elements which are of great importance in Aristophanic comedy: the fulfilment of a grandiose ambition by a character with whom the average member of the audience can identify himself, and its fulfilment by supernatural means which, although treated almost casually, overturn many of those sequences of cause and effect with which we are familiar in ordinary life. The gods are treated and portrayed not as the august beings worshipped in hymns and processions to temples, but as Pucks and Rumpelstiltskins drawn from the nursery-stories of an unusually sophisticated, confident and irreverent nursery. Iris, who is sent by Zeus to the bird-city to threaten destruction, is sexually insulted by the irrepressible Peisetairos and flies away in baffled rage. Prometheus comes secretly, a traitor to the kingdom of Zeus, to advise Peisetairos what demands he should make. The embassy sent by the gods to make peace consists of Poseidon, represented as a rather pompous aristocrat, Herakles, a bully and glutton (as in Greek folklore generally), and a gibbering foreign god. Peisetairos has been able to communicate with the birds in the first place because he sought out the hero Tereus, who according to legend was transformed into a hoopoe, and Tereus had taught the birds to speak Greek. Peisetairos meets Tereus on the ground, but the new city of the birds is unmistakably up in the air; what exactly it rests on is a problem which is never allowed to bother either the characters or the audience. Peisetairos and the human friend who accompanies him sprout wings when they have eaten a magic root of which the hoopoe knows (654f.), just as Odysseus in the fairy-tale world of the Odyssey makes himself safe against the spells of Circe by eating a magic plant which Hermes gives him. Basileia,[1] whom Peisetairos marries, is a deity invented for the occasion, a representation in tangible, personal form of the idea that Peisetairos acquires supreme power.

SELF-ASSERTION

Our own civilization is so accustomed to explaining in terms of general scientific laws the events of the world in which we live that we tend to assume that even the most intractable and complex events, including patterns of our own behaviour, are ultimately and in principle explicable in scientific terms; for us the question is not which events are acts of God, but whether there is a divine agent at all. When we look back in time two thousand years or more we make the acquaintance of cultures in which the boundary between 'act' and 'event' is quite different both in location and in nature. Fifth-century Greece produced some individuals of extraordinary intellectual penetration, who speculated on the structure and history of the universe in terms of natural, intelligible processes from which the acts of personal gods were excluded; but in the same city as such an individual, often perhaps in the same household, we should find a majority for whom a strong wind was a person who decided when he would blow, a blight on the crops the manifestation of a god's anger for a sacrifice promised but not performed, and a sudden bright idea the intervention of an unseen being in the mental processes of an individual human. The average Greek, in short, felt himself to be living in a world populated by superhuman agents (the term 'supernatural' would beg the question), and although he might exhibit a cheerful agnosticism if pressed to discuss the precise character and operation of any one such agent, he would not so

---

1 *Basíleiă*, 'queen' (known as a title of goddesses, e.g. *Peace* 974), not the abstract *Basiléiā*, 'monarchy'; this is plain from the scansion of lines 1537 and 1753.

cheerfully omit the inherited system of festivals, rituals, sacrifices and observances which in his view had for so long ensured the survival of his family and city.[2]

The Greek's relation with one of his gods was essentially the relation between subject and ruler. A ruler is a person whose actions and decisions cannot always be predicted or explained by his subjects; he can be placated, in normal times by normal tribute; he makes rules—which he himself does not necessarily obey—and punishes subjects who break the rules; but he does not concern himself with what lies outside the province of his rules, and a prudent subject will pay his tribute, obey the rules, and keep out of the ruler's way. But a subject needs something else: the opportunity to assert himself by ridiculing the ruler. Fifth-century comedy provided a notable outlet for this kind of self-assertion by depicting deities not only as worsted by aggressive humans, as in *Birds*, but also as stupid, greedy and cowardly; Dionysos at *Frogs* 479 faints and dirties himself in fright, and at the end of *Wealth* Hermes, hungry because now that men have acquired wealth for themselves they no longer feel the need to sacrifice to him, is treated disdainfully by the slave Karion (1113–1117):

> HERMES: Ever since Wealth recovered his sight, no one offers incense or bay or a cake or an animal—not a single thing—to us gods any more.
> KARION: No, and they won't, either. You gods looked after us pretty badly when you had the chance.

One rather important difference between ridicule of a human ruler and ridicule of a god is that one can ridicule the ruler behind his back, whereas a god is presumed to have eyes and ears everywhere; indeed, Dionysos is invoked to come and enjoy the dramatic festivals, and when he has come he finds himself and his fellow Olympians portrayed in a variety of discreditable predicaments. The apparent oddity of this procedure is justified by another very important difference: whereas the reaction of a human ruler to insults and mockery is predictable with virtual certainty, beliefs about the gods somehow evade truly empiri-

2 See M. P. Nilsson, *Greek Popular Religion* (New York, 1940; reprinted as *Greek Folk Religion* in 1960), especially chapters I, II, IV and V. Nilsson, who had very high scholarly standards and an incomparable knowledge of his subject, reacted with surprise and sorrow to some data, and these reactions have a distorting effect on some of his generalizations. We are likely to understand Greek religion better through the eyes, and with the working assumptions, of the anthropologist than with those of the metaphysician or theologian.

cal verification and so can be adjusted to the emotional and moral demands of society. To the ordinary Greek festive and ceremonial occasions were the primary constituent of religion; theology came a very bad second. He therefore continued in the religious observances which had developed over the centuries in response to human needs, but he did not ask himself 'What is the nature of a god who expects sacrifices but also accepts mockery?' This attitude may have been strengthened by the existence of essentially magical practices which only rarely come to the surface in literature, practices of control over a god by (e.g.) beating his statue when the crops have been unsatisfactory.[3]

If it is right to regard the treatment of the gods in comedy as a means by which man hits back at the superhuman powers which dominate the world, the religious standpoint and the political standpoint of comedy can be treated as two species of the same genus, and a certain contradiction in the traditional view of Aristophanes as simultaneously conservative and impious can be removed. It is in any case doubtful whether the label 'conservative', in the sense which it would bear in a modern state, can properly be attached to Aristophanes. In so far as comedy admitted political satire and invective, it could in theory have distributed its fire over three targets: the constitutional structure of the state, the style of politics, and individual political decisions. Aristophanes in fact spares the first of these three targets entirely, and all the evidence we have suggests that other fifth-century comic poets adopted the same standpoint as he did. It is not difficult to see why this should be so. The inherited constitution, established in essentials even before the grandfathers of Aristophanes and his friends defended Athenian freedom against the Persian invader, was fully democratic;[4] sovereign power lay in the hands of an assembly of all adult male citizens, and to this assembly all holders of judicial, military or administrative office were accountable. Revolution could come only from the extreme Right,

3 Theokritos 7.105ff. refers to an Arcadian custom of flogging the god Pan when game is scarce. A recently discovered inscription, of Hellenistic date, from Syedra in southern Turkey (G. E. Bean and T. B. Mitford, *Denkschriften der österreichischen Akademie der Wissenschaften*, Phil.-hist. Klasse, lxxxv [1956], 21f.) shows that when the Syedrians consulted an oracle on how to keep off aggressive raiders they were told to make a statue of the war-god, Ares, in chains and suppliant posture before Justice.

4 Democracy still had the character of a revolutionary movement in the fifth century; many major Greek states, including Sparta, Corinth and Thebes, restricted political power (in varying degrees) to a section of the citizen-body.

which believed in restriction of power to a certain part of the citizen-body; revolution of this kind succeeded briefly in 411 and again (with Spartan support) in 404, but it had no voice in practical politics at other times, and a comedy which implicitly advocated the exclusion of the poor from the sovereign assembly would have done its author about as much good as a modern comedy advocating the restriction of education to children with skins lighter than a prescribed point on a colour-chart. When an Aristophanic chorus or character talks affectionately about 'the old days' or 'as things used to be' the reference is not to a pre-democratic constitution but to a past period of security and prosperity contrasted with present discomfort and insecurity, and the length of time involved in the contrast may sometimes (as in *Peace* 572) be only a few years.

But the style of politics and the character of political leadership are a different matter. Of all the men whom we know from historical sources to have achieved political prominence at Athens during the period 445–385, there is not one who is not attacked and ridiculed either in the extant plays of Aristophanes or in the extant citations from the numerous lost plays of the period. Often the attack is on a grand scale: *Knights* is a prolonged and vicious assault on Kleon, Hyperbolos was ridiculed by several poets in a series of comedies (*Clouds* 551–559), and in the last years of the war Kleophon, the subject of some incidental scurrility in *Frogs*, had a whole play directed against him by the comic poet Plato, on the same occasion as *Frogs*. Perikles, who died two years before Aristophanes' first play, was similarly attacked during his life-time, and Aristophanes' own allusions to him and the part he played in bringing the war about are uncomplimentary in the extreme. All these leading men, and many minor politicians besides, are uniformly treated by the comic poets as vain, greedy, dishonest and self-seeking; and, wherever a wisp of smoke can be fanned into comic fire, they are represented also as ugly, diseased,[5] prostituted perverts, the sons of whores by foreigners who bribed their way into citizenship. One might have expected that when some eminent person actually did what a comic poet advocated he would have earned a compliment; but *Peace*,

5 The Greeks were not hampered by conventions of 'decency' in politics. Neokleides, prominent in political life during the first ten to fifteen years of the fourth century, is ridiculed for chronic eye disease, and in *Wealth* 716–747 we have a zestful description of his attempt to get a cure at Epidauros: Asklepios, the god of healing, put in his eyes substances which made him yell with pain and go away blinder than before.

performed early in 421 and composed (presumably) in 422, entirely ignores the successful efforts for peace made by Nikias during the winter of 422/1. It seems to be the business of comedy to grumble and slander, and to speak fair of a politician or general[6] would have been discordant with its function as a means by which the ordinary man asserts himself against his political or military superiors. It is a stock joke in Aristophanes and his contemporaries that *rhētores*, 'speakers', i.e. those who are influential in the assembly because they spoke cogently, were prostituted as boys; the chorus of *Peace*, welcoming the cessation of war, complains bitterly about military commanders who wear impressive plumes but run away on the battlefield and create despair and confusion by continually altering the call-up lists; and the chorus of *Clouds* claims the gratitude of the audience for causing by thunderstorms the postponement of 'senseless expeditions' (579f.).

This democratic spirit—democratic, at least, in the negative sense that it refuses to respect those who currently possess influence or authority—should not be confused with championship of the poor against the rich.[7] Since Athens was a slave-owning society, a citizen rarely employed another citizen, and there was no conflict between capital and labour within the citizen-body. A potentiality of conflict did exist between landowners and farmers on the one hand and the craftsmen, workmen and shopkeepers of the city on the other hand. The former, predominantly qualified by their property-ratings to serve as cavalry and heavy infantrymen, had at one time been, as in many Greek states they still were, that part of the population on which the physical survival of the city depended in a world of ceaseless wars. The latter, less often able to afford infantry arms and armour, were qualified only to serve as rowers in warships, and it was upon them (together with thousands of men who came to Athens as mercenaries from the Aegean islands) that the wealth and power of the Athenian Empire had in fact mainly depended since the Persian wars. The landowners and farmers lost their land when the enemy invaded Attica, but battles on land were less frequent, and involved a smaller number of men, than sea battles; up to two hundred rowers could die every time a warship

6 In an Athenian context, 'politician' means a man who is influential in the assembly, and 'general' means a man who in any given year is elected to high military command. There were no professional politicians and no professional soldiers. Cf. p. 95.

7 On the social, economic and political structure of Athens see A. H. M. Jones, *Athenian Democracy* (Oxford, 1957).

was sunk. No class likes to be devalued, and the heavy infantry who made up the middle and upper strata of the population, in addition to resisting with extraordinary success such tendency as there was towards tactical innovation, had little difficulty in maintaining their traditional status. They were assisted in this by being a class into which poorer men could hope to rise, and by a widespread feeling that maintenance of landed property in the same family for several generations is good evidence of divine favour. Aristophanes is willing enough to acknowledge the importance of the sailors when he makes Dikaiopolis in *Ach.* 161–163 reject with indignation the idea of paying two drachmai a day to Thracian mercenaries:

> For *them*—*two* drachmai—for those bare-knobs? What a fuss you'd
> hear from the top deck,[8] the men who keep the city safe!

But Dikaiopolis himself, like Trygaios in *Peace* and the choruses of both plays, is a farmer, and in both political issues are seen through the eyes of the farmers: men who think themselves as good as anybody, suspicious of political oratory and of commanders and officials. It seems probable that those members of Athenian society who were economically below the farming stratum nevertheless identified themselves sufficiently, and in sufficient numbers, with that stratum to constitute a single popular standpoint for the purposes of the comic poet. A contrast between urban and rural sentiment in the assembly is drawn in *Ass.* 431–434, and no doubt a farmer who disagreed with a decision could grumble that decent men of sense and substance (such as himself) had been deceived and outvoted by pale-faced shopkeepers, but he would not always have had good grounds for his complaint. During these years of the Peloponnesian War in which the rural population was concentrated in the city the farmers had the opportunity to attend the assembly in force, and when Dikaiopolis in *Ach.* 371–374 voices fears for his own fate if he pleads justification for making peace it is the country people (*ágroikoi*) whom he regards as easily fooled by self-seeking demagogues.

Comic revenge on authority is closely allied to revenge on intellectual superiority. When in *Birds* 992–1020 the mathematician and astronomer Meton comes to demonstrate how the city of the birds could be laid out symmetrically, Peisetairos, with dangerous politeness, advises him to go. The dialogue proceeds (1012–1020):

8   The Greek expression refers to the topmost and outermost line of rowers, not to officers.

METON: Why, what's the trouble?

PEISETAIROS: It's like Sparta; there's an expulsion of foreigners and a bit of a turmoil. A lot of violence going on in the city.

METON: Why, you don't say there's a civil war?

PEISTEAIROS: Oh, no, no!

METON: Well, what, then?

PEISETAIROS: There's a completely unanimous decision—to beat up every charlatan.

METON: Well, I'd better be going, then.

PEISETAIROS: Why, yes, because I'm not sure you'll be in time. (*Attacks him*) The violence is right on top of you!

METON: Ow! Ow! (*Exit*).

PEISETAIROS: Didn't I warn you at the start? Go and stick your rulers up against yourself somewhere else!

The scene seems to be showing us how to deal with an intellectual: hit him until he runs away. *Clouds* is, of course, the most elaborate ridicule of intellectual pretensions which has come down to us from antiquity; all kinds of scientific enquiry, represented without exception as futile or immoral or both, are blended in the pretentious, squalid, sly figure of Socrates, who at the end of the play is chased away, his school burned and demolished about his ears. The high-flown language of dithyrambic poets is also ridiculed, and they themselves are despised as parasites on rich patrons. The tragedies of Euripides and Agathon, which were felt to combine disturbing ideas with poetic innovations not to the taste of middle-aged, respectable, unreflecting men, are treated at times with patronizing affection, at times with 'criticism' which in substance is little more than a rude whistle. (cf. p. 147).

The violence with which Peisetairos treats Meton is a self-assertion not only of the plain man against his intellectual superiors but of the individual against the constraints imposed by society. Athenian law took violence seriously; a blow directed by one citizen at another could lead to a prosecution for *hýbris*, regarded as an offence not against the individual but against the community, and so even to the death-penalty, if the jury was satisfied that the striker intended to establish over his victim a moral and social ascendancy like that of a master over a slave. But Philokleon in *Wasps* is presented as somehow a better man, a more endearing old rogue than the characters, pompous or petulant or agitated, whom he has attacked and insulted in drunken gaiety. Whatever the law might say, and however severely *hýbris* might be analysed by a speaker in court as the very antithesis of the democratic spirit, the feeling that a real *man* lashes out on occasion could not be extinguished, and the outrageous behaviour of a character in comedy could provide an outlet for the spectator's feelings.

The seizure of sexual opportunity is felt even more strongly to be the hallmark of a man, and the complete absence of inhibition in sexual word and deed is one of the most striking features of Aristophanic comedy. Greek sexual language is composed of four strata: one corresponds to our 'four-letter' words, which have only a physiological or anatomical meaning and are never to be found in prose literature or in serious poetry; the second consists of slang, e.g. words normally meaning 'strike' but used also of sexual intercourse. Both these strata are characteristic of comedy. The third, 'proper' words, e.g. 'private parts', or 'be with', and the fourth, coy euphemisms such as 'we all know what', are characteristic of prose but very rare in comedy.

Sexuality is often expressed with roguish gusto, as in *Ach.* 263–279, where Dikaiopolis, celebrating at his farm a festival which includes the worship of Phales, the personification of the penis, sings of the delights of peace:

> O Phales, Phales,
> how much nicer
> to find your neighbour's pretty Thracian slave
> collecting wood, pinching it from your slopes,
> and seize her round the waist and lift her up
> and lay her down
> and stone her fruit,
> O Phales, Phales!

Often, however, sexual ideas and vulgar language are so distributed that they 'cap' a non-sexual joke or bring a passage to a climax, after which the prolonged laughter of the audience enables the subject to be broken off and a fresh line of dialogue started. So in *Thesm.* 30–36 Euripides and his old relation have arrived at the house of Agathon, a tragic poet who carefully cultivated an effeminate appearance:

OLD MAN: What Agathon's that? (*Pondering*) There *is* an Agathon . . . Ah! You mean the dark, strong man?
EURIPIDES: No, a different one.
OLD MAN: Never seen him. (*Pondering*) Ah! The one with the great bushy beard?

EURIPIDES: You've never *seen* him?
OLD MAN: No, never in my life, so far as I know.
EURIPIDES: Well, you've fucked him,[9] but maybe you don't know him! But let's get to one side, he's coming out.

In recent (but not very recent) times the gross sexual humour of Aristophanic comedy has been regarded as discordant with the subtle wit and literary parody with which it keeps company, and it has been suggested that the sexual humour, originating in primitive fertility-rites, was retained in the sophisticated era of Aristophanes only for its ritual character. I doubt whether we need attribute to the Athenians so emasculated a sense of humour, particularly when we take into account two facts: down to the middle of the fifth century the vase-painters (and I am speaking of the great artists, not of backstreet pornographers) clearly felt free to paint any subjects whatever, including not only ordinary sexual intercourse but male and female masturbation, and the tradition of iambic poetry created by Archilokhos (who had no more to do with fertility-rites than the vase-painters) was as uninhibited as comedy in using sexual subject-matter and vulgar language for humorous purposes. It seems reasonable to suppose that since Athenian society imposed a high degree of segregation on women and girls of citizen status and strict standards of decorum on the language used on serious public occasions the ordinary man enjoyed the sexuality of comedy as a channel for his own 'excess' sexuality.[10]

If 'pornography' is defined as writing of which the primary purpose is to arouse the reader's sexual desire, and if writing which achieves insight into sexuality or integrates sexuality with other aspects of life is not pornography, Aristophanes does not seem to me a pornographic writer. I doubt, however, whether our understanding of Aristophanic comedy (or of any other kind of comedy) is advanced by the distinction between 'belly-laughs' and 'sniggers' which is sometimes drawn in order to sustain the credo 'Aristophanes good, pornography bad'. Whether one laughs or sniggers depends less on the joke than on the circumstances in which it is made and on one's own degree of inhibition. There are, I think, passages in Aristophanes in which a sexual word

9   The Greeks sometimes, though not always, used the same words for homo-sexual as for heterosexual penetration.
10   The Greeks drew a sharper distinction, in respect of propriety of language, between humorous and serious utterance than is now customary; we might compare the difference in the nineteenth century between a male clubroom conversation and a public address to an upper-class mixed audience.

is inserted for the sole purpose of raising a laugh, and inserted in such a way that the poet seems to be nudging us and saying, 'Aren't I naughty!', e.g. *Ach.* 1088–1092:

> Get a move on! You've been holding up the dinner for a long time. Everything else is ready: couches, tables, cushions, rugs, garlands, scent, sweets—*the whores are there*—cornflour-cakes, flat-cakes, sesame-cakes . . .[11]

We reach perhaps a deeper level of self-assertion, one might almost say, of vicarious revenge on society, in the excremental humour of comedy. Serious Greek literature, by contrast, ignores the excretory processes almost as completely as the nineteenth-century novel; one of the rare exceptions is in Aiskhylos's *Choephori*, where a garrulous old nurse is permitted an allusion to the incontinence of the infant Orestes. A comic poet may suggest (as Aristophanes does in the opening scene of *Frogs*; cf. p. 58) that it is his rivals who have recourse to excremental humour, while he himself works on a more sophisticated level, but in such cases we do not have to believe him, any more than we believe an orator who disdainfully attributes to his adversaries rhetorical devices which we can see him employing himself. A scene in *Women in Assembly* (311ff.) depicts a citizen who has got up just before dawn with heavy-laden bowels and is looking for a secluded spot; his remark

> Anywhere's a good enough place in the dark

implies that he has no lavatory in his own house, and no doubt pigs, dogs and rats performed as useful a function as scavengers in a Greek city as they do today in an Asiatic village. Having squatted down, he finds that his motion is too hard, and he cannot expel it. He is interrupted by two neighbours the second of whom calls out,

> Hi, what are you doing? Having a shit?

—and thereafter the conversation takes a different turn, leaving our hero's physical problem unresolved, but not before it has been turned to humorous account with a prayer to the goddess of childbirth. References to excretion seem to the modern reader to be dragged in where the dramatic action does not require them. In particular 'fear' is more often expressed by (e.g.) 'dye yourself brown' than by any

---

11 Contrast *Frogs* 112–115, where Dionysos asks Herakles for information about the journey to the underworld: 'tell me the harbours, bread-shops, brothels, resting-places, turnings, . . .'

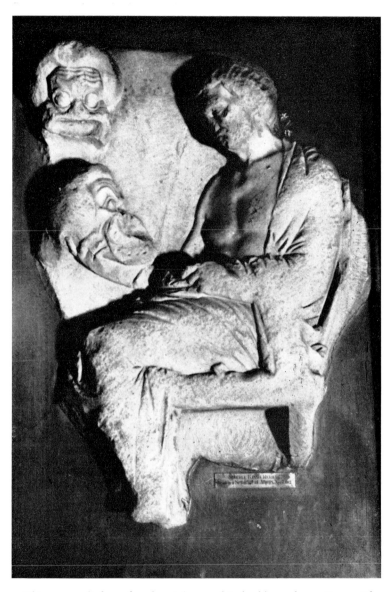

4 This grave-relief was found at Athens and is datable to about 380 B.C. The man portrayed, holding a comic mask in one hand and a papyrus roll in the other, is reasonably presumed to be a comic poet, and may be Aristophanes himself (T. B. L. Webster in *Studies Presented to David Moore Robinson*, St. Louis, 1951, vol. i, pp. 590–3).

5, 6 There is no doubt that these relief-sculptures portray comic choruses, but they belong to the time of Aristophanes' grandchildren, not to his own time so far, that is the nearest that the visual arts take us to the Aristophanic chorus.

other image or metaphor. As with sexual humour, excremental humour is often the climax to a run of dialogue, In *Clouds* 382ff., for example, Strepsiades has asked Socrates what causes thunder, and Socrates, having explained that it is the collision of clouds laden with water, goes on to an analogy:

> SOCRATES: Haven't you ever filled yourself up with soup at the Panathenaia, and a turmoil started in your belly, and all of a sudden there was a rumbling and bubbling all over it?
> STREPSIADES: Why, yes, and it makes an awful to-do straight away, and it's all in a turmoil; and the soup crashes like thunder, and roars away; quietly at first—pp! pp!—and then it steps it up—pppp!— and when I shit it's *thunder*—pppp PPPP!!!—just like the clouds!

We might have imagined that the Greeks, living as they did in conditions which we should regard as intolerably insanitary, would not have welcomed such frequent reminders in comedy of dirt and discomfort. But the humour of excretion seems to belong to all cultures; indeed, the noisy expulsion of gas from the bowels has as good a claim as anything in our experience to be absolutely and unconditionally funny. That is presumably due to the fact that the small child, having begun with a natural sensual enjoyment of defecation, is then restrained from making a mess or a bad smell where adults do not want it, and is thus provided with a channel through which he can later retaliate on society, even if only vicariously, by identifying himself with characters shouting vulgar words in comedy. There are far fewer jokes about urination than about defecation, and even fewer about expectoration; both, I imagine, were treated very casually by Greek society.

The argument of this section is that devaluation of gods, politicians, generals and intellectuals may be taken together with ready recourse to violence, uninhibited sexuality, frequent reference to excretion and unrestricted vulgarity of language, as different forms of the self-assertion of man against the unseen world, of the average man against superior authority, and of the individual against society. The next section will examine the rather dreamlike character of the processes by which this self-assertion is realized.

CAUSE AND EFFECT

In *Acharnians* Dikaiopolis, fed up with the war and with the unwillingness of his fellow-citizens to take any practical steps towards ending it, achieves a *private* peace, applicable to himself and his family alone, and thereupon opens a private market to which traders from enemy countries can bring the desirable imports which he has missed for six years. He is able to make this peace-treaty because an immortal, Amphitheos by name, turns up at a meeting of the assembly with the announcement that he has been commissioned by the gods to negotiate an end to the war. He is thrown out of the assembly, but Dikaiopolis has a word with him and provides him with what the gods have forgotten, the travelling expenses necessary for the negotiations. Amphitheos flies away and returns with peace for Dikaiopolis within the space of forty-five lines of continuous dialogue. We are not encouraged to ask why the gods wanted peace to be made or why Amphitheos needed travelling expenses for a job so quickly done. Again, when a Megarian and a Theban arrive at Dikaiopolis's private market, we are given no indication of how they learned that he was at peace with them or how they managed to cross part of Attica in wartime to reach him. Aristophanes, in short, has started with an 'if only . . .' construction and has filled it in with those elements alone which are necessary to complete a sequence of events at 'if only . . .' level. Practical questions which would arise at once if the fantasy were to be translated into real terms are admitted only to the extent that they can be exploited for humorous purposes; which is to say, most of them are excluded altogether.

A practical question of this kind, likely to be contemplated by the modern reader but not raised by the poet, is posed by the first scene of *Lysistrata*. The heroine of the play proposes to end the war by an international sex-strike, and for this purpose representatives of the women of all the chief belligerent cities meet her in Athens. How they got there, and how they will get home again, we are not encouraged to ask. But there are much larger problems than that in the basic concept and the whole development of the play. The reason why the women are tired of the war is that they never see their menfolk, who are away on campaigns for months at a time; they all assert this (99–106). So Lysistrata propounds her scheme for a sex-strike. But how does a woman go on such a strike against a man who is not there? In fact, once the strike has begun, the absence of the men is never mentioned again. Myrrhine complained that her husband has been away at Pylos for seven whole months, but by the time the strike is six days old we see Myrrhine's husband, tormented by insupportable desire, clamouring for her return home. He says nothing about having been away; and in any case, why does he speak of her *return* home? Lysistrata's original plan was (149–154, 160f.):

LYSISTRATA: If we stayed at home with our make-up on, and came in wearing a see-through dress, nothing else, and shaved down below in a nice triangle, and our husbands got a stand and wanted a bash, and we didn't say yes but kept away, they'd soon make peace, I know that.

. . .

KALONIKE: But suppose they pull us into the bedroom by force?
LYSISTRATA: Hang on to the door.

She goes on to explain that the old women of Athens have been given the task of seizing the Akropolis, where the state's reserve of money was kept. We might have imagined that this division of labour will be maintained: the women young enough to retain their sex-appeal will stay at home to torment their husbands, while other necessary steps will be left to those too old to be attractive. But this is not so, for at the end of the first scene a cry of triumph is heard; Lysistrata explains that 'the women' (she does not now say 'the *old* women') have seized the Akropolis, and after telling the Spartan representative to go back and set the plot in motion at Sparta she says (245f.):

And we'll go in and join the other women on the Akropolis and bar the gates with them.

Then for the rest of the play, until peace is made, Lysistrata and the wives on strike remain on the Akropolis.

Plays in which men have to disguise themselves as women or women as men furnish interesting examples of the 'selective' treatment of reality. In *Women at the Thesmophoria* the old man who is disguised as a woman naturally has to have his beard shaved off and to be dressed in women's clothes, and he also promises (267f.) to talk in a woman's voice. Nothing is said about his complexion, although this was an important distinction between men and women, since a deep suntan was admired in men and a fair skin in women. In *Women in Assembly*, on the other hand, the women who are disguising themselves as men have taken great trouble to acquire a tan, in addition to making false beards, but nothing is said about their voices. The man who has attended the assembly and has not penetrated their disguise describes one of the speakers as 'a good-looking, *pale* young man' but makes no comment on the speaker's voice! In both plays a systematic attempt to account for every element in the disguise would slow things down too much; a selection is therefore made, and the selection is not quite the same in both cases. One might say that in *Thesm.* the women are not allowed to notice the old man's colour, and in *Ass.* the men are not allowed to notice the women's voices. The reason why the old man, Euripides' kinsman, goes to the meeting of the women is that Euripides himself would be recognized (189); but when Euripides comes disguised as Menelaos (871) he is not recognized. The disguised old man sends his female slave away when the women gather for the meeting, on the grounds (294) that slaves may not be present at it; but some of the women have slaves with them, as we see later (609, 728). Similarly, in *Frogs* 630–673 the slave Xanthias, disguised as Herakles, and his master the god Dionysos, whom Xanthias alleges to be his slave, are beaten to discover which of them is a god, for a god will not feel pain. In fact, both of them feel pain and utter cries, which they explain away as not due to the blows. But in 657 Xanthias says that his own cry of pain was occasioned by a thorn in his foot. This would actually show that he is not a god, if anyone noticed the implication, but no one does. Again, in *Wasps* 230–394 Bdelykleon and his slave are allowed to sleep peacefully through the entry of the chorus and the dialogue between the chorus outside the house and Philikleon inside.

It is only to be expected that selection and combination of elements which may prove on scrutiny hard to reconcile with cause and effect as we recognise them in ordinary life would also affect the consistency with which an individual can be characterized, and Socrates in *Clouds* provides an example of such inconsistency. Aristophanes' purpose in that play is to combine and exploit *all* the popular allegations made at different times and in different circumstances against scientists, philosophers, and rhetoricians. Since intellectuals spend time indoors thinking, they are pale and weedy, and the youths who follow their teachings will be similarly poor specimens. Since they do nothing that a decent man would regard as real work, and are too high-minded to trouble themselves with the comforts and pleasures of respectable citizens, they are poor, they live by stealing, and they live in squalid and verminous conditions. At the same time they take fees for teaching men how to cheat creditors and adversaries at law. When Strepsiades is enrolled as a pupil he is told that he must be prepared for a hard training (415–419):

... and if you don't grow tired, standing or walking, and don't mind too much being cold, and don't want your lunch, and keep off wine and gymnasia and nonsense of any other kind, and think that the greatest prize—as a smart man ought to think—is to win in action and counsel and in battle with the tongue.

Strepsiades, a tough old Attic farmer, has no hesitation in declaring that he has just the right qualities; they are, indeed, precisely the qualities—down to the word 'lunch'—that the Greeks admired in soldiers. But when, later in the play, the personification of abstract Wrong presents as attractive a picture as he can of himself to Strepsiades' son Pheidippides, we hear no more about hardship, but rather (1071–1073, 1077f.):

> Consider, my boy, all that there is in 'decency', and how many pleasures you're likely to be deprived of (sc. 'if you follow what Right calls "decency"'): boys, women, party-games, good food, drink, giggles. And what's the point in your living, if you're deprived of all that?
>
> .   .   .
>
> If you associate with *me*, you can do what your nature tells you to, skip, laugh, regard nothing as shameful.

It does not quite resolve the contradiction to say that the Socratics offer an ascetic means to a sensually abundant end, for where does Socrates himself stand in relation to Wrong? He is careless of comfort, going without shoes, but why does he stay poor and dirty when it is his trade to teach pupils to attain the opposite condition? We are accustomed to the idea of pupils who attain wealth and worldly success while the teacher to whom they owe so much remains poor and obscure, but the position of the professional teacher in our own social structure is quite different from that of the late fifth-century sophist. The eminent sophists who associated with some of the wealthiest men of their day were not in fact tough, impoverished ascetics, and Aristophanes combines in the Socratics two quite contradictory strands of behaviour and attitude.

IMAGERY AND PERSONIFICATION

When Amphitheos comes back to Dikaiopolis with a private peace, he brings not a document but some samples of wine: 'five-year', 'ten-year' and 'thirty-year' wine. The reason for this is that libations of wine were poured to the gods as part of the ceremony of making a truce or treaty, and so *spondái*, 'libations', meant also 'truce'. Aristophanes has here transformed a concept into a material object by taking an appropriate sense of the word for that concept.[12] At the *Knights* he

12   This does not mean that the Greeks liked wine thirty years old; it is simply that age in years is a factor in the quality of wine, and duration in years is the most important aspect of a peace-treaty.

plays a different trick with *spondái* by presenting them as live young women; their acceptance by Demos ('People') represents in tangible form the making of a thirty-year peace treaty by the Athenian people.

Personification is one of the oldest and most pervasive characteristics of Greek literature, and it is hard on occasion to decide whether the treatment of an abstract entity in personal terms reflects a genuinely personalizing outlook on the world or merely exemplifies a traditional form of linguistic expression. Euripides, for example, in *Bacchae* 370–373 makes his chorus cast the sentiment 'the words of Pentheus are unholy' in the form:

> Holiness, mistress among the gods,
> Holiness, who over the earth
> fly upon golden wing,
> do you hear these words of Pentheus?

It is therefore entirely in keeping with poetic practice, however different from tragedy in detail, when the chorus of *Acharnians* sings of War, who has brought about the destruction of the vines in Attica, as an unmanageable guest at a party, and apostrophizes Reconciliation in terms of sexual passion (979–987, 989–994):

> Never shall I welcome War into my house,
> nor shall he ever lie[13] in my company and sing the Harmodios-song,
> for he's a violent man in drink.
> All was well with us when he came rioting in,[14]
> and he made all go wrong—upsetting, spilling,
> fighting, and what's more, when I kept on inviting him,
> "Lie down, have a drink, take this loving-cup",
> he got worse, and burnt the vine-props in the fire,
> and spilt—we couldn't stop him—the wine out of our vines.
>   . . .
> O Reconciliation, companion of beautiful Aphrodite and the beloved Graces,
> what a pretty face you have, and I never knew it!
> If only a love-god would unite you and me,
> as he is in paintings, wearing a crown of flowers!
> Perhaps you're sure I'm an old man and past it?
> Why, with you in my arms I think I could still manage three in a row!

13   The Greeks lay down to eat and drink.
14   The reference is not to ill-disposed entry, but to a social usage: at a certain stage of drink a party would sometimes set out to pay a hilarious and noisy visit to houses where (it hoped) it would be welcome.

The remainder of the song to Reconciliation appears to describe the planting and cultivation of vines, figs and olives, but nearly all the words chosen are also slang words for the male and female genitals and so constitute a description of some details of sexual intercourse.

We meet War as a speaking character in *Peace*, and Reconciliation as a mute personage in *Lysistrata*. The personified Right and Wrong in *Clouds*, who conduct an argument against each other, have often (and rightly) been compared to the personification of the Laws in Plato's *Crito*, and the way is prepared early in the play for their eventual appearance as persons by Strepsiades' saying (112f.) that both arguments are 'with' the Socratics; the preposition used here, *pará*, is similar to the French *chez*, and what Strepsiades says is not quite the same as saying 'the Socratics know how to use both arguments'. But the Greeks also spoke of *X*-ness (e.g. health, wealth, poverty) as being 'with' someone in the ordinary sense of the English 'with', as a way of saying that that person is *x*. This is the idiom which underlies the whole plot of *Wealth*. The divine person Wealth is traditionally blind, i.e. undeserving people are often rich and deserving people are often poor. Khremylos is guided by an oracle to a poor blind old man, whom he identifies as Wealth himself; he takes the god to Epidauros to have him cured of his blindness, and thereafter 'he has Wealth in his house'—i.e. 'he has wealth in his house'—i.e. he is wealthy (the distinction between capital letters and small letters was not known to the ancient Greeks). Wealth speaks indifferently in terms appropriate to a person and in those appropriate to a thing, e.g. 237–244:

> If by chance I go into a miser's house, straightway he buries me down in the ground; and if some friend of his, an honest man, comes and asks for a little bit of money, he denies he's ever set eyes on me. If by chance I go into a crazy man's house, I'm up against whores and gambling and in no time at all I'm thrown out of the door naked.

Khremylos and his friend Blepsidemos have just agreed on the desirability of taking Wealth to Epidauros when a hideous old woman checks them with menacing language (437–443):

> POVERTY: No, I am Poverty, who have been dwelling with you both many years.
> BLEPSIDEMOS: Oh, my God, my God, let me out of here! (*Starts to run away.*)

KHREMYLOS: Hi, what are you doing? Yellow! Chicken! Stay with me, won't you?

BLEPSIDEMOS: Not on your life!

KHREMYLOS: Stay here! We're *men* and there are two of us; are we going to run away from one woman?

BLEPSIDEMOS: Why, you fool, she's Poverty. There's no more dangerous creature anywhere on earth.

The concept that Poverty 'dwells with' a poor man recurs in a passage of Menander's *Dyskolos*, seventy-two years after *Wealth*, and here it is casual idiom, not visible presence on stage:

I've been wasting a lot of time looking after things here, and Knemon's digging all alone. I must go and join him. Ah, curse you, Poverty! Why are you such a burden to *us*? Why do you sit indoors and live in our house year after year, so long a time?

So also in Menander's *Epitrepontes* a girl about to embark on a plan which calls for plausibility cries (379f.):

Dear Persuasion, be with me as my ally and cause all that I say to succeed!

The idiom is alien to us, but wholly Greek. Perhaps the nearest we come to it nowadays is the personification of cars and boats; the Greeks would have taken that for granted too, to judge from Strepsiades' words in *Clouds* (1494) as he sets fire to the roof of Socrates' house:

It's your job, torch, to give a good flame!

IV

Illusion, Instruction and Entertainment

THE PARABASIS

In each of the earlier plays of Aristophanes we find that at a certain point the progress of the action requires all the characters to be off-stage—for example, at *Knights* 497 the Paphlagonian has run off to denounce the Sausage-seller to the Council, the Sausage-seller has run after him to win the Council over to his own case, and the Slave goes into the house. At such a point the chorus addresses itself directly to the audience for about a hundred lines, and during this section (the 'parabasis') the sequence of actions and events which constitute the plot of the play is suspended. The dramatic status of the chorus is also ambivalent: they remain Acharnians, knights, birds, waspish jurymen, clouds, etc., but they speak and sing not as if they were involved in a fictional situation with Dikaiopolis and his private peace-treaty or Bdelykleon and his father's mania, but as if they were visiting Athens on the occasion of a Dionysiac festival. The parabasis has a recognizable structure[1] which occurs in full or in part in several plays, and each of its parts tends to have special functions of its own. The complete structure is as follows:

(i) Valediction to the departing characters; here the chorus begins with words appropriate to the plot, but may move within this same part to the less dramatic role required for part (ii). Thus in *Knights* 498–506:

> Go on your way, and good luck go with you,

[1] The major units of a Greek play exhibit formal structures of a kind more familiar to us in eighteenth-century music than in modern drama. The same can be said of other genres of Greek poetry, and even of prose; but no structure was so rigid as to resist innovation, and innovations tended to be substantial and periodic rather than gradual.

and may you prosper as I hope . . .
And you (*i.e. the audience*) attend to our anapaests . . .

(ii) The 'anapaests', which are recited by the chorus-leader. They are named after its usual rhythm, of which the basic unit is ‿‿ — ‿‿ —, but other metres are sometimes used (e.g. in *Clouds*). The reason for believing that the chorus-leader alone utters this part is that the same metre is often used elsewhere for dialogue between individual characters, and we know that when the chorus is indicated as taking part in dialogue only the chorus-leader speaks, for he may be addressed in the second person singular. It appears, however, from a quite explicit address to a piper in *Birds* 676–684 that the recitation of the anapaests in the parabasis was accompanied on a pipe. The poet most commonly uses the anapaests to praise his own work and denigrate his rivals in a vigorous but essentially playful way, and in a style full of images and conceits. Thus in *Acharnians* the theme of the anapaests (626–664) is: It's a shame to slander our poet by saying that he insults the Athenian people; he speaks his mind and saves you from being cheated; when the king of Persia was approached for help by the Spartans, he wanted to know which side in the war has a poet who'll lambast them and turn them into better men, for that's the side that will win; and when the Spartans demand Aigina back, it's because our poet lives there; but don't you let him go, because he'll never give up telling you what you should be told; so to hell with Kleon! In *Clouds* Aristophanes uses the first person singular with reference to himself throughout the anapaests, so that the chorus becomes no more than a mouthpiece for his direct personal communication with the audience. In *Birds* this self-advertisement is omitted and the chorus is allowed to speak about the superiority of birds to men, maintaining its dramatic role to an abnormal degree.

(iii) The 'ode', which is addressed to gods, inviting them to join the festival, is sung by the whole chorus and is composed in lyric metres. There may be a certain relationship apparent between the gods selected and the character of the chorus; thus, for example, the ode in *Knights* is addressed to Poseidon as the god of horses and of the sea. In *Acharnians*, on the other hand, although the ode is introduced formally as an appeal to 'the Acharnian Muse' for inspiration, its real subject is rustic feasting.

(iv) The 'epirrhema', recited by the chorus-leader in trochaic tetrameters (a metre occasionally used also for dialogue). This consists of advice uttered in character by chorus to audience; in *Acharnians* and *Wasps*, for example, the standpoint of old men is adopted (in the former case indignant and pathetic, in the latter proud and fierce), in the *Knights* that of young cavalrymen (representing themselves as champions of the tradition of courage and self-sacrifice, and asking for tolerance), in *Clouds* that of clouds complaining that even an eclipse did not warn the Athenians off electing Kleon to high office.

(v) The 'antode', which in metrical form responds exactly to the ode and may continue the invocation of the ode. In *Acharnians*, exceptionally, it continues the theme of the epirrhema.

(vi) The 'antepirrhema', in the same metre as the epirrhema and of the same length, is similar to it in theme but may be lighter and less didactic in tone. In *Clouds*, for example, the chorus brings a message from the Moon, complaining that the Athenian calendar has got out of step and the gods are muddled by not knowing when to expect festivals.

We find a modification of this structure introduced as early as *Peace*, where the parabasis which begins at 729 has only anapaests, ode and antode, the epirrhema and antepirrhema being postponed to a later stage in the play and appearing there (1127–1190) with a fresh ode and antode, so as to constitute a second parabasis. Even plays which have a full parabasis in the centre may have a shorter second parabasis towards the end (*Knights* 1264–1315, *Clouds* 1115–1130, *Birds* 1058–1117). After *Birds* the traditional form seems to dissolve fairly rapidly; in *Lysistrata* the division into two mutually hostile choruses until line 1042 necessarily reduces the parabatic element to vanishing-point,[2] and in *Women at the Thesmophoria* lyrics of the kind we would normally associate with the parabasis are postponed until 947–1000 and 1136–1059, leaving the central parabasis (785–845) without any lyrics at all. In *Frogs* the anapaests are transferred to the long complex of songs and recitation performed by the chorus of initiates at its first arrival, and in the two fourth-century plays, *Women in Assembly* and *Wealth*, the parabasis has gone altogether.

Whether the chorus-leader in the recited parts of the parabasis speaks explicitly on behalf of the poet or on behalf of the category of persons or beings portrayed by the chorus, he describes some of what he has to say as 'blame', 'criticism' or 'complaint' against the Athenian people or (e.g. *Frogs* 686f.) as 'good advice' or 'good teaching' (though it

---

2 There is a hint of it in the women's chorus at 648 ('Isn't it my business to give the city some good advice?'), but after the two choruses are united there is a deliberate repudiation of what might have been expected. ('We are not preparing to say a single unkind word of any citizen'.)

must be remembered that *didáskēn*, in addition to 'teach', means 'tell ... how to ...', 'tell ... what to do', 'explain'). A long tradition of the poet as moralist underlies this usage. Many of the archaic poets addressed their poems to their fellow-citizens and were regarded essentially as preachers who chose poetic form in order to promote wisdom, justice and courage; among them Archilokhos, capable of vindictive passion and scurrility as well as of more subdued sentiments, used language and imagery which have much in common with Attic comedy. Modern readers (or some modern readers, at any rate) may be surprised to find that in *Frogs* 1007–1012 the ghosts of Aiskhylos and Euripides, competing before Dionysos for the throne of poetry in the underworld, agree on the principle that a poet should be admired above all for the good effects of his moral teaching on his fellow-citizens.[3] With such a tradition behind him, the comic poet was in a privileged position when he used the parabasis as a medium for offering advice and admonition to the audience, whether he spoke openly *in propria persona* or from some other defined standpoint. We might have expected to find him using this privilege in order to preach directly whatever lesson the rest of the play implies; but this is just what he does *not* do. The parabasis of *Acharnians* is not about war and peace, nor is that of *Knights* about Kleon (who, instead, is attacked in the epirrhema of the parabasis of *Clouds*, a play which otherwise does not mention him). The parabasis of *Wasps* enlarges on an aspect of 'waspishness'—ferocity in battle—which stands to the waspish severity of jurors as the obverse of a coin does to the reverse; the parabasis of *Women at the Thesmophoria* does not criticize Euripides (the main subject of the play), and only marginally defends the character of women (otherwise represented throughout the play in a very unfavourable light), for it is primarily concerned to mock the men for not living up to the standards of integrity and intelligence expected of Athenians. The 'good advice' offered to the community by an Aristophanic parabasis, when it is not extolling the merits of the poet himself at the expense of his rivals, tends always to be advice which is acceptable at the level of popular sentiment, even if not always accepted and put into practice. It is acceptable because of its essentially conciliatory character, promoting that *homónoia*, 'community of mind', which was regarded as strengthening the city

3   Though they are speaking of 'poets' in general in the context of a dispute about *tragic* poetry, it is not impossible that Aristophanes has his tongue in his cheek in making the characters describe as the highest function of poetry that function of *comedy* which he emphasizes in his own parabases.

against external enemies. The clearest example is the least jocular of parabases, *Frogs* 686–705 and 718–737, where a plea is made for the re-enfranchisement of individuals who came from old families with good patriotic records but had been involved, through varying degrees of malice or miscalculation, in the oligarchic revolution of 411; it may well be that popular sentiment was already moving in that direction at the time of *Frogs*, and one of the first reactions to the disastrous Athenian defeat at Aigospotamoi a few months later was a decree of sweeping re-enfranchisement.

Despite the position of moral and intellectual superiority which the poet assumes in a parabasis, his language is in some ways more temperate than that of serious didactic verse (e.g. Kallinos fr. 1, 'When will you be valorous,? Are you not ashamed...?') or of the philosophical writers who blend sorrow and anger in contemplating the ignorance of their fellow-mortals (e.g. Parmenides fr. 6, Empedokles fr. 11). Intemperate abuse of the Athenian citizenry as a whole, excluded from parabases, is admitted in dialogue, where the sudden rupture of illusion is intended to have comic effect. In *Frogs* Dionysos crosses the lake at the edge of the underworld in a boat, while Xanthias has to run round it. When they meet, Dionysos asks Xanthias if he saw the sinners undergoing punishment, of whom Herakles had told them (274–276):

DIONYSOS: Did you see there the parricides and perjurers that he told us about?

XANTHIAS: Why, didn't *you*?

DIONYSOS: I certainly did—(*with a gesture towards the audience*) and I can see them now!

Or again, when Trygaios has returned to earth from his flight to Olympos (*Peace* 821–823):

You were small to look at from up above. *I* thought, from the sky, that you were a really nasty lot; but from here you're much nastier!

PROLOGUES

The parabasis is the most sustained suspension of the dramatic action that occurs regularly in the course of a comedy, but there are two other points at which we may expect to find the personages of the play speaking to us rather than to one another: at the end, to tell us that the play is over, and at the beginning, to explain to us what it is about. The end is sometimes a mere formula: so in *Clouds* 1510f.,

Lead on out; we've done our stint of dancing for today.

The opening scene, however, is anything but a formula. Both tragedy and comedy had several ways of beginning a play: it is possible (as Sophokles shows us) to begin with a dialogue so constructed that the audience is given the greatest possible amount of information about the characters and their situation in the shortest possible time. Alternatively, a play can begin with a soliloquy which, while ostensibly an expression of emotion which the speaker cannot keep to himself, assumes the character of an exposition to the audience. Or again, the pretence of soliloquy can be virtually discarded and a prologue uttered by a deity who in some cases will not appear again in the course of the play; this method is sometimes adopted by Euripides, and except that it does not explicitly recognize our presence by saying 'you' or 'spectators', it comes nearer than anything else to breaking the dramatic illusion which is otherwise the rule in tragedy. Aristophanes shows some ingenuity in conveying the dramatic situation to us in the opening scene. The first eighty lines of *Clouds* are fundamentally an expository prologue, but the dangers of formality and monotony are avoided by beginning with Strepsiades' outburst of emotion, passing to his reading aloud from his account-book, with interruptions from Pheidippides (crying out in his sleep and then momentarily waking) and from the slave when the lamp goes out. Everything is designed to encourage us not to notice that Strepsiades is confiding more and more in *us*, and if by any chance our interest has flagged it is rekindled by his saying (75–77) that he has thought of a way out of his troubles but not actually telling us what it is. In *Knights*, *Wasps*, *Peace* and *Birds* we begin with dialogue and are told the situation by one of the participating characters only after we have been stimulated into trying to infer it for ourselves. Thus at *Knights* 35, after we have seen that the two slaves on stage are contemplating desertion to escape torment at the hands of the 'newly-bought Paphlagonian':

A: Would you like me to explain to the audience what it's all about?
B: Not a bad idea. But let's make one request of them, to make it clear to us by their expressions if they're pleased by the verses and the situation.
A: I'll tell them now, then. We two have a master . . .

—and the exposition takes up thirty-two lines.

The corresponding section of *Peace* is remarkably skilful. One slave, outside the house, is working at a big kneading-trough, apparently kneading bread, but with his head strangely averted from his work. A second slave rushes out of the house-door and cries:

Give me a loaf for the beetle, quick!

As he takes a large brown lump from the other, we realize that the beetle of which he speaks must be one of those sturdy, busy beetles which build and roll along a ball of dung, and the slave at the trough must be up to his elbows in dung. This realization gives rise to a rather disquieting question: how big is a beetle that needs a couple of slaves to keep it fed? Suspense is heightened as the slave from the house runs to and fro with fresh supplies, and at one point (29ff.) the slave from the trough, peeping cautiously through the door, describes how the monster is stuffing itself. Instead of being told outright what the situation is we are deliberately teased (43–63):

> SLAVE A: So by now some young man in the audience, with a good opinion of himself as a critic, will be saying, 'What's this all about? What's the beetle for?' Then an Ionian sitting next to him says, 'Ay think it's an allewsion to Kleon—he's a shit-feeder, and not ashamed of it'.
>
> SLAVE B: Well, I'll go in and give the beetle a drink[4] (*Exit*).
>
> SLAVE A: And I—I'll explain the plot to the boys and the little fellows and the men and the real *men* and all the really, really *top* people here. My master's crazy in a strange way—not the way you are, but a different way, quite strange. All day he looks up at the sky with his mouth open, so, and slangs Zeus and says, 'Zeus, what are you intending? Put down your brush, don't sweep the Greeks away.' Ah! Quiet! I think I can hear his voice.
>
> TRYGAIOS: (*from within*): Zeus, whatever are you going to do to our people? Before you know it you'll have squeezed every country to a pulp.

Not until the next stage of the slave's exposition do we learn that Trygaios has fattened up a dung-beetle in order to fly on its back to heaven and try to make Zeus change the course of events.

THEATRICAL REFERENCES

By contrast with tragedy, the chorus or the characters in a comedy may

---

4 i.e. to urinate. The line has an additional humorous point in that one would normally go out, not in, to urinate; cf. *Peace* 1265f., where the boys come out for that purpose.

at any moment step half out of the dramatic roles which they are sustaining and make an explicit reference to the theatre, the audience, or some other aspect of the festival. It is fair to call this 'rupture of dramatic illusion', and to observe that no such rupture occurs in tragedy, provided that by 'illusion' we do not mean visual ingenuities of production (in which the Greeks had naturally not advanced very far) but simply the uninterrupted concentration of the fictitious personages of the play on their fictitious situation. The comic poet breaks illusion quite deliberately for humorous effect, as, for instance, in *Birds* 445–447. The Hoopoe has there restrained the chorus of birds from killing Peisetairos, and Peisetairos has demanded the security of an oath from the birds, to which the chorus-leader agrees. A common formula in oaths is: 'if I abide by my oath, may my fortune be good in every way, but if I break it, may all evils befall me!' The birds, oath is:

> CHORUS-LEADER: I swear it, as I hope to win first prize with a unanimous verdict of judges and audience.
> PEISETAIROS: That will surely happen!
> CHORUS-LEADER: But if I break my oath, may I win by one judge's verdict only!

—a reference to the judges at the festival in which the play was competing, and nicely turned so as to suggest that a victory by a majority of one is the very worst that Aristophanes can expect. (He was disappointed; *Birds* came second.)

In *Clouds* 323–327, where the chorus of clouds is just about to make its entrance, a reference to the layout of the theatre has considerable comic effect:

> SOCRATES: Look now this way towards Parnes.[5] Now I see them slowly descending.
> STREPSIADES: Where? Tell me! Show me!
> SOCRATES: Here they come, a great host of them, across valleys and thickets, here, at the side!
> STREPSIADES: (*Peering*) What do you mean? I can't see them.
> SOCRATES: (*Exasperated*) *In the wings!*
> STREPSIADES: Ah, now, yes, I can just make them out!

5 If one actually looks towards Mount Parnes from the theatre, the whole bulk of the Akropolis completely blocks the view; we have to regard Socrates as saying something which would naturally be said of approaching clouds at almost any other point in Athens.

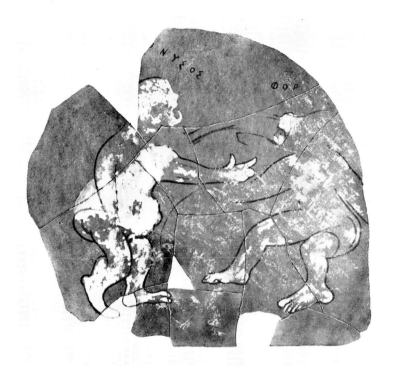

7 Fragments of an Athenian vase, about 400 B.C. (the photograph shows not the original fragments, but a watercolour painting of them, which clarifies the outline of the figures). The person on the left is Dionysos, and the one on the right, Phor[, *may* be Phormion; *if* he is, the vase appears to 'illustrate' Eupolis's *Taksiarkhoi* (cf. p. 217).

8 These dancers dressed as birds are portrayed on a vase over 100 years earlier than Aristophanes' *Birds*. The vase does not 'illustrate' Aristophanes; it demonstrates the antiquity of the 'animal-chorus' characteristic of so many comedies.

9 A modern performance of Aristophanes' *Wasps* at Athens. Philokleon is being encouraged by the chorus to lower himself on a rope from the upper window (cf. p. 125).

SOCRATES: Well, you can certainly see them *now*, unless you've got pumpkins stopping up your eyes!

Similarly, an economic necessity is turned to good account in *Peace* 1019–1022. Prayers have been uttered to Peace, and it looks as if at the next moment a sheep is going to be killed as a sacrifice to her. But the slave says, 'It isn't right' and goes on to explain:

> Peace, I'm sure, takes no pleasure in bloodshed. 'The altar runs not red'.

Trygaios says:

> All right, take the sheep indoors. Sacrifice it there, cut out the thighbones, and bring them out here. That way, the manager saves a sheep!

So the sheep, a live stage-property, lives to be eaten another day, and a cheaper property, old thighbones, is substituted.

Acharnians offers a special and complicated case of rupture of illusion. Within the story which is being enacted, Dikaiopolis has to convince the angry Acharnians that he was justified in making a private peace-treaty. To excite their pity he decides to dress himself in rags, and goes to the house of Euripides to borrow one of the sets of rags in which (according to a repeated allegation in comedy) Euripides liked to present some of his tragic characters. Dikaiopolis explains (377–382):

> I know what happened to *me*—I know what Kleon did to me because of last year's comedy. He dragged me into the council-chamber, slandered me, swamped me with lies ...[6]

Therefore he asks Euripides (414–417):

> By your knees I entreat you, Euripides, give me a rag from that old play of yours. I have to make a long speech to the chorus (*he does not say 'to the Acharnians'*), and it means my death if I don't speak well.

Having got his rags, he goes on to a further request (437–444):

> Euripides, now that you've done me this favour, give me something else that goes with the rags—the little Mysian cap to put on my head.
>
> > 'Today I must be thought a beggar-man,
> > be who I am, but seem not to be so'.

6   On the nature of the feud between Aristophanes and Kleon see pp. 99f.

The audience must know who I am, but the chorus must stand there gawping, so that I can take the mickey out of them with a bit of speechifying,

And when Dikaiopolis finally makes his speech, he addresses it not to the chorus but to the audience (496–505):

Don't be angry with me, you audience, if, although I'm a beggar, I set about speaking of the city before the Athenian people when I'm doing comedy. Even comedy knows what's right, and what I'm going to say may shock you, but it's right. Kleon won't accuse me this time of slandering the city in the presence of foreigners, because we're by ourselves; it's the Lenaian festival, and no foreigners are here yet.

Here it seems to be the individual character (not, as in the parabasis, the chorus) who is speaking on the poet's behalf; possibly we should think rather of Dikaiopolis as the comic 'hero' appearing (like Charlie Chaplin) in many different years under different names and in different situations, but if we do we must not overlook the fact that the verb in the expression I have uneasily translated as 'doing comedy', *trygōidían poōn*, is the verb regularly used of the writer.[7]

The opening scene of *Frogs* exploits rupture of illusion not to expound the situation to the audience (which is done later, in dialogue) but to suggest the poet's superiority to his rivals. The two characters who enter are Dionysos, wearing the lionskin associated with Herakles, and his slave Xanthias, who is riding on a donkey but carrying the luggage slung over his shoulder (not in panniers on the donkey). The play begins (1–18):

XANTHIAS: Am I to say one of the usual things, master, that make the audience laugh?
DIONYSOS: Why, yes, whatever you like—except 'I'm hard-pressed'. Keep off that. It's really very irritating by now.
XANTHIAS: And nothing else smart?
DIONYSOS: Yes, except 'I'm squashed'.
XANTHIAS: (*Eagerly*) Well—can I say the *really* funny bit?
DIONYSOS: Why, yes, don't hesitate. (*As if struck by second thoughts, warningly*) But there's just one thing you must *not* say!
XANTHIAS: (*Crestfallen*) What's that?
DIONYSOS: Shift your load and say that you want a shit!

7   The word is coined from *trýks*, 'lees of wine'.

XANTHIAS: (*Pleading*) Nor this—that seeing that I'm carrying such a burden, if someone doesn't take it away—(*Gleefully*) *I'll fart it off*!
DIONYSOS: Oh, for God's sake, no, except when I want an emetic.
XANTHIAS: What's the point of my carrying all this luggage, then, if I'm not going to do any of the things that Phrynichos and Lykis and Ameipsias do? There's always luggage-carrying in their comedies.
DIONYSOS: Just don't do it! When I'm in the audience and see any of those *coups de théâtre* I leave at the end with a good year on my life.[8]

At the same time as Aristophanes criticises other poets for excremental humour, he takes full advantage of all the vulgar words to raise the same kind of laughter himself.

DISCONTINUITY OF CHARACTERIZATION

One common consequence of the incompleteness of dramatic illusion in comedy is that characters may say things which in real life would draw a puzzled or indignant reply from their interlocutors, or things which they themselves would not even want to say in a situation at all like that which is being enacted as part of the play. When, for example, Kalonike in *Lys.* 112–114 answers the question

> Would you be willing, if I could find some way, to join me in putting an end to the war?

by the enthusiastic answer

> Oh yes, I would indeed, even if I had to pawn my best dress—and drink the proceeds the same day!

she is saying herself what could be realistically represented as:

> KALONIKE: Oh yes, I would indeed, even if I had to pawn my best dress!
> A CYNICAL SPECTATOR: (*Aside*) Huh! If you did that, I bet you'd drink the proceeds the same day!

No one in fact takes any notice of what Kalonike has said; Myrrhine and Lampito continue respectively 'Yes, and so would I, even if...'

---

8 A human being who said this would lay himself open to ridicule, since the dramatic festivals were *annual*, so that between one Dionysia and the next, or one Lenaia and the next, he would necessarily put on a year's age. That it is said by Dionysos gives it a different point: gods did not age.

and 'Yes, and I'd even . . .'. The utterance by a character of words
which someone else might say about him is an important element
throughout *Knights*, where the Paphlagonian slave (Aristophanes'
way of presenting Kleon) takes for granted all the obnoxious features
in his own character which Aristophanes attributed to Kleon, features
to which Kleon himself (or a Paphlagonian slave, if it comes to that)
would have been reluctant to admit. Similarly a character may say
something which in reality would defeat the purpose of his speaking,
and the character to whom it is said may react as he would to a
different utterance.[9] In *Thesm.* 936–938 the old man asks a favour
of the prytanis:

> OLD MAN: Prytanis, I beseech you, by your right hand—which you
> are wont to hold out palm upwards, when anyone offers you money
> —grant me one little favour, though I am doomed to die.
> PRYTANIS: What favour do you want of me?

Sometimes humorous passages isolate themselves as self-contained
jokes which may not arise very naturally out of the preceding dialogue
and may also be dropped at a point where, if by any chance they arose
in a real dialogue, they would be very unlikely to be dropped. When
Strepsiades in *Clouds* 193 has been told by his student-guide that some
students who are bending right over, with their heads to the ground,
are 'investigating Tartaros', he asks:

> Why's their arse pointing up to the sky, then?

Not a very sensible question, for the obvious reply would be 'because
their heads are down to the ground', but it is simply a 'feed' for the
answer:

> It's learning astronomy on its own!

Later, just as Strepsiades is about to enter the school as a pupil, he asks
Socrates (500–502):

> Tell me this, now: if I'm diligent and put my heart into learning,
> which of your pupils shall I become most like?

A curious, artificial question, and a feed for a joke which the Athenians
possibly found funnier than we can (503–504):

9   This technique was taken to extremes by the Marx Brothers; people seldom
react to Groucho's insults except by a fleeting expression of indignation, and it
is often possible to tell how long the script-writer has allowed for the audience's
laughter before the next line is uttered.

SOCRATES: You'll turn into a replica of Khairephon.
STREPSIADES: Oh Lord! I'll be a living corpse!

When Kalonike, near the beginning of *Lysistrata*, asks Lysistrata why she has summoned all the women to a meeting, the dialogue runs thus (23–25):

KALONIKE: What's it all about? (*Literally, 'what is the thing to be done?'* or *'what is the business?'*) How big? (*A normal Greek way of saying 'how important is it?'*)
LYSISTRATA: Big (*i.e. 'important'*).
KALONIKE: Aha! And thick, too?
LYSISTRATA: Yes, very thick.
KALONIKE: Well, why ever aren't we all here, then?
LYSISTRATA: (*Impatient*) That's not how it is at all. (*Bitter*) We'd have lost no time in meeting, if it had been.

'Thick' (*pakhý*) is not an adjective which could normally qualify *prâgma* ('business', 'activity', 'thing to be done') and if a real Kalonike had put such a question Lysistrata could only have asked 'What on earth do you mean?', but Lysistrata is made by the poet to accept the adjective for the sake of the sexual joke.

In *Wasps* 1219–1249 Bdelykleon, preparing his father Philokleon for social life, tests him on the drinking-songs in which guests were expected to play their part after dinner. Suppose, he says, that I'm Kleon, and I sing the first words of the Harmodios song. Philokleon sings as the next verse not the actual words of that song, but words insulting to Kleon. Bdelykleon is horrified; but when he goes on to two other songs, the first imagined as begun by a certain Theoros, and the next by Aiskhines, and Philokleon plays exactly the same trick on both occasions, Bdelykleon allows it to pass without reproof or comment; for Aristophanes does not want to bore us with repetition of the same joke, and he does want to ridicule Theoros and Aiskhines. The whole sequence ends with Bdelykleon commending Philokleon (1249),

Well, you understand *that* pretty well!

for doing precisely what he had told him not to do in the first instance. Bdelykleon steps out of the role of a man trying to turn his reprobate father into an acceptable member of refined society, and becomes for the moment the mouthpiece of the poet inviting us to applaud a joke against a well-known contemporary.

Discontinuity of characterization for humorous purposes has a more positive side: there are times when the participants in a scene seem to enlarge on its humorous possibilities for its own sake. A case in point is *Wasps* 169–195, where Philokleon, confined to the house by Bdelykleon and by the household slaves (who take their orders from Bdelykleon), attempts an absurd means of escape.

PHILOKLEON: (*from within*): I just want to take the donkey and sell it, along with its panniers. It's the first day of the month.
BDELYKLEON: Surely *I* could sell it, couldn't I?
PHILOKLEON: Not like I could.
BDELYKLEON: No, I dare say; I'd do it better.
PHILOKLEON: Well, bring the donkey out, anyway.
XANTHIAS: What an excuse he dangled in front of you—butter wouldn't melt in his mouth!—so that you'd let him come out.
BDELYKLEON: Well, he didn't catch anything that way. I realized the trick he was up to. I think I'll go in and bring the donkey out, so that the old man doesn't even have a chance to peep out again. (*Bdelykleon opens the door and leads out a model donkey on rollers,*[10] *with its panniers; underneath it is Philokleon, hanging on to the panniers like Odysseus escaping from the cave of the Cyclops by hanging underneath a great ram.*) What are you making a fuss about, donkey? Is it because you're going to be sold today? (*This is meant to remind us of the blinded Cyclops asking the ram why it lags behind.*) Get a move on! What are you groaning for? Carrying Odysseus, or something?
XANTHIAS: Why, good God, it *is* carrying someone curled up underneath!
BDELYKLEON: What? Let's see!
XANTHIAS: There!
BDELYKLEON: What ever's this?

We might imagine that Bdelykleon's recognition of his father would follow at once, but the recognition is delayed in order to fit in a joke modelled on the Odysseus story; Odysseus had cunningly told the Cyclops that his name was *Outis*, 'No-man'.

BDELYKLEON: Who on earth are you?
PHILOKLEON: Why, I'm Noman.
BDELYKLEON: Noman? Where from?
PHILOKLEON: From Ithake (*like Odysseus*), son of Runaway. (*Asked*

10 I assume a model rather than a real donkey, for the smooth running of the scene, and I do not know whether the Greeks ever thought of the modern pantomime animal, two men inside an imitation animal-skin.

for his name in full, a Greek would give his own name, his father's name, and his nationality.)

BDELYKLEON: Well, you're a Noman who'll regret it, I can tell you. (*To Xanthias*) Pull him out from underneath! What a louse, getting under there! He's exactly like a summoner's foal (*klētér*, '*summoner*', *was also a slang word for* '*donkey*').

PHILOKLEON: If you don't let me be, we're going to have a fight!

So far, so good; once the grotesquerie of the idea is admitted, the interaction of the characters is realistic. But Bdelykleon's next question is a 'feed' for a humorous answer which the real Philokleon could only give if his anger had wholly evaporated and he were laughing at himself.

BDELYKLEON: Why, what'll you fight us about?

PHILOKLEON: A donkey's shadow.

This was a proverbial expression for an illusory cause of a quarrel. Bdelykleon continues with:

You're a bad old man, well on in trickery and up to anything.

Philokleon takes 'bad' and 'well on' in a different sense, and interprets *parábolos*, 'ready to try anything'[11] as if it were 'past' (*par-*) the age of 'a young animal which has not yet shed its first teeth' (*ábolos*). He turns the point into a joke of a kind which would be made by an amused observer rather than by an angry old man thwarted in his attempts to escape.

PHILOKLEON: Bad, me? No, no, don't you know I'm at my best now? Maybe you'll know it when you've eaten an undercut of old juryman!

Hypogástrion, literally, 'bit under the stomach', carries with it an allusion to his own posture under the donkey, and possibly we are meant to remember that Odysseus would have been eaten by the Cyclops if he had not escaped.

A further example is *Acharnians* 764–796. A Megarian has disguised his daughters as pigs and is trying to sell them to Dikaiopolis. Aristophanes exploits the ambiguities of the word *khôiros*, properly 'young pig' but also in slang, 'cunt'.

11 There are some uncertainties in the interpretation of *parábolos*. The word I have translated 'bad' means, when applied to meat, 'of poor quality', not 'decomposing'.

DIKAIOPOLIS: What have you brought with you?

MEGARIAN: *Khôiroi* for the Mysteries. (*Pigs were the characteristic sacrifice at the Eleusinian Mysteries.*)

DIKAIOPOLIS: That's good! Show me them.

MEGARIAN: They're really lovely. Touch, if you like. See how lovely and fat it is! ('*It*' *here refers to one of the girls.*)

DIKAIOPOLIS: (*Perceiving at once that he is being shown not a pig but a girl wearing trotters and a snout*) Why, what on earth is this?

MEGARIAN: A *khôiros*, of course.

DIKAIOPOLIS: What do you mean? What kind of *khôiros* is this?

MEGARIAN: Megarian. *Isn't* this a *khôiros*?

DIKAIOPOLIS: It doesn't seem so to *me*.

So far Dikaiopolis has taken *khôiros* consistently in the sense 'young pig', and he is simply (and rightly) denying that the girl is a pig. In real life—if we can imagine a trick such as the Megarian's in real life—the next step would be for Dikaiopolis to drive away the Megarian, saying 'Get away with you! Trying to make a fool of me!' But now the Megarian tries to trap Dikaiopolis, by exploiting the anatomical sense of *khôiros* (which I will label *khôiros$_2$*), into admitting that the girl is a pig (*khôiros$_1$*).

MEGARIAN: What an idea! (*Appealing to the audience*). Such a mistrustful man! He says this isn't a *khôiros$_1$*. All right, if you're willing, I'll bet you a bag of thyme-salt that this (*he points between the girl's legs*) is what every Greek calls *khôiros$_2$*.

DIKAIOPOLIS: But it's a human being's! ('*It*' *here* = *khôiros$_2$*).

MEGARIAN: Yes, of course it is, it's mine. Whose do you imagine it is? ('*It*' *here* = *khôiros$_1$*)

The Megarian has won his verbal game, but it is not a game that in real life makes people pay out money for a pig that is no pig. However, Aristophanes does not allow Dikaiopolis to lose patience. The dialogue continues:

MEGARIAN: Would you like to hear them make a noise?

DIKAIOPOLIS: Indeed I would.

MEGARIAN: (*To one of the girls*) Quick, speak up, piggy! (*Hisses threateningly in her ear*) You don't want to? Struck dumb, damn you? I swear I'll take you back home again!

GIRL: (*Frightened by his threat, because home means starvation*) Eek! Eek!

MEGARIAN: Well, is it a *khôiros$_1$*?

A squeak is hardly enough to convince a shrewd Attic farmer that the girl is a pig after all, but now Dikaiopolis enters, as it were, into the spirit of the game. He accepts the girls as pigs for the simple reason that if he did not a series of jokes which depend on his acceptance could not be made. At the same time, some of the things he says about the 'pigs', and some of the Megarian's answers, take their point solely from play on the other sense of *khôîros*.

DIKAIOPOLIS: Now it *does* seem to be a *khôîros*. But when it's grown up it'll be a twat! (*The second sentence only makes sense if* khôîros *in the first sentence is taken in retrospect as* khôîros$_2$; *but that first sentence was an answer to the question,* 'Is it khôîros$_1$?'.)
MEGARIAN: In five years, I can tell you, it'll be exactly like its mother.
DIKAIOPOLIS: But this one isn't fit for sacrifice!
MEGARIAN: What do you mean? How isn't it fit for sacrifice?
DIKAIOPOLIS: It hasn't got a tail. (*A sacrificial victim could not, as a rule be a deficient or deformed animal.*)
MEGARIAN: That's because it's young. When it's a bit older it'll have a big, thick, red one (*i.e. its mate's penis*) If you want one to bring up (*as opposed to an animal to be eaten young*), this one (*pointing to the other girl, as a seller of real animals would*) is a lovely *khôîros*.
DIKAIOPOLIS: (*Having inspected the other girl*) Its twat's absolutely the twin of the other!
MEGARIAN: Yes, because they have the same mother and they're from the same sire. But if it fattens up a bit and gets a covering of hair it'll be a really lovely *khôîros* to sacrifice to Aphrodite.
DIKAIOPOLIS: But a *khôîros* isn't sacrificed to Aphrodite. (*There were several deities to whom pigs were not sacrificed.*)
MEGARIAN: Not a *khôîros* to Aphrodite? Why, *only* to her! (Khôîros$_2$, *and metaphorical 'sacrifice', for Aphrodite was the deity who presided over sexual pleasure, and* khôîros$_1$ *was certainly sacrificed to some other deities.*) And the flesh of these *khôîroi* is absolutely delicious when it's skewered on a spit (*i.e. penetrated by the penis*).

For the rest of the scene the 'pigs' are accepted as pigs, and the play on words is dropped. While it was going on, the progression of the comic story, the selling of disguised girls by a Megarian to Dikaiopolis, was virtually suspended, and the two characters exploited to the limit the humorous possibilities offered by the ambiguity of *khôîros*.

V

Structure and Style

CONTEST AND EPISODES

In *Acharnians* the essential issue, Dikaiopolis's achievement of his private peace and his success in persuading the Chorus to agree with him, is settled halfway through the play; that is to say, the crisis of the play is located not at or near the end, but before the parabasis, and all that follows the parabasis (*a*) illustrates the consequences of the settlement of the issue and (*b*) at the end, pushes the consequences to the point of a noisy triumph without introducing any significant element of surprise or suspense. Each of the first four illustrative episodes brings on new characters who serve a purpose in relation to that episode only: first, the Megarian and an informer; second, the Theban and another informer (named as Nikarkhos); third, a farmer from the Parnes foothills; fourth, a messenger from a bridegroom. The two remaining episodes involve Lamakhos, whom we have met earlier in the play. This pattern, crisis—parabasis—illustrative episodes, recurs in *Peace*, where the plot leaves no room for any genuinely new development in the second half of the play, and in *Birds*, where the issue settled is the building of the birds' city but we still wait to see *how* the gods will be made to surrender and what extent of the birds' victory over them will be. In *Women in Assembly* and *Wealth*, although there is no parabasis to serve as the hinge of the play, it remains true that the latter part of the play illustrates, with the help of new characters in self-contained scenes, the consequences of the resolution of crisis to which the earlier part builds up. *Wasps* is a little different in so far as the resolution is essentially negative, and the appearance of new characters (the people assaulted by Philokleon) of subordinate importance.

Both in these plays and in most of the remainder, which have their crisis much nearer the end, Aristophanes utilizes for the resolution of an issue (whether *the* issue of the play or a subordinate issue) a formal structure which admits of subdivision and classification in rather the same manner as the parabasis (cf. p. 49). A scene which has this structure is commonly designated nowadays by the Greek term *agṓn*, but there is no very good reason for not calling it by the English term 'contest'. The full structure of the contest can be seen twice in *Clouds*, in the argument between Right and Wrong and in the later argument between Strepsiades and Pheidippides about the treatment of parents, and in the first of the series of contests between Aiskhylos and Euripides in *Frogs*. Its ingredients are:

(i) The two contestants enter, quarrelling.

(ii) The chorus sings a lyric stanza, which despite its often elaborate language is a sort of introduction of the contestants 'from the chair'.

(iii) The chorus addresses to one of the contestants two lines, in the same metre as that contestant will use for his speech, exhorting him to state his case.

(iv) The first contestant speaks, normally with interruptions from the other and sometimes, if a third character is present, with comments and asides from that character.

(v) The end of the contestant's speech is in the same rhythm as the body of the speech but in shorter and more loosely organized metrical units than the equal and regular lines of the speech.

(vi) The chorus sings a lyric stanza responding to (ii) and serving as a comment on the performance of the first contestant.

(vii), (viii) and (ix) serve the same function as (iii), (iv) and (v), but all in relation to the second contestant, who may use a different metre from the first contestant.

The plot does not always allow the chorus to act as an impartial chairman in a contest of this kind; in *Wasps*, for example, the chorus hopes that Philokleon will win, but to make the contest possible it has to agree to treatment of the issue in rational terms, and in *Lysistrata* the Proboulos is supported in his contest with Lysistrata by the men's chorus while the women's chorus naturally supports Lysistrata. In *Knights* the chorus supports the Sausage-seller against the Paphlagonian, and instead of a formal speech by one contestant balancing a formal speech by the other we have in effect a pair of quarrelsome dialogues. Although all such contests may be called 'rational', in so far as they are composed of coherent words and not of stone-throwing and cries, and one contestant may persuade the chorus that he is right (as Bdelykleon does in *Wasps*), the arguments used are as unequal in their cogency or intellectual honesty as those of a speaker in a lawcourt, and it is not normally to be expected that either of the contestants should admit to the error of his former ways. The contest may indeed end with vulgar abuse from the victor and expressions of rage and indignation from the vanquished; thus, for example, Poverty in *Wealth* is defeated in her attempts to persuade Khremylos and his friend Blepsidemos of her own importance and of the evil consequences of a universal distribution of wealth (598–600, 608–612):

> KHREMYLOS: Anyway, get lost, and don't you murmur another syllable. You're not going to win the argument, even if you convince me.
>
> . . .
>
> POVERTY: The day will come, let me tell you, when you'll send for me to come back.
> KHREMYLOS: *Then*, you'll come back; but *now*, get lost. It's better for me to be a rich man, and your heart can bleed for all it's worth.

Although the elements of the structured contest exist in *Wealth*, they happen to be absent from the earliest extant play, *Acharnians*, where Dikaiopolis's persuasion of the chorus follows quite different lines. The structure may have been developed before Aristophanes, but it is difficult to be sure about this when we do not have his first two plays; his very first play, *Babylonians*, certainly contained some kind of contest between a moral and an immoral young man, which he himself regarded as similar in character to the contest between Right and Wrong in *Clouds*. We can at any rate observe the influence of the contest-form on scenes which are not strictly speaking contests at all, but expositions by a character to a listener who is at times incredulous or critical but is not positively pressing a rival view; Peisetairos's exposition in *Birds* contains all the ingredients (ii)–(ix) listed above, but he plays the roles of both 'contestants', (viii)–(ix) serving to explain what follows from what he has said in (iv)–(v).

LYRIC STANZAS

In addition to the circumstances already mentioned, stanzas of lyric poetry sung to music occur between episodes or between major sections of longer scenes. They are normally sung by the chorus, but sometimes by leading characters, and a stanza broken up into lyric dialogue between chorus and character is not unknown. The last two plays, *Women in Assembly* and *Wealth*, show a departure from fifth-century practice in that some of their lyrics were not included in the written text which went into circulation and may therefore not have been composed by Aristophanes himself; the transmitted text indicates by the one word *khorô* ('of the chorus') the points at which such lyrics would have been sung on the occasion of performance, and with the decreasing importance of the chorus later in the fourth century this indication became standard practice.

As will have been gathered from references in earlier chapters, the forms of Greek verse were not patterns of stress but patterns of quantity, any given syllable being treated as 'long' or 'short'. If we jumbled in a hat half a dozen tokens representing long syllables and another half dozen representing short syllables, and then laid them out in the random order in which we removed them from the hat, it would be possible to ask whether the resulting pattern is a *known* Greek verse-form, and possible to answer this question from a survey of all extant Greek poetry; but it would not make sense to ask whether the result was a *possible* Greek verse-form, for no one can say of any pattern that it *could* not occur in Greek poetry. However, most lyric passages of Aristophanes are composed of patterns which are common, some of them very common, in comedy and tragedy alike.[1] Even a stanza comprising a dozen different types of verse subsumable under two or more main rhythmic genera is likely to have a structure which recurs in other plays: for example, three verses of the form — ᴗ — ᴗᴗ — ᴗ — rounded off by its 'clausular' or 'catalectic' form — ᴗ — ᴗᴗ — —, then a run of the rhythm — ᴗᴗ — ᴗᴗ . . ., then four verses of the form — ᴗᴗ — ᴗ — ᴗ — (a simple variant on — ᴗ — ᴗᴗ — ᴗ —) rounded off by its catalectic form — ᴗᴗ — ᴗ — —. Lyric passages which do not conform to familiar patterns and structures may not be susceptible of an entirely uncontroversial 'metrical analysis', but an attempt at analysis is not a mere academic exercise; it is an attempt to answer an aesthetic question by re-creating the rhythmical design of the passage as the poet conceived it.[2]

---

1 This does not mean that there are no metrical differences between tragedy and comedy; for example, the 'dochmiac' metre, common in tragedy at moments of high emotion, is used in comedy almost entirely for parodic effect, (for the exception, see p. 172), and extensive runs of pure 'cretic' (— ᴗ —) or 'paeonic' (— ᴗ ᴗ ᴗ) rhythm are peculiar to comedy.

2 *Lys.* and *Thesm.* present more serious and more numerous problems of metrical analysis than the remaining plays.

Many lyrics consist of a pair of stanzas in 'responsion'; that is to say, the pattern of the first stanza (the 'strophe') is exactly repeated in the second (the 'antistrophe'). The antistrophe need not follow the strophe immediately, but may be separated from it by a substantial passage of dialogue; thus in *Knights* 303–408 the strophe 303–313 finds its responding antistrophe in 383–390 and the strophe 322–334 its antistrophe in 397–408. The same principle of response applies when the stanza is divided between chorus and character; so *Acharnians* 1008–1017 is a strophe to which 1037–1046 responds:

CHORUS: I envy you your wisdom
              and even more the feasting,
              my friend, which you enjoy.
DIKAIOPOLIS: What will you say, then, when you see
              the thrushes being roasted?
CHORUS: That promise too I welcome.
DIKAIOPOLIS: (*To a slave*) Stir up the fire!
CHORUS: You hear how like a *cordon bleu*,
              a banqueteer,
              he serves his appetite?

(Then, after Dikaiopolis has turned away a farmer who had implored his help)

CHORUS: By making peace he's managed
              to get his wish, and no one,
              it seems, will have a share.
DIKAIOPOLIS: (*To a slave*) Pour the honey on the sausage,
              and fry the cuttle-fish.
CHORUS: You hear those proclamations?
DIKAIOPOLIS: (*To slaves*) Roast the eels!
CHORUS: You'll slay me with that hungry smell,
              the neighbours too,
              with your Do this, Do that.

Occasionally response on a larger scale produces something like a poem written in short stanzas: sets of four are to be found in *Ach.* 836–859 and *Frogs* 814–829, and in *Frogs* 417–443 we have no less than eight very short stanzas in responsion, of which the last three are dialogue, and the set is introduced by a stanza which is almost, but not quite, identical in metre. There is some evidence that a limited range of abnormalities unacceptable in tragedy was accepted in comic responsion, there are, at any rate, some cases, well distributed over the first nine of Aristophanes' plays, in which *n* units in one verse may respond to *n*–1 in the equivalent verse of the antistrophe, and in all these cases neither the grammar nor the sense justifies emendation.

The language of Aristophanes' lyrics may sometimes be indistinguishable, in its majestic compound words with heroic and religious associations, from the language of the serious lyrics of tragedy; the strophe and antistrophe sung by the clouds, before they come into sight, in *Clouds* 275–290 and 298–313, are the most impressive example, 'Eternal Clouds, let us arise . . .' and 'Maidens who bear the rain, let us go . . .'. More often the vocabulary and ideas of lyric passages are closely akin to those of comic dialogue, but the expression is more concentrated. Just as a passage of dialogue may lead to a humorous climax which is not completed until the last word or phrase of the passage, so the 'punch' of a lyric stanza may be delayed until the very last word. Thus in *Frogs* 534–541 the Chorus, complimenting Dionysos on his change of disguise with Xanthias, uses the analogy of a man experienced in sea-travel who knows which side of the ship to go to in bad weather; the song ends:

> A change of course
> into a comfortable berth
> takes a really clever man,
> by nature a Theramenes.

Theramenes, to whom other allusions are made in *Frogs*, had managed in 411 to emerge in safety from the collapse of the oligarchic revolution, having ditched his friends, and in 406 he again displayed a remarkable capacity for self-preservation when he successfully evaded the blame for failure to carry out an order to rescue men clinging to wreckage after a sea-battle and turned the Athenians' anger against the generals who had given the order. In this song, the listener might have begun to suspect how it would end, but in some songs the very last word can produce an unexpected twist. In *Ach.* 1150–1161 the Chorus has pronounced an elaborate curse against a certain Antimakhos, and in the antistrophe (1162–1173) a second curse is expressed thus:

> That's one curse on him; now for another, by night.
> I hope that on his homeward way from riding,
> sweating with fever, a crazy drunken footpad
> will crack him on the head;
> and, looking for a stone to throw, in darkness

his fingers close on a new-shitten turd;
he'll charge and shoot his bolt,
and miss,
and hit
Kratinos.

PARODY

Comedy, alone of Greek literary genres, combines all the registers of
Greek utterance which are known to us: at one extreme a solemnity
evocative of heroic warfare and gorgeous processionals, at the other
a vulgarity inadmissible in polite intercourse. The predominant register
of dialogue is common to comedy, prose literature and documents; but
even comic dialogue is poetry, and the comic poet does not deny himself the freedom of all poets to play with language. A special way of
doing this is the concoction of large compound words, to which the
Greek language lends itself very readily; when Philokleon (*Wasps* 1357),
complaining of his son's meanness, calls him *kymīnopristokardamoglýphos*,
the word is easily dismantled and understood as 'a man who is so mean
that he saws cummin-seed in half and carves bits off cress', and the
giant word in the closing song of *Ass.* (1169–1174), containing twenty-
six components each of which denotes a dish to be served at a feast, is no
harder to understand than the equivalent list of twenty-six words
would have been. At other times, however, a word is created to fit a
context and would not be intelligible in isolation. When Strepsiades
has been told (*Clouds* 156–164) of Socrates' explanation of how a gnat
buzzes through its lower bowel, he congratulates him (166) on his
dientéreuma, 'going through the gut', modelled on *énteron*, 'gut' and
words with the prefix *dia-* in the sense 'thorough', 'from end to end'.
Verbal allusions of this kind tax the translator's ingenuity, but fortunately many of them are designed for contexts in which the humour is
derived from excretion or sex, and these are fields in which modern
languages have a very large vocabulary. In *Birds* 65–68, when the two
Athenians have been frightened out of their wits by the apparition of
the hoopoe's slave, they swear that they are birds, not men, and the
slave asks them what kind of birds they are.

EUELPIDES: I? I'm a *hypodediɔ́s*, an African bird.
SLAVE: Nonsense!
EUELPIDES: Well, ask what's at my feet! (*Fear relaxed his bowels*).
SLAVE: And he—what bird is he? (*To Peisetairos*) Go on, tell me!
PEISETAIROS: I'm an *epikekhodɔ́s* pheasant.

Hypodediṓs means literally 'a bit afraid', and *epikekhodṓs* 'having shat on . . .' (as so often, the vulgar word is climactic, the second of a pair or the third of a trio). We might translate 'trembrel' and 'shittern', if we could rely on readers who had heard of whimbrels and bitterns. In *Knights* 1391f. old Demos, presented with a thirty-year peace treaty personified as beautiful young women reacts like any lusty Athenian to a personified female abstraction in comedy and asks:

Do tell me—is it all right for me to *katatriākontōtísai* them?

—literally 'to thirty-yearize down them'; it is one of those cases where, given the context, *any* word which occupies the space in 'can I . . . them?' will be taken in the sense 'fuck', and we might translate (e.g.) 'can I slip them a good long armistice?'

But comic confections of this kind are less conspicuous than the use of language deliberately taken from serious poetry or from technical literature. All such usage is conveniently, though perhaps a little misleading, brought under the general heading of 'parody', and a very large part of parody is 'paratragedy', since contemporary tragedy was its most obvious source. Parody has two quite distinct purposes, which may be realized simultaneously but can also be realized in isolation from each other. One purpose is to hold up the serious poetry itself to criticism and ridicule; parody suggests, by selection and exaggeration, (e.g.) '*this* is what Euripides is like'. That kind of parody is to be found in the latter part of *Frogs*, where Aiskhylos and Euripides produce grotesque but very funny parodies of each other's lyrics, and in the first scene of *Thesm.*, where the fact that we no longer possess the tragedies of Agathon does not prevent us from seeing that the lyrics which Aristophanes puts into Agathon's mouth must be a linguistic and metrical parody of that poet's tragic style.[3] The second, and commoner, purpose of parody is to exploit the humorous potentialities of incongruity by combining high-flown tragic diction and allusions to well-known tragic situations with vulgarity or trivial domestic predicaments. The effect of incongruity may be achieved by a word or

3 By far the best modern parallel known to me is Anthony Lover's short film *De Düva* (1968), in which motifs from *The Seventh Seal* and *Wild Strawberries*, with dialogue in mock-Swedish, are used to parody Ingmar Bergman. For modern taste, as for Aristophanes, parody has to be kept short, or at least (as in Stella Gibbons' *Cold Comfort Farm*) divided into discontinuous portions. Fielding's *The Tragedy of Tragedies, or the Life and Deaths of Tom Thumb the Great*, which is parody on the grand scale, depends for much of its effect on incongruities.

two, as in *Clouds* 30, where Strepsiades, having discovered from his account-book that he owes Pasias twelve minae, turns back to the book and asks himself:

atàr tí khréos ébā me metà tòn Pāsíān?

If we took this a word at a time, we could restore the phonology of ordinary speech by changing *khréos* to *khréɔs* and *ébā* (admissible in Attic only in lyrics) to *ébē*, giving the sense 'But what debt came to me after Pasias?' But in tragic language *khréos*, unlike the ordinary word *khréɔs*, can mean 'thing', 'requirement', 'involvement', and *tí khréos* is little more than a tragic expression for 'what?'; and although in tragedy one could say (as here, *ébā me*) 'came me' for 'came to me', prose or comic dialogue would require the preposition. The word-group *tí khréos ébā me* thus has intense tragic colouring, creating the maximum of incongruity in the context of a farmer reckoning up his debts. A more spectacular incongruity in a more extended context occurs in *Lysistrata* 706–719, where Lysistrata is having some difficulty in making all the women of Athens keep their oath to abjure sex:

CHORUS-LEADER: Queen of our great design and enterprise,
                tell me, why hast thou come so frowning forth?
LYSISTRATA: The female heart and deeds of evil women
                cause me to walk despondent up and down.
CHORUS-LEADER: What say'st thou?
LYSISTRATA: Truth! Truth!
CHORUS-LEADER: What is amiss? Tell it to us who love thee.
LYSISTRATA: 'Tis shame to speak and grievous to be silent.
CHORUS-LEADER: Do not, I beg, conceal the ill we suffer.
LYSISTRATA: We need a fuck. Such is my tale in brief.
CHORUS-LEADER: Ah! Zeus!
LYSISTRATA: Cry'st thou on Zeus? Anyway, that's how it is. So I can't keep them any longer away from their men. They're slipping off in all directions.

When Trygaios in *Peace* is seen rising into the air on his beetle, one of his children addresses him in dactylic rhythm, he replies in the same rhythm, and the two of them conduct a dialogue of question and answer in high tragic style (124–153) with beautifully-timed lapses into comedy, e.g.

(127f.)   What is thy purpose, that thou tak'st the reins
            and rid'st a beetle to the heavens, pa?
                  · · ·

(136f.)   Shouldst thou not ride on wingéd Pegasos?
          The gods would think it more like tragedy.

Such use of tragic poetry to create humorous incongruity is a kind of
'devaluation' of tragedy,[4] and akin to the depiction of gods, politicians
and intellectuals in degrading situations (cf. pp. 32ff.). But in recognizing
that it has this effect, whether we like it or not, it would be unreasonable
to suppose that the effect was always Aristophanes' primary intention.
The temptation to make use of some recent and spectacular tragedy
which had become a talking-point must often have been irresistible
to a comic poet, even if he himself had been impressed and moved by
the tragedy in question, and I would be inclined to accept at their surface value (which is high enough, in all conscience) the parodies of
Euripides' *Helen* and *Andromeda* in *Thesm.* 846–928 and 1017–1135. In
the latter passage the Old Man, who attended the festival Thesmophoria disguised as a woman, has been detected, arrested, and imprisoned in the portable stocks, guarded by a policeman (who, like all
the police at Athens, is a 'barbarian', a public slave of Scythian origin).
Euripides comes to rescue him, playing the part of Perseus, while the
Old Man plays the part of Andromeda, who was chained to a rock but
saved by Perseus before she could be devoured by a sea-monster. The
parody is highly topical, since the tragedy had been first performed the
year before. The Old Man begins his lament:

> Maidens, my dearest maidens,
> could I but escape,
> unseen by the Scythian!

Then he addresses the echo which Euripides had introduced into the
original scene:

> Do you hear me, O voice that respond in the caves?
> Give your consent, allow me
> to go home to my wife.

The first, second and fourth lines belong wholly to the tragedy (indeed,
'maidens' and 'caves' are no part of the Old Man's predicament), the
third and sixth wholly to the comedy, and the fifth is an adaption of
the original:

4   In *Birds* 786–789 (cf. p. 146) the chorus suggests that an audience might find
tragedy tedious but be glad to return to the theatre for comedy. Kratinos fr. 306,
the opening words of a comedy in which the audience is told to wake up and
'clear its eyes of the rubbish of ephemeral poets', *may* be a similar joke.

> Cease your voice, allow me
> my fill of lamentation with my friends.

When in the parabasis of *Birds* the chorus expounds the origins of the universe and the hatching of the first birds from the union of Eros and Chaos, a certain devaluation of poems such as Hesiod's *Theogony* and later prose theogonies is necessarily involved, in so far as if we can laugh at X, and X resembles Y, it is difficult thereafter to take Y quite as seriously as we used to: but it would be wrong to imagine that Aristophanes' primary purpose is to ridicule theogonies. The humour lies in the adaptation of a familiar literary form to a novel purpose, and the effect is heightened by exaggeration of the style of the original (687f., 693):

> Wingless creatures of a day, luckless wights, men like unto dreams, attend to us . . .
> In the beginning there was Chaos and Night and black Erebos and broad Tartaros . . .

Parody of non-dramatic poetry is rare in comedy, since its greatest practitioners were long since dead, but one particular type of doggerel was a very vulnerable target for ridicule. This was the oracles, cast in the metre and language of heroic poetry, which existed both in oral tradition and in (commonly private) collections, often attributed to allegedly inspired figures of the past. From the manner in which Aristophanes ridicules them it is a fair inference that they were sometimes used by interested parties in debates about national policy, and Thucydides viii 1.1 mentions 'seers and reciters of oracles' among those who had filled the Athenians with high hopes at the time of the despatch of the Sicilian expedition. In *Peace* 1043–1126 Trygaios's sacrifice to Peace is interrupted by the arrival of a certain Hierokles, who soon begins to spout menacing oracles in the riddling style characteristic of the genre. Trygaios replies in the same metre, e.g. 1075–1079a:

> HIEROKLES: 'Not yet is 't pleasing to the blessed gods
>   t' abate the moil, till wolf take sheep to wife.'
> TRYGAIOS: And how the hell can wolf take sheep to wife?
> HIEROKLES: 'As the gas-beetle flees and farts his worst,
>   and the bell-finch in haste hatches blind chicks,
>   then 'twere not yet the hour that peace be made'.

The fundamentally irreverent attitude displayed in the parodying of oracles extends to the adaptation for humorous purposes, sometimes obscene, of formulae associated with religious ritual.

In Aristophanes' time a number of technical languages were in process of development: first, perhaps, in architecture and administration (both commonly overlooked in modern discussions of the growth of philosophical and scientific language, since the relevant evidence is epigraphic and not literary), then in medicine, intellectual speculation in general, and—more fluid and more idiosyncratic than the rest—literary and rhetorical criticism. Much of the striking imagery used in *Frogs* with reference to tragic poetry may be parodic in character, based on the terminology currently in fashion among connoisseurs of the theatre. A brief passage in *Knights* (1377–1380) satirizes the creation of new words in *-ikós* (our *-ic* and hybrid *-ical*) by young men discussing the style of a political orator, and in *Clouds* 327f. Socrates uses a series of abstract nouns in *-sis* to denote processes of intellectual apprehension and discussion. It would be wrong to suggest, however, that all the words and word-formatives which occur in Aristophanes but are alien to unspecialized prose must be either comic confection or parody and in either case humorous. Linguistic enterprise is characteristic of the fifth century as a whole, and much of the colour in Aristophanes' language is best explained by the assumption that the comic poet, no less than practitioners of other literary genres, was inventive, subtle and sensitive to combinations of associations.[5]

5 Such forensic and political oratory as survives from the fifth century strongly suggests that conventional distinctions between 'prose' and 'poetic' vocabulary were less rigidly maintained than in the fourth, and also that greater experimentation with word-formation was acceptable then than later. See my article 'Lo Stile di Aristofane', *Quaderini Urbinati di Cultura Classica* ix (1970), 7–23.

VI

Acharnians

Produced in 425, at the Lenaia, and awarded first prize

SYNOPSIS

The Peloponnesian War has lasted for nearly six years, and during that time the population of Attica has been concentrated within the perimeter of Athens, Peiraieus and the walls connecting the two. Their farms have been burned and their vines and olive-trees cut down by invading Peloponnesian armies each summer; but control of the seas and the coasts by Athenian naval power has not been impaired or even effectively challenged. In this situation an Athenian farmer, Dikaiopolis, has decided that he would rather be at peace than at war, and he has come to the assembly to make as much fuss as he can. He gets no comfort from the proceedings of the assembly. A certain Amphitheos, who declares himself immortal and of divine ancestry, announces that the gods have given him the job of making peace between Athens and Sparta; he is at once removed from the assembly by the police, and the assembly shows itself interested only in how to increase the scale of the war. An Athenian embassy sent to Persia twelve years earlier, with a stipend of two drachmai a day for each member, brings back an envoy ('the King's Eye') from the King of Persia and a promise (to which the envoy's pidgin-Greek gives the lie) of gold; Dikaiopolis, outraged, pretends to expose the envoy and his attendant eunuchs as Athenian impostors.[1] Another Athenian, Theoros, returns from a Thracian

---

1 It is not necessary to believe that a particular embassy to Persia is satirized in this scene, still less that one had actually been sent in 437 and had only just returned. The possibility of getting money from the King of Persia was seriously considered by both sides, but it is in keeping with Dikaiopolis's attitude that he should regard any exploration of this possibility as a misdirected waste of public money, profiting only those who were sent as ambassadors. The passage also exploits humorously the vast scale of the Persian Empire and the stories about it propagated in Herodotos.

king with an army of mercenaries—who demonstrate, by stealing Dikaiopolis's lunch, that their only interest is in plunder. But in the meantime Dikaiopolis has commissioned Amphitheos to go off to Sparta and get him a peace-treaty on a purely private basis. Getting no satisfaction from the assembly, Dikaiopolis declares that he has felt a drop of rain; this is a 'sign from heaven' that continuation of the meeting is inauspicious, and it is accordingly adjourned. Now Amphitheos returns with sample treaties (*spondái* ; cf. pp. 45f.); Dikaiopolis chooses the thirty-year treaty and goes off to his farm with the intention of celebrating the Rural Dionysia. Amphitheos runs off to escape pursuit by the old men of Akharnai, who have got wind of him on his way here; Akharnai, a thickly populated area north of Athens, had suffered particularly heavy damage in the first Peloponnesian invasion, and the Acharnians were for that reason determined to fight a war of revenge to a successful conclusion.

Dikaiopolis goes into a door in the skene (202), which thereupon represents his farm; up to that point, we had to imagine the scene as the Pnyx, where the assembly met in Athens, and the skene did not represent anything. The chorus of old Acharnians now arrives, singing an angry song, exhorting one another to the pursuit, lamenting the years which have made them slow, threatening the man who has dared to make peace. They hear Dikaiopolis calling, inside his house, for silence, and they back to one side. Out comes Dikaiopolis, organizing his household in a celebration of the Rural Dionysia; his daughter carries the basket of offerings, a slave carries the big model phallos, his wife watches from the roof, and he himself utters a prayer to Dionysos and a happy song to Phales. Suddenly the chorus attacks, stoning him.[2] The procession is broken up and the family flees indoors. Dikaiopolis does his best to keep the Acharnians at bay with argument, but this only angers them more; suddenly he turns the tables on them by producing a charcoal-basket which he threatens to 'kill' if they harm him. Charcoal-burning is one of the characteristic activities of Akharnai, so that the basket is the 'fellow-demesman' (334) of the Chorus; the threat to kill it is a parody of Euripides' *Telephos*, in which Telephos secured a hearing by seizing the infant son of Agamemnon as a hostage (cf. p. 164, on *Thesm.*).

2 According to tradition, some individuals whose impiety or treachery was felt too monstrous for ordinary execution had been stoned to death; cf. Demosthenes xviii 204 on a certain Kyrsilos, who had advocated surrender to the Persians in 480.

Now the chorus has to agree to hear Dikaiopolis's case, but first he wants to dress up as a beggar, to exploit their compassion. This too is parody of *Telephos*, and Dikaiopolis visits Euripides to borrow the beggar's rags in which Telephos had appeared in the play. Euripides is rolled out of the house on the trolley which was used in tragedy to reveal interior scenes, and Dikaiopolis, adopting the tone of a wheedling, importunate beggar, secures from Euripides' store of 'properties' the complete rig-out of the disguised Telephos. So dressed, he delivers to the chorus a long speech in which he suggests that the war was begun for no good reason and that he has done the sensible thing in opting out of it; the speech combines parody of Euripides with parody of Herodotos and with a good deal of comic rhetoric. Half the chorus is convinced, the other half incensed; the two halves are on the point of coming to blows, when a new character appears—Lamakhos, invoked by the belligerent half-chorus. Lamakhos was a man who had made a name for himself as an elected general,[3] and therefore a man who stood to gain by continuation and enlargement of the war. Dikaiopolis makes a fool of him, pretending to be frightened to death, then switching to coarse mockery, then fiercely indignant, and indignant on the chorus's behalf; people like Lamakhos get good jobs and high pay all over the place, but when have these decent, hard-working old Acharnians ever been sent on embassies? Considering how many Athenian generals were killed in action (as Lamakhos was, eleven years later), and considering that it is prudent to appoint to embassies those who will do the job best rather than those who could do with the money, the argument is senseless, but (like many senseless arguments) it works. Lamakhos is defeated and the whole Chorus is convinced.

The parabasis follows, the issue between hero and chorus being now resolved, and after the parabasis come two scenes illustrating the consequences of Dikaiopolis's creation of a private market in which he will trade with enemy nations. In the first scene a Megarian comes to sell his daughters, whom he disguises as piglets. Megara, Attica's small western neighbour, had been very hard hit by the war, but there is no suggestion in the play that it was not humane to hit so hard; cheerful and self-satisfied humour is extracted from the desperate hunger

---

3 We should not imagine Lamakhos as the red-faced white-moustached 'colonel' of modern mythology; Dikaiopolis calls him a young man (601), and we should think of him as the kind of man who becomes a divisional commander before he is forty.

(751–763, 797–810) to which father and children have been reduced,[4] and when an informer comes to make trouble about the presence of enemy goods on Attic soil Dikaiopolis drives him away for inter- ference with *his* well-being, not with the Megarian's. In the second scene a Theban comes laden with all the good things to eat that Boeotia produces. He is in quite a different position from the Megarian, and cannot offhand think of anything he wants from Attica. Dikaiopolis has the bright idea of selling him an informer, a characteristic Attic product, and one such (named as Nikarkhos) arrives opportunely; he is packed up in shavings, like a vase, and exported to Boeotia.

Time has flown by; earlier in the play we saw Dikaiopolis cele- brating the Rural Dionysia, and now it is time for another festival, the Anthesteria. Lamakhos sends Dikaiopolis some money for delicacies, but his messenger is sent away empty-handed. A farmer whose oxen have been taken by a Boeotian raiding party comes to beg for 'a drop of peace', but gets none; Dikaiopolis does not propose to share with his benighted fellow-citizens the advantages he has gained by his private initiative. A messenger from a newly-married bridegroom is similarly rejected, but a messenger from the bride, who comes with him, fares better; the bride 'doesn't deserve to suffer from the war' (1062),[5] and Dikaiopolis gives her peace in the form of an ointment which (as if it had magical properties) she can put on her husband's penis to keep him safe from call-up.

Now a messenger comes for Lamakhos, bringing an order from the board of generals; he is to watch the passes over Parnes in the snow and guard against Boeotian raiders. A second messenger summons Dikaio- polis to a feast with the priest of Dionysos. The luckless and the lucky make their preparations simultaneously; Lamakhos's slave brings out the accoutrements of war, Dikaiopolis's brings out delicacies for a great hamper. Both go off their very different ways. After a choral interlude, we see them return: Lamakhos wounded and limping, supported by his slaves, Dikaiopolis drunk, randy and hilarious, supported by two girls. Lamakhos is taken off in one direction to the surgery, and the

4 The only reference in comedy to the Athenian massacre and enslavement of the inhabitants of Melos in 416 is *Birds* 186, where Peisetairos promises the hoopoe that the birds will 'destroy the gods with a Melian hunger', i.e. starve them out.
5 The text says *tô polémō t' ouk aksíā*, 'and not deserving of the war'; it is not uncommonly emended to ... *aitíā*, 'and not responsible for the war'.

chorus follows Dikaiopolis off in the other direction, echoing his cries of triumphant victory.

PRODUCTION

The first scene of the play is potentially spectacular, which is not to say that it was actually produced in a spectacular manner. It represents a meeting of the assembly, and probably a group of mute performers entered as the *prytánēs*, the body of fifty which presided over the assembly, sitting, perhaps, on the step(s) forward of the skene, but it is not impossible that both in describing the behaviour of the prytanes (40–42) and in addressing them (56–58. 167f.) Dikaiopolis is actually looking and gesturing towards the audience, which is thus forced into playing a role as unexacting as it is appropriate.

The number of speaking characters in this scene and the timing of their exits and entrances pose an interesting problem. Prima facie the text points to the following:

(1) Dikaiopolis: on stage throughout, 1–203.
(2) The herald of the assembly: entrance 40–42, exit 173.
(3) Amphitheos: entrance 45, enforced exit 55; reappearance 129–132; entrance 175, exit 203.
(4) The Athenian envoy who has returned from Persia: entrance 64, exit 125.
(5) The 'King's Eye': entrance 94, exit 125.
(6) A certain Theoros, back from Thrace: entrance 134, exit 173.

No other scene in comedy needs six speaking actors, or even five; can we reduce the number needed for this scene to four? If we give the parts of Amphitheos, the envoy from Persia and Theoros all to one actor we can effect the reduction on paper, but it means a change from Amphitheos to envoy during 56–63, back to Amphitheos during 126–128, then to Theoros during line 133, and back to Amphitheos during 174. Changes of this speed are not credible, and it seems that we are necessarily committed to five actors. This can be managed if we treat the King's Eye as an extra who has only two lines to speak, one of pseudo-Persian and one of pidgin-Greek, and give the roles of the envoy and Theoros to one actor. The time available to him for the change of role can perhaps be extended from the interval 126–133 allocated above on prima facie grounds; at 110 Dikaiopolis exclaims

Get away! I'll put some questions to him (*i.e. to the King's Eye*) by myself (*mónos, lit. 'alone'*).

If at this point he threatens the envoy with his stick and drives him out of the theatre with shouts and blows,[6] the time available for a change of costume into the part of Theoros is extended to twenty-four lines.

In the last two hundred lines of the play we appear to be looking at two doors, one representing the house of Dikaiopolis and the other the house of Lamakhos. Each of the two men orders his own slave to 'bring out' (1097f., 1109, etc.) the items which he needs. If only one door is available, it does not consistently represent anybody's house, but only the point of transition from the property-store to the area in view of the audience (cf. p. 21); but in that case it is surprising that both before and after that scene clear (and, one would have thought, unnecessary) reference is made to Lamakhos's house. In 1071, when the messenger arrives to give Lamakhos the order to guard the Parnes passes, Lamakhos's first words, in tragic style, are:

Who makes resound the palace faced with bronze?

And when Lamakhos returns wounded, he is preceded by a servant who declaims, also in tragic style (1174f.):

O servitors of Lamakhos's house,
heat water, water!—in a casserole.

Again, almost the last words of Lamakhos after his return are (1222f.):

Carry me out from home
to Pittakos's surgery
with hands of healing.

Thus *if* one door is in use during the frantic scene of preparation, we are given every encouragement, on either side of that scene, to identify it as Lamakhos's door. Yet before that—before Lamakhos's reference to his 'palace faced with bronze'—it seems to be identified as Dikaiopolis's door, behind which great culinary activity is going on; the chorus says nothing to suggest that it sees the food being cooked, but twice refers (1015, 1042) to hearing Dikaiopolis's orders as he dispenses to his slaves the delicacies bought from the Theban. All this points to the use of two doors, one of them consistently Dikaiopolis's house from 202 to the end of the play, the other Euripides' from 395 to 479 and Lamakhos's from 573 to the end; and, as we shall see, there is an even stronger case for two

6   It must be admitted that a similar line in *Thesm.* 626 is no more than a command to stand aside, for the character so addressed is required nine lines later.

doors in *Clouds, Peace* and *Women in Assembly*. But the evidence bearing upon the staging of comedy is rarely free of complications and uncertainties, and the present case is no exception. When Dikaiopolis acquires a splendid Boeotian eel from the Theban, he says (887–894):

> Servitors, bring the oven and the fan out here to me. Look, boys, upon the noblest of eels—at last she's come, after five years, and how we've missed her! Salute her, children; and I'll give you charcoal in honour of this guest. Well, take her in. Never may I be parted, even death, from you (*sc. the eel*) in your garnishing of beetroot![7]

Why does he ask for the oven to be brought out, as if to cook the eel on the spot, and then send the eel indoors? It could plausibly be argued that this is a preparation for all the cooking that is to come later; that the cooking will all be done *outside*, in and around the oven brought out at 888; and that the door in the skene will not thereafter represent Dikaiopolis's house, but alternately Lamakhos's and the indeterminate 'source of properties'. But if that is the poet's purpose, why does he make Dikaiopolis tell a slave to 'take in' the eel? I do not think that a wholly satisfactory inscenation of *Acharnians* has yet been propounded; to come off the fence in favour of one door or two—so far as *this* play is concerned—is possible only if we shut our eyes to at least one of the relevant data and thus conceal from ourselves the nature of the problems with which the study of Aristophanic comedy habitually confronts us.[8]

PEACE AND WAR

Neither in *Acharnians* nor anywhere else in Aristophanes does the question of 'pacifism' arise, if by that term we mean the willingness to endure, or to see inflicted upon others, any suffering whatsoever in preference to committing the sin of homicide. The issue which does arise is the utility of continuing war for uncertain and marginal gain when it is possible to make peace at a trivial cost. Aristophanes and his audience were perfectly aware that on the whole peace is more enjoyable than war, but there is no sign that anyone, except some right-wing

7 The oddities of the English translation reflect paratragic words and phrases in the original.

8 At the beginning of the scene of preparation, according to the manuscript text, Dikaiopolis says to his slave *sýnkleie*, which would normally mean 'shut up the house'; but a different interpretation of the word is possible, and so is an emendation *sýnklāe*, which would be addressed to Lamakhos and would have a completely different meaning, consonant with the preceding line.

extremists who would have accepted alien rule if it maintained their own class in power within Athens, would have been willing to sacrifice for the sake of peace the wealth and dominant position which Athens derived from her rule over the Aegean islands and the coastal cities of Asia Minor. In the closing scene of *Knights* Demos (the personification of the Athenian people) gladly accepts a thirty-year peace-treaty, but the chorus at the beginning of the scene has hailed him as 'monarch of Greece and of this land' (1330) and as 'king of the Greeks' (1333).

A speaker in the introductory portion of Plato's *Laws* is made to say (626A):

> What most men call peace is only a word; in fact there exists by nature a state of unproclaimed war between every city and every other city.

Although by no means all Greeks would have put the matter so in-compromisingly, they were more inclined than we are to regard war as part of the fabric of nature, on a par with bad weather. Thucydides (iv. 64.3) represents a Syracusan in 424 as trying to persuade all the Greek states of Sicily to ward off the threat of Athenian intervention:

> We shall have our wars, no doubt, from time to time, and we'll make peace again by discussions among ourselves; but if we are wise we shall combine to repel alien attack.

Between small and equally-matched cities, especially in the less sophisti-cated parts of the Greek world, war was something of a seasonal occupa-tion. It could be more serious; from time to time a city would destroy one of its smaller neighbours, killing the adult male population, selling the rest into slavery, and razing the city to the ground. This was one of the facts of life which Aristophanes and his audience recognised, but in the early years of the Peloponnesian War it would not have occurred to many of them that there could be any real danger of such a fate to a city as large and powerful as Athens. In any case, the turning of the other cheek did not occupy a conspicuous place in the moral scheme of Greek society; it was manly to return evil for evil, and pusillanimous to choose safety in preference to glory. Three generations later it is remarkable to observe the great emphasis laid by Demosthenes, in justifying the foreign policy which he had advocated, on that kind of national honour which is maintained by a readiness to fight. One can-not accuse the Athenians of romanticizing war from a safe distance; they knew from their own experience what hacking and piercing with sharp metal was like.

During 432 and the winter of 432/1, when Sparta's allies prodded her into beginning hostilities against Athens, one of the issues was the 'Megarian Decree', a measure by which the Athenians, in retaliation for what they considered unfriendly behaviour on the part of Megara, debarred Megarians from access to Athens and the states of the Athenian empire.[9] At one point during that winter the Spartans went so far as to say that 'if the Athenians repealed the Megarian Decree there would be no war' (Thucydides i.139.1). This demand created in some quarters at Athens a feeling that repeal was a reasonable price to pay for the maintenance of peace. Perikles insisted that if Athens yielded to Sparta on this issue she would suffer a lasting moral defeat and more serious demands would follow. His advice prevailed, but the minority which thought the decree not worth a war did not necessarily change its mind; in the second summer of the war, when Athens had been stricken by the unforeseen disaster of the plague, there was a temporary majority in favour of negotiations for peace, and in popular tradition Perikles and the Megarian Decree became firmly established as 'the cause' of the war. This is to be seen not only in *Acharnians* 509–556 and *Peace* 603–614 but also in our evidence for the lost *Dionysalexandros* of Kratinos, which satirized Perikles as 'having brought the war upon Athens' (cf. p. 217) and in a fourth-century view (Andokides iii. 8) that the war broke out in 431 'because of the Megarians'.[10] If, therefore, it were possible to translate Dikaiopolis's speech to the chorus into the terminology of a judiciously expressed political tract, it would amount to this: courage in the interests of one's own city is admirable, and it is to be hoped that Sparta will suffer an earthquake which will pay her back for the damage she has done to Attica, *but* Athens was too hasty in embarking on the present war over an unimportant issue, and it would be both agreeable and safe to try to stop fighting now. Reasonableness, sympathy, understanding and magnanimity were all recognized by the Greeks as virtues, and it would not have been difficult in 425 to argue that these standards of behaviour indicated peace negotiations rather than war *à outrance*. To make such a case it might have been necessary to retain at least one of the evasions of the speech itself (535–539):

9   The extent and nature and purpose of the debarment are all controversial, but the details of the controversy are not relevant to the present discussion.

10   Thucydides, who lived through the Peloponnesian War and wrote a history of it, regarded it as all one war from 431 to 404, but this was not the prevailing view at the time or for quite a long time afterwards. The fourth-century orators thought of the ten years' war from 431 to 421 as distinct from the subsequent fighting.

Then the Megarians . . . asked the Spartans that the decree should be repealed; and we were not willing, although they asked repeatedly. (*Who asked whom repeatedly? The Megarians the Spartans, or the Spartans us?*)

But what is most striking is how much would have to be changed in translating from humorous to serious level. In order to justify his private treaty to the chorus Dikaiopolis borrows rags from Euripides, dresses himself up like Euripides' tragic hero Telephos, and then delivers a speech which begins and ends as a close parody of Telephos's famous speech, thus directing our attention away from the content of the argument to the incongruous humour of parody. Moreover, inside the parody of tragedy lies another parody; Herodotos's history of the conflict between Greeks and Persians, which was put into circulation three or four years before *Acharnians*, opens with myths (Io, Medea, Helen) of the seizure of European women by Asiatics and Asiatic women by Europeans, and it is difficult not to see an allusion to Herodotos in *Ach.* 524–529:

Some young men who'd had too much to drink went off to Megara and kidnapped the prostitute Simaitha. This hurt the Megarians and really roused them, so in retaliation they kidnapped two of Aspasia's prostitutes. So that was how the war burst on the whole Greek world, all from three whores.[11]

In *Peace* 603–614, which shares with Dikaiopolis's speech the treatment of the Megarian Decree as the final blow to peace, the nature of the events leading up to it is entirely different, so that we can hardly treat the story of the kidnappings as the standard popular version of the causes of the war. Aristophanes could conceivably expect us to perceive and assess a serious argument for peace wrapped in a double layer of amusing parody, but whether he did expect this depends on our interpretation of the framework into which the parody is fitted.

It cannot be too strongly emphasized that Dikaiopolis does not concern himself even with the interests of his own city, let alone those of the Greek world; in this respect he is strikingly different from Trygaios in *Peace*. He wants his own comfort and pleasure, and escapes by magical means from his obligations as a citizen subject to the rule of the sovereign assembly and its elected officers. It is not easy to read into his behaviour the implication that Athens would be a better and safer place

11   See also note 1 above on Herodotos.

if everyone else followed his example, for not only does he reject the idea of sharing the benefits of peace with anyone else, he operates on a supernatural level, exempt from the operation of real causes and effects, to which others cannot follow him simply by a wish or a decision to do so. Having got his peace, he does not think of going out to preach to the Acharnians, or to anyone else; it is they who pursue him, intent on punishing him, and everything that he says to them is designed in one way or another to save him from that punishment. One way is plausible argument; another is trickery, hence the beggar-costume and the Euripidean style (440–444); and a third is confident, noisy bluster. Only half the chorus is persuaded by his speech; what wins over the other half is his outrageous mockery of Lamakhos and his successful arousal of old men's prejudices against distinguished younger men.

In sum: *Acharnians* is not a pill of political advice thickly sugared with humour, but a fantasy of total selfishness, exploiting, among much else, political views and arguments which existed at all levels, from the most casual grumbling to the most thoughtful analysis, as ingredients of the contemporary situation.

VII

Knights

Produced in 424, at the Lenaia, and awarded first prize. It was the first occasion on which Aristophanes acted as his own producer. 'Knights' is the traditional English translation of *hippês*, which means 'cavalry', 'horsemen'; it has a point, in that the cavalry of a Greek state was recruited from the wealthiest class, which could afford to keep horses, so that the ordinary Athenian would think of *hippês* as we think of cavalry officers or Guards officers, not as troopers or guardsmen.

SYNOPSIS

The play is an allegory of an unusual kind. *Dêmos Pyknítēs* is the head of a household; his name is the ordinary word for the Athenian people in assembly and the made-up demotic *Pyknítēs* (every Athenian inherited from his father a 'demotic' signifying his ancestral locality) is a reference to the Pnyx (*pykn-* in the oblique cases), where the assembly met. He has recently bought a Paphlagonian slave, who has become his master's favourite and terrorizes the other slaves. This 'Paphlagonian' is a thin disguise for Kleon, who since Perikles' death in 429 had risen to a dominant position in Athenian political life; representation of him as a Paphlagonian is designed to suggest, in accordance with the common forms of political antagonism, that he is not of true Athenian origin, and also to remind us of *paphlásdēn*, 'bluster'. The play begins with two slaves lamenting the ill-treatment which now falls upon them and contemplating desertion as the only remedy. How relationships within the household of Demos reflect political relationships is indicated by 54–57, where one slave says:

I'd kneaded a Lakonian loaf at Pylos; but *he* skipped round somehow,

in a really dirty way, and snatched it from under my nose and served
it up himself—the loaf that *I*'d kneaded!

Kleon and Demosthenes had together mastered the Spartan garrison on
the island of Sphakteria, lying off Pylos, which Demosthenes had
captured before Kleon was sent out; and although Kleon claimed the
credit, it was open to those who did not like him to play down his
responsibility. Aristophanes contrives to refer to the Pylos affair ten
times in the course of the play.

Having decided that they cannot hope to desert successfully, the two
slaves steal some wine in the hope of inspiration, and no sooner have
they taken a drink than they pluck up courage to steal from the snoring
Paphlagonian some of the oracles (cf. p. 76) which he carefully guards.
These oracles reveal to them that the Paphlagonian is destined to be
overthrown by a sausage-seller; and sure enough, along comes a
sausage-seller on his way to the market. They pounce on this bewildered man, assure him that he is destined to rule over the whole
Athenian empire, and by sonorous recitation of the oracle persuade him
that his destiny is inescapable. He is terrified at the prospect of conflict
with the Paphlagonian, but they assure him that a thousand knights
will be on his side. When the Paphlagonian wakes up and storms out of
the house roaring and threatening, the Sausage-seller starts to run, but
the situation is saved by the slave's cry to the knights—and the chorus
comes charging into the orchestra with a rousing song based rhythmi-
cally on the cry actually uttered in a charge, *paîe paîe*, 'Strike! Strike!'

The Paphlagonian, beset by this furious attack, cries in vain for 'old
men of the juries' to help him, then equally vainly tries to flatter the
chorus. The Sausage-seller, whose courage never deserts him from this
point onwards, embarks on a slanging-match in which he trumps every
threat or boast of the Paphlagonian with more shameless boasts, more
bloodthirsty threats or coarser ridicule. In the course of the scene all
the stock forms of political smear and charge are satirized, and at 475
the Paphlagonian declares he will go to the Council and denounce the
Sausage-seller, the slave and chorus as conspirators against the security
of the city. Off goes the Sausage-seller after him to outface him in the
Council.

The parabasis is performed during their absence, and after it the
Sausage-seller, ecstatically greeted by the chorus, returns with the news
that he has won the day. He describes the proceedings in a long narrative speech, vulgar and hilarious, with little or none of the parody of

tragic messenger-speeches which we might have expected. He tells how he crashed into the Council with the news (642–645) that he had 'never seen whitebait cheaper'. The Paphlagonian countered with the proposal of a 'good-news sacrifice' of a hundred oxen to Athena (i.e. like most festivals, an orgy of beef within the formal framework of a religious ceremony), but the Sausage-seller outbid him at once: two hundred oxen, and a vow of a thousand goats to Artemis next day if anchovies came down to a hundred for an obol. The Council wouldn't stay to listen to the Paphlagonian (667–673):

> He entreated them to wait just a little, 'to hear', he said, 'what the herald from Sparta says, because he's come to discuss an armistice.' [1] But they with one voice shouted, 'An armistice, *now*? Why, it's because they've heard that whitebait are cheap here! We don't want any armistice; let the war go on!'

No sooner has the chorus acclaimed this tale than the Paphlagonian arrives, full of fury, and threatens to haul the Sausage-seller before the assembly (*dêmos*). They both call old Demos out of his house and declare themselves his rival 'lovers'; in Thucydides ii.43.1 Perikles is portrayed as calling on the Athenian people (in 431/0) to be 'lovers' of their city— for lovers try to outbid one another in generosity to the person whom they love—and it is possible that it was Perikles himself who had popularized the image. The contest which follows has the formal structure which we meet repeatedly in Aristophanes from this play onwards (cf. p. 67), except that neither side is allowed an uninterrupted presentation of his own case. Their flattery of Demos is gross, and, reaches its nadir in 909f.:

> SAUSAGE-SELLER: Look, here's a hare's tail to wipe round your eyes with!
> PAPHLAGONIAN: O Demos, when you blow your nose wipe your fingers on my head!

Eventually Demos regards the Sausage-seller as victor and demands back from the Paphlagonian the seal-ring which he held as the trusted steward of Demos. We might think that this has settled the matter, but the contest just completed is in fact only the first of three stages (the three successive throws required for a victory in wrestling, influential

---

1 In other contexts (e.g. 1388–1395) Kleon is depicted as hostile to the idea of making peace, but in the present context it is necessary for him to speak of an armistice in order that the short-sightedness of the Council may be demonstrated.

on Greek imagery, may be relevant here). The Paphlagonian asks Demos to hear his oracles; the Sausage-seller declares that he has even better oracles. The battle of oracles ends, like the previous stage of the contest, with Demos deciding in favour of the Sausage-seller. The third and final stage is to decide which of the two contestants does more for Demos and has more to offer him. Their efforts to press dainties on him leave him a little bewildered, and the Sausage-seller achieves final victory in an unforeseen way (1211–1224):

> SAUSAGE-SELLER: I'll tell you! Come and take my box—don't say anything—and check what's in it, and then the Paphlagonian's. And don't you worry, you'll decide between us easily enough.
> DEMOS: Well, let's see, what's in it?
> SAUSAGE-SELLER: (*Showing Demos inside his box*) Don't you see it's empty, dad? I brought everything in it to you.
> DEMOS: This box has the right democratic ideas!
> SAUSAGE-SELLER: Now come here to the Paphlagonian's. See?
> DEMOS: (*Looking in the other box*) Why, all the good things it's full of! What a damn great cake he stowed away—and he cut off a tiny little bit and gave to me!
> SAUSAGE-SELLER: That's how he treated you earlier, too. He gave you just a little of all he got, and he served up the biggest share to himself.
> DEMOS: (*To the Paphlagonian*) You bastard, is that how you stole and cheated me?

Demos now demands of the Paphlagonian his 'crown'—the crown put on by a speaker in the assembly—that he may transfer it to the Sausage-seller. The Paphlagonian fights one last delaying action, claiming that an oracle foretells by whom, and by whom alone, he is to be worsted. Item by item he discovers, to his horror, that the Sausage-seller is the man of destiny. His increasingly dramatic exclamations and his despairing farewell to his crown are modelled on a variety of tragic passages.

The Sausage-seller's name, 'Agorakritos', is now revealed. Demos is rejuvenated, restored to the majesty he enjoyed in the days of the Persian wars. He confesses with shame how easily he has been bamboozled in the past, and, instructed by Agorakritos, promises to behave better in future. The Paphlagonian is carted off to take up the squalid trade of a sausage-seller. No other Aristophanic play ends without either a song of exultation or a plain reference to the fact that the play is over, and it is reasonably suspected that the original ending of *Knights* is lost. We would have expected a line or two of song from the chorus while the unhappy Paphlagonian is removed, and it is hard to think of any good reason why Aristophanes should not have written them.

ALLEGORY

The idea of presenting Demos as master of a household and politicians as his slaves is a brilliant idea, but it is not carried through consistently; purely domestic relationships and purely political relationships run side by side throughout the play, and we have to be prepared for constant shifts from one level to the other. Even in the speech of the slave who 'kneaded the Lakonian loaf' the addition of the words 'at Pylos' takes us outside the domestic context which the rest of the speech maintains. The oracle which foretells the overthrow of the Paphlagonian by the Sausage-seller is not presented as an oracle foretelling the displacement of the slave-steward within a household, but as a succession of men who 'will have the administration of the *city*' (130): first an oakum-*seller*, then a sheep-*seller*, thirdly a *seller* of hides (Kleon), where we would have thought it possible to say 'house' instead of 'city' and substitute specialized skills (such as appear in lists of slaves) for trades.[2] But the central theme of the play, the displacement of the Paphlagonian by the Sausage-seller, is itself in conflict with the household allegory, for the Sausage-seller is a free citizen and therefore not in competition with a slave of Demos. Similarly, whereas 'appeal to the assembly', coming after the Paphlagonian's lack of success in denouncing the Sausage-seller to the Council, can be portrayed as an appeal to the individual Demos, there is nothing in domestic relationships corresponding to the Council. When the Paphlagonian and the Sausage-seller go off to the Council, we have moved right outside the allegory with which the play began, and the 'appeal to Demos' represents a partial move back. Only in the final scene is the allegory wholly discarded; there, Demos is the personification of the Athenian people and Agorakritos a comic hero who has set everything to rights.

The name of Kleon is used only once in the play, at 976, where the

2 The ancient commentators, drawing on some other allusions in comedy, identified the oakum-seller as Eukrates and the sheep-seller as either Kallias or Lysikles. There is no historical evidence for the political domination of Athens by any of these men between the death of Perikles and the rise of Kleon, and presumably Aristophanes has exaggerated, for the sake of the oracular climax, whatever part they played in politics.

choral song preceding the contest of the oracles says '. . . if Kleon perishes'. Consistent reference to him elsewhere as 'the Paphlagonian' is not entirely for maintenance of the domestic allegory, but to be hurtful.

PRODUCTION

One interesting feature of *Knights* is that it can be performed by only three actors. From the entry of the chorus until the parabasis there are only the three roles of the Paphlagonian, the Sausage-seller and the Slave, and after the parabasis again only three, Demos replacing the Slave. In the opening scene the second slave leaves at 154, just after the dialogue between the two slaves and the Sausage-seller has begun, and the Paphlagonian does not enter until 235; the intervening dialogue has been conducted by the one slave and the Sausage-seller. The only problem arises at 234, where someone cries out:

Oh, my God! The Paphlagonian's coming out!

The manuscripts give this line to the second slave, but it is hard to believe that for the sake of this one moment Aristophanes had no alternative but to convert a three-actor play into a four-actor play. It is reasonable to suppose that the actor who took the part of the second slave, and is now dressed as the Paphlagonian and ready for entry a moment later cried out this line, in the slave's voice, from inside the skene. Both in tragedy and comedy there are occasions on which cries of fear or pain are uttered by characters whom we do not see.

The only door needed can represent the house of Demos, at least down to 755, where we 'adjourn' to the Pnyx for the contest. Thereafter the same door may serve as the point of transition from an indeterminate 'inside'. In 997f. both the Paphlagonian and the Sausage-seller 'bring *out*' their piles of oracles; in 1110 the Paphlagonian says that he is going *in* to get food for Demos, and he speaks of bringing *out* a chair in 1164. The Sausage-seller must surely be imagined as bringing all *his* contributions out of the skene, not from somewhere in the wings, and since in 1151 he is told by the Paphlagonian to 'get out of the way', and retorts in the same style, it looks as if both of them are using the same door, barging each other on their way in and out.

Knights is the only play which makes an explicit allusion to masks, in terms discussed on p. 28, and we naturally wonder whether the two slaves in the opening scene were indentifiable by portrait-masks as eminent citizens. There is no doubt that we are meant to think of the slave who expounds the situation to us as Demosthenes—his reference to 'the Lakonian loaf' ensures that—but considerable doubt on the identification of the other slave. A possible candidate is Nikias, whose refusal to accept responsibility for bringing the Sphakteria affair to a quick conclusion led directly to Kleon's appointment. The relevant ancient hypothesis to the play says:

> *It seems* that the character who speaks first is Demosthenes . . . *They say* that of the two slaves one is Demosthenes and the other Nikias, *to make* both of them politicians.[3]

This interpretation is reflected in the dramatis personae and the sigla of the medieval text, but the manner of its expression shows that it is interpretation, not continuous tradition, and it may not be justified. It must also be emphasized that the identification of the second slave and the supposition that either slave wore a portrait-mask are separate questions. Recognizable portraiture was not necessarily reconcilable with the requirements of a comic mask unless the individual portrayed had something very unusual about the shape of his head or the colour of his hair (cf. p. 28). Some element of dress displaying a symbolic association with an individual cannot, of course, be ruled out.

POLITICAL LEADERSHIP

A distinction has been drawn (p. 33) between criticism of political structure, criticism of political style, and criticism of individual decisions on policy. The only significant ways in which the Athenian democracy of the 420s could be changed structurally were by a restriction of power to something less than the total citizen body and by a diminution in the accountability of magistrates. *Knights* contains no suggestion, either explicit or implied, that changes of this kind ought to be made; indeed, by portraying Demos as master of a household and politically or militarily important individuals as his servants Aristophanes takes essentially the same point of view as the fourth-century orators who operate within the framework of the democracy and cannot afford, in the interests of their own political careers, to incur suspicion of anti-democratic sentiments. Aristophanes' Demos has been lazy and obtuse and too easy-going, and has allowed politicians to

---

3 The word used by the hypothesis is *dēmēgóroi*, 'men who address the assembly'—a useful reminder that since the Athenians had no professional army and men elected to military office needed to address the assembly the modern distinction between 'soldier' and 'politician' does not apply to ancient Athens.

cheat him while they line their own pockets and victimize their personal enemies; the reformation of Demos at the end of the play is a
realization of the need to exercise more vigilantly and conscientiously
the power that belongs to him. The fourth-century orators, again in
tune with *Knights*, naturally do not suggest that the Athenian people
is by nature incapable of exercising sovereign power responsibly; it is
ingenuous, tolerant and compassionate, led into error by the dishonest
rhetoric of self-seeking politicians but capable of instantaneous reformation if it reasserts by an act of will the shrewd and heroic qualities
which it truly possesses. This judicious blending of reproof and re-
assurance, commonplace in the fourth century, may be summed up in
two Aristophanic passages, One is *Knights* 1355–1357:

> DEMOS: I am ashamed of what I did wrong before.
> SAUSAGE-SELLER: But *you* weren't to blame—don't you worry about
> that—the men who deceived you are to blame.

And in *Clouds* 587–594 (from the epirrhema of the parabasis) an item of
practical advice is introduced with an allusion to a myth about the
destiny of Athens:

> All the same, you did elect Kleon. They say that the taking of bad
> decisions is an attribute of this city, but that the gods bring all the
> mistakes you make to a happier conclusion. And we'll easily explain
> how this mistake too can turn out all right. If you convict Kleon. . . .

The type of political leadership which is defeated in *Knights* is characterized by: gross flattery of the demos and extravagant protestations
of loyalty, backed up by enthusiasm in prosecuting individuals who
could be accused of unpatriotic conduct; promotion of measures which
offered short-term economic advantage to a lot of people, with insufficient regard for long-term security; and the emergence of the
leader himself from industrial and commercial circles, not from the
land-owning families which had a long and distinguished tradition of
generous patriotic service.[4] All these aspects of demagoguery are
explicitly condemned by the fourth-century orators, not least by those
orators who actually exhibit them to a marked degree. The author of
the prosecution of Aristogeiton in 325/4 (Demosthenes xxv), precisely
one hundred years after *Knights*, refers to the 'watchdog' image which

4 Hyperbolos is several times ridiculed in comedy as a 'lamp-seller'; but it is
interesting that in *Peace* 680–692 his association with lamps yields a joke which
is not primarily directed against him.

we find in the 'oracle' of *Knights* 1015–1035 and the domestic trial-scene of *Wasps* 891–1008:

Well, what *is* Aristogeiton? Some people declare he's the watchdog of the people. What kind of dog? The kind that doesn't bite those whom he accuses of being wolves, but himself eats up the sheep he claims to be guarding.

Demosthenes, according to his own account (xxvii 9), inherited from his father two workshops stocked with thirty slaves who were skilled knife-makers and twenty who were carpenters specializing in beds and couches. His political adversary Aiskhines sneers at him (ii 93) as 'the knife-maker's bastard'; Demosthenes retaliates by depicting Aiskhines as a subordinate clerk who had spent his boyhood cleaning up the schoolroom for his schoolmaster-father ('You', says Demosthenes in a snobbish and patronising passage, 'taught reading and writing, but *I* was a pupil', implying 'you had to earn a living, but my father was rich enough to send me to school'). Andokides (i 146) refers to Kleophon, the prominent politician of the last years of the Peloponnesian war, as 'the lyre-maker', but some recent evidence[5] indicates that Kleophon's father, whatever the family's associations with musical instruments, had been elected general in 428 and was politically prominent fifteen years earlier. It is of the greatest importance to remember that derogatory references to manufacture and commerce belong just as much to democratic political practice, where the mass audience is the arbiter of issues, as to comedy, and their occurrence in Aristophanes does nothing to align him with a right-wing 'party'. The same is true of allegations of barbarian ancestry, imperfect acquaintance with the Greek language, or improper enrolment on the citizen registers; Aiskhines calls Demosthenes a 'Scythian', on the strength of a rumour about his mother's origins, and Demosthenes claims that Aiskhines' father was really a slave.

Aristophanes might have depicted a defeat of the noisy, vulgar, un-educated, upstart 'Paphlagonian' by a dignified, cultured representative of an aristocratic house, but he chose instead to make the victor a sausage-seller, of 'bad' parentage (185f.), almost illiterate (188f.), trained in the 'school of life' to steal and lie (1235–1239) and accustomed to earn a bit on the side as a male prostitute (1241f.). The displacement of the Paphlagonian by the Sausage-seller, who can shout louder, insult

5 See Russell Meiggs and David Lewis, *A Selection of Greek Historical Inscriptions to the End of the Fifth Century B.C.* (Oxford, 1969), 41f.

more promptly, lie harder and flatter more grossly, is represented as the bottom of the slope down which political leadership at Athens has rolled with increasing momentum.[6] What, then, of the future? If it is bad that the political scene should be dominated by a man like Kleon, it ought to be worse if dominated by the Sausage-seller; yet at the end of *Knights* Demos is admonished, and the man who has defeated Kleon by outdoing him in Kleonism shows no further desire to exercise the power which now lies within his grasp. An interpretation of the play which sees irony and despair in its last scene deserves serious consideration, but it is not the only alternative open to us. If Aristophanes wished to do three things—to satirize political practice for humorous purposes, to exalt the fundamental good sense of the Athenian people in a manner consonant with the festive tradition of comedy, and to take personal revenge on Kleon—it was necessary for him to create a vulgar, self-confident, resourceful 'hero' who would re-establish the people in the rightful exercise of its own power by getting the better of Kleon, who had increasingly usurped that power. If he really did intend irony and despair, he marred his own intention by the lyric interchange between the chorus and Demos in 1111–1150, where Demos, reproached for being too easily flattered and misled, declares that he knows very well what is going on; he likes to keep (*tréphēn*, 'maintain', 'support', one's children, a maiden aunt, a dog, etc.) one 'champion' at a time, and strike him down when he's 'full'. The chorus congratulates Demos on his wisdom in feeding politicians until they are ready for sacrifice, and Demos changes to a different image in his reply (1145–1150):

> I watch them every time, although
> appearing not to see them steal.
> And then I make them vomit up
> all that they ever stole from me,
> sticking a funnel down their throat.

(The 'funnel', *kēmós*, is that of the urn into which the votes were cast in the lawcourts.) If Demos really knows what he's doing, there is less danger that he will surrender everything to the Sausage-seller; of course, his boast is not really in keeping with his shame and shock when he is told (1335–1355) of his follies, but contradictions must appear—in

6 The chorus does not pretend that the Sausage-seller is *nobler* than the Paphlagonian, but rejoices that the Paphlagonian is being worsted by someone *viler* (*miarốteros*, 329).

Aristophanes' time, in Demosthenes' or in ours—when we try to push to extremes *both* satire on the style of democratic politics *and* an expression of faith in the intelligence and integrity of ordinary people.

Despite the implied association of honest political leadership with land-owning families, many elements in the play seem designed to promote a sentimental unity of classes against leaders like Kleon. In the parabasis the chorus invokes Poseidon in two different divine roles (551–564): as god of horses and chariot-racing (and thus especially dear to the highest economic class) and as god of the sea, of special concern to the rowers, the lowest economic class. Speaking as cavalrymen, the chorus praises the Athenian tradition of unstinting service to the state without any reward save tolerance (578–580):

> And what's more, we don't ask for anything except one single thing: if peace returns one day and we cease from our labours, don't mind our wearing our hair long and looking as if we'd just come from the bath.

(Similarly in fourth-century oratory a wealthy speaker parades his readiness to sacrifice everything for the Athenian people and to expect no favours in return.) The antepirrhema of the parabasis extracts humour from the ships designed as horse-transports; it imagines the horses as rowing themselves and camping and foraging on shore. In the second parabasis the triremes are imagined (1300ff.) as talking to one another indignantly about grandiose projects for Athenian naval intervention far afield. In the anapaests of the main parabasis the poet's reluctance to act as his own producer in previous years is described metaphorically in terms of recognition that one should serve first as a rower, and then in the prow, before venturing on the duties of a helmsman. Add that the reformed Demos promises (1366f.) to ensure that rowers are paid their wages promptly and fully, and it may well seem that having chosen one end of the social scale for the chorus of *Knights* Aristophanes deliberately emphasizes its community of interests with the other end.

In later years Aristophanes spoke of *Knights* as a victory over Kleon; *Clouds* 549f.:

> I hit Kleon in the belly when he was at the height of his power, but I didn't go so far as to jump on him when he was down.

Whether or not it was really a victory which in any sense put Kleon 'down', Kleon seems to have been the aggressor in the feud. After

Babylonians at the City Dionysia of 426 Kleon indicted the poet for injury to the community, since the play had ridiculed holders of Athenian magistracies before an audience containing (as normally at the City Dionysia) many representatives from the subject-allies. Whether Kleon indicted Aristophanes himself, who wrote the play, or Kallistratos, who produced it and will have been regarded as the author in the official record, is uncertain and (for present purposes) unimportant. The indictment was clearly a serious enough threat, but it does not seem to have issued in a successful prosecution; Kleon, as self-appointed watchdog of the people's interests, was perhaps barking more often and more loudly than anyone wanted him to. In *Acharnians* Aristophanes felt able to express himself frankly and uncompromisingly on the subject of the attempted indictment, and thereafter he set about composing this 'blow in the belly', *Knights*. The judges liked it and gave it first prize. A few weeks later the Athenian people elected Kleon one of the ten generals for the year 424/3.

VIII

Clouds

Produced in 423, at the City Dionysia; it was placed third out of
three by the judges. The *Clouds* which we possess is not the original
play, but a version partially revised by Aristophanes (cf. p. 103).

SYNOPSIS

The principal character of *Clouds* is an Attic farmer called 'Strepsiades',
similar in status and tastes to Dikaiopolis but gullible, muddle-headed,
and given to alternation between too much self-assurance and too little.
He married a woman of city-bred, aristocratic family, and their only
son, Pheidippides, has been encouraged by that side of the family to
indulge in the expensive sports of well-to-do young men, horse-racing
and chariot-racing. In consequence, Strepsiades is hopelessly in debt
and hard pressed by his creditors. He has heard of a school run by a pair
of intellectuals, Socrates and Khairephon,[1] at which young men may
learn all the tricks of forensic argument, and he hopes that if he puts his
son through this school he will be able, with the son's help, to defeat his
creditors in court and escape paying his debts. Pheidippides, however,
recoils at the idea of becoming a pallid scholar, and Strepsiades, despite
his misgivings about his advancing years and bad memory, decides that
there is nothing for it but to attend the school himself.

His first impressions, the anecdotes told him by the student who
admits him, the sight of the students at work, and the strange scientific
instruments which they use, arouse in him amused astonishment as
well as uncritical enthusiasm, but the latter prevails, and when he

1 Although Khairephon, who is known from Plato as an intimate friend of
Socrates, is mentioned at the beginning and end of the play as if he were joint
principal of the school, he does not appear as a character.

finally meets Socrates (suspended in the air, because one thinks better about difficult problems when removed from the moist air of ground-level) he begs to be taken on as a student. Socrates 'initiates' him in a ceremony modelled on religious initiation, and invokes the deities to whose worship the school is devoted, the Clouds. Strepsiades is most impressed by the appearance of these majestic creatures (who constitute the chorus of the play), and all his traditional beliefs about the phenomena of nature and the government of the universe by Zeus fall like ninepins before the scientific theories promptly and confidently expounded by Socrates. He promises for the future to worship only the novel deities presented to him by Socrates—Void, Clouds and Tongue—and in return the Clouds promise him that if he is an assiduous student he will become a distinguished 'consultant' to whom his fellow-citizens will bring their legal problems.

His ability, however, does not match his optimism, and he has neither the wit nor the patience to understand or remember any of the basic training in philology which Socrates tries to give him. Socrates then requires him to lie in a bed and give his imagination free reign (a certain analogy with the 'free association' technique of psychotherapy must occur to modern readers, but the purpose of the exercise is rather different), in the hope that he may think of ingenious ways of escaping the legal actions brought by his creditors. The bed is painful, for vermin profit by the school's high-minded disregard of the good things of ordinary life. Even so, Strepsiades manages to concoct a few far-fetched ideas, but he over-reaches himself, Socrates loses patience, and Strepsiades is expelled.

Reduced to his original condition of despair, Strepsiades plucks up courage, fortified by half-baked recollections of what little he has learned, to insist that Pheidippides become a student. Pheidippides, a little afraid that his father has gone mad, and not quite able to defy him (for Greek society set a high standard of filial obedience), allows himself to be presented to Socrates, who sees in him a better prospect than in Strepsiades. Father and son become spectators of a set-piece contest between Right and Wrong,[2] two abstract characters who emerge from

2 In the sigla, hypotheses and scholia these characters are called *díkaios lógos* and *ádikos lógos*; *lógos* is 'account', 'exposition', 'speech', 'argument', 'principle', and *díkaios* and *ádikos* are respectively 'just', 'honest', 'righteous' and the opposite. In the text of the play it appears that we are meant to think of them as *kreíttōn lógos* and *hḗttōn lógos*; *kreíttōn* and *hḗttōn* are respectively 'superior', 'stronger', and 'inferior', 'weaker'.

the school, that they may choose at the end whether Right or Wrong is to have charge of the son's education. Right praises the culture and morality of earlier generations, and speaks of contemporary youth in terms essentially familiar in our own day. Wrong cross-questions Right, setting easy traps into which Right falls, and paints a lively picture of the pleasures, success and security open to the young man who is equipped to talk his way through anything. Strepsiades is overjoyed, and Pheidippides, grumbling, is handed over as a pupil to Wrong.

His course completed, he seems at first to have fulfilled his father's hopes, and Strepsiades, in this euphoric state, drives away two creditors who come to ask him for their money. They retreat angered and insulted by the old man's bizarre mixture of mockery, violence and incoherent scraps of ideas borrowed from Socrates and Pheidippides. But then matters take a new turn. Strepsiades and his son quarrel after dinner about poetry, for Pheidippides despises the old poets on whose work Strepsiades has been brought up, and Strepsiades cannot stomach the immoralities of Euripides. Pheidippides simply knocks his father down; and quarrelsome though the Greeks were, they regarded with horror the ill-treatment of parents by their children. Strepsiades now wishes that he had never sent his son to Socrates' school, and his distress is only increased by the argument in which Pheidippides suggests that the long-standing traditions of society are not rationally defensible. Repenting now of that dishonest desire to cheat his creditors which has led him to disaster, Strepsiades, helped by one of his slaves, sets fire to the school and drives Socrates and the students away.

THE REVISION OF THE PLAY

In the anapaests [3] of the parabasis the Chorus serves as the mouthpiece of the poet; the first person singular throughout that passage means 'I, Aristophanes'. The poet has a complaint to make against the audience (521–525):

> I thought you were a bright audience, and that this was my most brilliant comedy, so I thought you should be the first to taste it. But I was repulsed, worsted by vulgar rivals, though I didn't deserve that.

A play cannot, on the occasion of its first production, refer to its own

---

3   The metre of this part of the parabasis is not anapaestic in the strict sense but a metre favoured for the same purpose by several comic poets and named by late metricians 'eupolidean' after the poet Eupolis.

failure in the past; what we are reading, therefore, must be a revised version. This becomes clear also towards the end of the anapaests, where (549–559) the poet complains that whereas he himself, after 'hitting Kleon in the belly' (i.e. in *Knights*, produced in 424), did not return to the attack, other poets continue to attack Hyperbolos, taking their cue from Eupolis's play *Marikas*. *Marikas* was the first produced in 421, and since there were only two occasions each year on which comedies could be produced it follows that Aristophanes cannot have written this passage of *Clouds* before 418 or, at the earliest, 419.

One of the seven hypotheses transmitted with the text of the play states that a revised version of *Clouds* was put on in 422, but this statement must be false, for the Alexandrian scholars who spotted the oddity of the reference to *Marikas* observed that the records of the Athenian dramatic festivals mentioned *Clouds* once only, under the year of its original production, 423. It seems that we are dealing with a revised version which Aristophanes put into circulation as a written text but did not succeed in putting on stage. Further examination shows that the revision was not completed and we shall also see (p. 105) that the version we have could not have been performed under Athenian theatrical conditions.

One indication of incomplete revision is that the epirrhema of the parabasis speaks of Kleon as still alive (591–594):

> If you convict that cormorant Kleon of corruption and embezzlement and clamp the stocks on his neck, then whatever you may have done wrong in the past will turn out all right, back to how things used to be.

Kleon was in fact killed in battle in 422, so that this passage could never have been uttered on the same occasion as the reference to Eupolis's *Marikas* and plays about Hyperbolos. A further indication of incomplete revision lies in the context of Right and Wrong. Before they enter, Socrates says (886f.):

> He will learn for himself from the Arguments themselves; I shan't be here.

He does not explain further the reasons for his absence, but we can supply one: since both Strepsiades and Pheidippides will remain on stage throughout the contest of Right and Wrong, there will be four actors on stage, and the actor who has played Socrates will be required

for the role of Right or of Wrong. But as matters stand this actor has
no time to change his costume, for only one and a half lines intervene
between Socrates' words 'I shan't be here' and the first words of Right
to Wrong. On the analogy of other plays, as was observed by ancient
commentators, we should have expected a choral song to intervene. It
looks as if Aristophanes has removed the song but has not written a
substitute; and, quite apart from formal considerations, there is a
scholion on 889 which supports this idea. The scholion tells us that the
two Arguments were brought on in cages, like fighting-cocks. In the
entire contest there is not a single image to suggest this idea, and the
scholia on Aristophanes afford no other example of a theatrical interpretation which cannot be derived from the text itself. My own opinion
is that in the original version of *Clouds* a choral song preceding the entry
of Right and Wrong used imagery derived from cock-fighting, and
that the scholion on 889 was ultimately derived from an interpretation
of that song.[4]

There is some evidence (which seems to me cogent, but not to everyone) that a text of the original *Clouds* survived into the Hellenistic
period.[5] If it did, statements made in the hypotheses and scholia about
the differences between the two versions have to be taken seriously and
cannot be dismissed as guesswork. These statements refer not only to the
parabasis and to the recruiting of the contest of Right and Wrong but
also to the last scene of the play, in which Strepsiades sets fire to the
school. Unfortunately, no one tells us how the original version ended,
and there is room for speculation; but we have no grounds for thinking
that it took a significantly different view of Socrates and of the moral
and social issues raised by un-traditional education.

4   It may be added that after the lyric antistrophe 804–809, which responds to
the strophe 700–706, there come a further two lyric verses to which nothing in
the strophe responds. Although certain abnormalities of responsion are well
attested in Aristophanes, there is no parallel to an abnormality on this scale. I am
inclined to think that two verses which originally stood after 706 were deleted
by the poet but not replaced.
5   Since I discussed this question in my commentary on *Clouds*, H. Erbse,
'Über die ersten "Wolken" des Aristophanes', *Opus Nobile: Festschrift zum
60 Geburtstag von Ulf Jantzen* (Wiesbaden, 1969), 35–41, has offered a new
interpretation of one of the items of evidence which I regarded as supporting
the survival of the first version of the play. On the other side, a fragmentary
ancient book-list (*Oxyrhynchus Papyri* xxxlii [1968], no. 2659) contains the titles
'*Wealth* I' (cf. p. 14) and '*Clouds* II' and I find it very hard to believe that our
Clouds would have been specified as '*Clouds* II' in Roman times unless possession of '*Clouds* I' had been a practical possibility.

PRODUCTION

As has been observed above, four actors are required for 814–1112: Strepsiades and Pheidippides are on stage throughout, Socrates from 868 to 887, Right and Wrong from 889 to 1112; on the assumption that there was originally a choral song between 888 and 889, and that there would have been a new one there if the revised play have ever been produced, either Right or Wrong can be played by the actor who played Socrates. At the end of the contest, the manuscripts represent Socrates as suddenly reappearing (1105) to press Strepsiades for a decision and to take over Pheidippides, but it is implied by a scholion and by one of the hypotheses that these lines are spoken by Wrong, not by Socrates. This makes sense and avoids any problem of casting. One abnormality remains: there is no other play in which it is *necessary* to give so large a part to a fourth actor, and if as a general rule the fourth actor had much less work to do than the other three this abnormality may be connected with the fact that the *Clouds* which we have was not completely revised for performance.

This fact, however, cannot usefully be invoked to explain away the complexities of staging presupposed by the text—two doors and a movable set—given that similar complexities are presupposed by some other plays. When the play begins, Strepsiades and Pheidippides are lying in their beds, *as if* inside their house but *in fact* in front of the skene. It is not easy for us to imagine them as sleeping out of doors, for (a) the young man is 'wrapped up in five blankets' (10), i.e. the weather is not to be thought of as hot, (b) the streets of Athens were not particularly safe at night even for a man wide awake, the stealing of clothes being a common crime (cf. *Ass.* 668f.), and (c) even if we are to think of Strepsiades' house as being in the country, anyone who slept in the open would naturally do so in the interior courtyard rather than outside the house altogether. I presume that the beds and their occupants are brought on before our eyes and placed in front of the skene before the play can begin, and that the question 'where exactly are they supposed to be sleeping?' is not one which anyone in the audience wishes to ask. When Strepsiades has woken Pheidippides and is trying to persuade him to enrol in Socrates' school, he points to the school and to its door (92); by this time both men must be on their feet, and the beds can be removed by slaves any time from now on. We have seen (p. 24) that the wording of the text presupposes that Strepsiades' house and the school are represented by different doors.

A further complication arises at the end of the conversation between Strepsiades and the student who has opened the door to him. Strepsiades cries (181):

> Come on, come on, open the Reflectory,[6] and show Socrates to me, quick as you can. I'm bursting to learn! Come on, open the door!

The situation which we have to imagine is that the student now takes Strepsiades inside. What we actually see—somehow or other—is a group of students absorbed in their work, to whom after a few lines the guide-student says (195–199):

> Go *in*, so that He doesn't find you here.

The students duly go in, leaving the guide-student and Strepsiades alone with the scientific instruments which are part of the school's equipment. Much later, when Socrates has agreed to admit Strepsiades as a pupil (505–509):

> SOCRATES: Don't talk so much; follow me this way—come on, get a move on!
> STREPSIADES: Put a honey-cake into my hand first; I'm frightened at going down inside, like going into the Cave of Trophonios.
> SOCRATES: Go *on*! Why do you keep on poking and peering round the door?

Somehow what was presented to us at 184 as an interior scene has become an exterior scene eleven lines later, and the door which was opened to admit Strepsiades at 183f. is a door which he has still to enter at 509. It is not easy to suppose, for the reasons given on p. 25, that the interior scene is revealed by pushing out the theatrical trolley. It could be that when the guide-student opens the door at 183f. the students come out and take up their positions, carrying all those objects with them, and leave the objects behind when they go in at 199. A third possibility is that a movable screen, containing a small door, stood in front of one side of the skene at the beginning of the play. This would be the house and door to which Strepsiades points at 92, and where he knocks at 132. The guide-student could come out of it to talk to him

6 This is one of the traditional English translations of *phrontistḗrion*, coined from *phrontísdēn*, 'think', 'worry', on the analogy of *dikastḗrion*, 'lawcourt' in relation to *dikásdēn*, 'decide a lawsuit', and other words in -*ḗrion* denoting places of work.

during 133–183, and at 183 men concealed behind the screen could walk
off with it out of the theatre. The students and instruments thus revealed would be in front of the permanent skene, and when told to go
in the students would enter the skene through a door which for the rest
of the play would represent the school.

There is a passage towards the end of the play which points to the
consistent use of two separate doors for Strepsiades' house and Socrates'
school. In the course of expounding the universe to Strepsiades Socrates
says that the governing force is not Zeus but *Dínos* ('Vortex', 'Whirl',
'Circulation': 380), and this is one scrap of teaching which Strepsiades'
memory retains. When he is finally disillusioned, and Pheidippides has
rejected his appeal to respect 'Zeus of the Family' with the assertion the
Dinos is now the ruler, Strepsiades cries (1472–1474):

> No, he hasn't driven out Zeus. That's what I thought—*because of
> this dínos.* Oh, what I fool I was, when I thought that you, made of
> earthenware, were a god!

It seems certain that Strepsiades addresses these last words to an actual
dínos (a kind of large pot). Where does it come from? Does he dive for
a second into the skene to get it, or does a slave rush out and thrust it
into his hands? A few lines later, when Pheidippides has gone off,
Strepsiades appeals to the god Hermes for forgiveness, and pretends
(1483–1485) that the god whispers advice into his ear. When we remember that a herm, representing Hermes, normally stood at an
Athenian's front door, it seems plausible to suggest that two doors are
in use: one, flanked by the conventional herm, represents Strepsiades'
house, and the other, flanked by a *dínos* type of pot, symbolising the
Dínos in which the Socratics believe, represents the school. This second
door will have been revealed at the moment when the screen was taken
away (184), and the symbols of the old and the new religions will have
been the background of the action from then onwards.

The suspension of Socrates in the air was no doubt effected by the
theatrical crane (used also in *Peace*, cf. p. 26), so that the attention of the
audience should not be distracted from the jokes made in 184–217. I
suspect that Socrates was not immediately revealed on the 'opening' of
the school at 184, but swung into sight just before Strepsiades calls
attention to him at 217. At the end of the play, where Strepsiades and
his slave batter off the tiles of the school and set fire to the rafters, it is
hardly possible for us to say how much Aristophanes envisaged would
really be done in performance.

SCIENCE, RHETORIC AND MORALITY[7]

The material for the play is provided by the confluence of two important developments in the culture of the fifth century and by their collision with the traditional beliefs and practices of Greek society. Both developments were the product of the intellectual curiosity which distinguished the Greeks from many other peoples. One was scientific speculation on the structure of the universe. This speculation attempted to explain as natural events, subject to intelligible physical laws, astronomical and meteorological phenomena which had traditionally been regarded as the unpredictable acts of supernatural persons. Such explanation left little room for the traditional gods; whether it implicitly denied their existence, or divested them of personality and removed them to a remote stratum of being, or simply drew attention to the fact that mythology was a mass of conflicting tradition which did not admit of rational proof, its spirit was not easily reconcilable with the intimate personal association characterizing the Greek's relations with the gods of his household, locality and city. The hostility of the ordinary man towards scientific speculation was not simply due to his normal distaste for abstract reasoning or to the somewhat dogmatic form of exposition, inadequately supported by empirical evidence, which was often favoured by Greek intellectuals. The ordinary man regarded his own life as dependent on the goodwill of the gods, who caused his crops to grow and his animals to increase, and it was well known that gods might punish a shipful of men, even a whole city, if one blasphemer in it were allowed to go unpunished. Moreover, some of the best things in life—singing, dancing, dressing up, eating, drinking—were a conspicuous part of festivals in honour of the gods, and inculcation of scepticism cast a shadow over physical enjoyment. For these reasons alone a certain tension between the intellectual and the ordinary man was inevitable, and it was heightened when critical scrutiny was extended from the elements of nature to the institutions of society. It is hardly possible to be seriously interested in how the earth took shape without ever stopping to wonder how (for example) rules against incest took shape, and intellectuals in the fifth century did in fact interest themselves in speculation on prehistory, anthropology and sociology. The Greek noun *nómos* and the verb *nomísdēn*, often translatable respectively as 'law' and 'think', denote the customary usages of a

7 On the subjects discussed in this section see W. K. C. Guthrie, *A History of Greek Philosophy*, volume III (Cambridge, 1969), Part One.

given society, including the constitution, written law, religious cult, administrative procedure, assumptions, beliefs, etiquette, generally accepted values and even linguistic usage. All critical speculation whatsoever, whether directed upon nature or on man, was bound to find itself in some degree in conflict with *nómos*; that is to say, it was bound to be felt by the ordinary unthinking man as threatening his security.

The second cultural development of the period which is relevant to *Clouds* is the growth of a systematic interest in the techniques of persuasion in lawcourts and political assemblies.[8] The Greeks had always enjoyed public speaking, and had always listened to speeches as to an art-form, with the keen ear of a connoisseur, not to mention a keen eye for stance and gesture. No doubt, too, men who knew themselves to be grossly in the wrong had always put up the most ingenious arguments they could devise and had exploited any weakness they could spot in the pleas of their honest adversaries. In the fifth century the success enjoyed by really convincing speakers in democratic assemblies, the obvious fact that attainment of political power turned so much on the ability to persuade, and the impossibility of drawing a sharp dividing line between what we would call 'politics' or 'administration' and the prosecution of a rival for an alleged political or administrative offence, led to scrutiny and study of the oratorical means to political ends. A man who applies, for the purpose of inciting irrational prejudices and misleading an uneducated audience by arguments which he knows to be fallacious the logical skills which in science and philosophy serve to distinguish valid inferences from invalid may fairly be accused of intellectual prostitution, but prostitution of any kind flourishes where the demand is high and the rewards great. Protagoras, who spent much of his time at Athens and was a contemporary and friend of Perikles, was especially interested in the technique of presenting an equally strong case for and against the same proposition; the 'Tetralogies' ascribed to Antiphon, in which the author has composed both the prosecutors' and the defendants' speeches in imaginary cases of homicide, illustrate how this technique could be applied to the lawcourts. Gorgias, who taught pupils the practice of forensic and political oratory, was equally ready to tackle metaphysical propositions. The fact that in some cases scientific and philosophical interests really were combined with rhetoric encouraged the ordinary man to associate all intellectual pursuits with

8   On the growth of forensic 'consultancy' see my *Lysias and the Corpus Lysiacum* (Berkeley and Los Angeles, 1968), chapters VIII and IX, and George Kennedy, *The Art of Persuasion in Greece* (London, 1963), chapters I–III.

the desire of clever and wealthy young men to be taught the techniques of attaining political power and a degree of immunity from prosecution for civil offences. *Young* men, in particular, because ingenious and persuasive argument was the one means by which the experienced judgment of old men could be devalued; *wealthy* young men, because those intellectuals who took pupils—intellectuals who were coming to be called *sophistaí*, our 'sophists', a word which at an earlier date had a much wider and more complimentary meaning—charged very high fees; and *clever* young men, because they were prepared to use their brains in a way unfamiliar to most of the older generation. Traditional Athenian education trained boys in skills and arts useful to the community in war and peace, such as gymnastics, throwing the javelin, reading and writing, singing and playing stringed instruments, but there was no respect in which it encouraged a boy to think critically; education was a matter of passing on traditional techniques from one generation to the next. The sophists did not directly substitute one kind of education for another, since they did not teach mere boys, but they fed an intellectual appetite which a young man's previous education had done nothing to satisfy or even to stimulate. How this cultural movement could be regarded is best illustrated by *Clouds* itself, where we see that as a basis for the rhetorical training which is Strepsiades' reason for seeking out Socrates and entrusting his son to the school Socrates is imagined as studying astronomy, meteorology and geology, experimenting in entomology, analysing metre and rationalizing grammar. Pheidippides emerges from the school not only skilled in word-play but with a taste for challenging *nómos* by speculative reconstruction of prehistory (1421f.) or by appeal to that antithesis between *nómos* and 'nature' which was one of the really important intellectual discoveries of the fifth century. It may seem surprising that a culture which had itself made so many innovations in the arts and in political organization should have reacted with such undiscriminating hostility against innovations in morality and religion. The Athenians, however, tended to play down their own innovations; devoted to their ancestors, conscious of the continued ghostly presence of those ancestors, they were more inclined to postulate the existence of a kind of prehistoric democracy on Attic soil than to claim credit for having devised a political system unknown in earlier times. There was, moreover, a widespread and deep-seated belief in the divinity of Justice, and this forms the rational connection (as the versatility of the sophists forms the fortuitous connection) between new theories of meteorology and the desire of a debtor to cheat his creditors. Hesiod had described Justice as the rule which Zeus had laid down for the life of human society, and personified her as the minister of Zeus. Popular morality was tenacious of the idea that the unjust man, the perjurer, the defaulting debtor, even if he escapes human detection and punishment, nevertheless meets with his deserts at the hands of the gods; or, if he dies secure and happy, his descendants pay the penalty after him; or again (as was coming to be believed increasingly in the fifth century [cf. p. 208]) his soul pays the penalty in the underworld. To criticize the divine genealogies propounded by the poets and to attribute the working of the universe to impersonal physical forces uninterested in human behaviour was to lift from the ingenious and the aggressive fears which were believed to have constrained them to obey the law.

The moral framework within which the plot of *Clouds* is presented is as stark as that of an evangelical tract. Strepsiades begins with a dishonest intention; he is easily persuaded by Socrates to reject the traditional gods; and he looks forward with excitement to a successful career of dishonesty. Pheidippides learns from Wrong a nonchalant, selfish nihilism which is portrayed as deserving far greater condemnation than the almost equally selfish extravagance by which he had impoverished his father. There is no suggestion that anything which Socrates has to offer is of any value to society or of any interest to a decent citizen. In the last stage of his quarrel with his son Strepsiades turns to the audience with three lines of ponderous moralizing (1437–1439):

You men of my age, I think what he says is right, and I'm all for agreeing with the honest side of his case. It's fair enough that we should be beaten if we don't do right.

Horrified by Pheidippides' offer to demonstrate that it is permissible to strike one's mother as well as one's father, Strepsiades turns in despair to the chorus, and they reveal their true nature and purpose in a passage of tragic rhythm (1453–1464):

STREPSIADES: It's all through you, Clouds, that this has happened to me. I put my troubles in *your* hands.
CHORUS: You are the cause of your own suffering,
            bending yourself into the ways of evil.
STREPSIADES: Why then did you not warn me from the first, but led me on, a poor old countryman?

CHORUS: This is our wont, whenever we discern
a man who is in love with evildoing,
until we cast him into misery,
that he may learn to fear the gods in heaven.
STREPSIADES: Oh, it's cruel, Clouds, but it's just! I ought never to
have tried to get away without paying the money I'd borrowed.

So the ambiguities in the role of the clouds are resolved; they are
genuine divine beings, but under the government of Zeus and the
Olympians, and they have punished Strepsiades for his dishonest intentions by answering the invocation of Socrates and inciting Strepsiades to enrol as a student. Their secret was well kept from the audience
as well as from the characters. Although during the parabasis they behave like any other comic chorus and invoke the traditional gods to
take part in the festival, within the plot they give us no hint of what is
to come until 1114, which makes a vaguely menacing suggestion that
Strepsiades will come to regret Pheidippides' enrolment. It is only in
1303–1320, immediately before the quarrel between father and son,
that the clouds take their stand unambiguously on the side of traditional
morality.

For all this, we have to remember that Athenian society was by
Greek standards open-minded and tolerant of unconventional beliefs,
and it contained, especially in the ranks of its wealthy aristocracy, an
unusually high proportion of men who were intellectually alive. Those
whose speculations and skills undermined traditional assumptions were
not conspirators or spies who sowed the seeds of intellectual revolt and
escaped under cover of darkness before the respectable citizenry could
catch them, but what we would nowadays call 'controversial figures',
distinguished, attracting as much admiration on one side as mistrust on
the other, and in danger only if they became involved fortuitously or
peripherally in political crises which were not of their making.

It is difficult for the modern reader to understand how a writer as
sensitive and subtle as Aristophanes could have taken the field with such
vigour on the side of the philistines against that spirit of systematic,
rational inquiry which we regard as an essential ingredient of civilization. Perhaps we underrate the extent to which aesthetic sensibility and
devotion to the perfecting of artistic technique can be divorced from
abstract or scientific reasoning.[9] It is possible that in many of the greatest

9 A comparable gulf can exist between professions which one might have
supposed to be akin. A lawyer once seriously asked me whether Mr X (he
named a very distinguished classicist) was 'quite right in the head'. The reason

Greek artists and poets (Pindar, for example) the divorce was complete; and in the comic poets a predilection for artistic creativity rather than systematic analysis naturally have been reinforced by a temperamental inclination to mock what is new and difficult from the standpoint of the man in the street. A man could hardly have become a comic poet without this inclination. Popular humorous writers in our own time do not hesitate to ridicule Freud or Picasso although they neither know nor care what Freud actually said or why he said it and have perhaps never troubled to look at a modern painting except in a newspaper photograph. Aristophanes at least had more excuse; exciting though some Greek philosophical and scientific speculations now seem to have been, viewed as an early stage in the intellectual history of Europe, they were not always expressed in a way which would necessarily make them appear, even to a rational man, more plausible than Hesiodic myths.

Aristophanes' ability to see that aspect of anything which lends itself most readily to comic exploitation substantially modifies in detail the simple and inflexible moral rigour suggested by the outline of *Clouds*. The contest between Right and Wrong is not in fact a contest between right and wrong. Right has no weapon against the sharp criticisms of Wrong except bad temper, and his picture of the boys of an earlier generation as uniformly tough, disciplined, bashful and obedient adheres too closely to the standard contrast (in all ages) between present and past to be accepted as anything but a vivid comic caricature of a familiar constant. The peculiar feature conspicuous in Right's exposition, which would be absent in a serious and sympathetic presentation of a similar exposition today, is that his interest in boys is strongly focussed on their genitals. Athenian society in Aristophanes' time was 'bisexual' in the sense that men were sexually aroused at least as much by handsome boys as by pretty girls; it was taken for granted that this arousal was natural and normal, and if an Athenian said that he was 'in love' it could not be known without asking him (and he would not mind being asked) whether he was in love with a boy or with a girl. Although Aristophanes' characters are predominantly heterosexual, there is no suggestion anywhere in his work that they would find

for his question was that he had attended a college dinner at which he had heard Mr X and another classicist spend a full twenty minutes in discussing the meaning of a passage in the *Agamemnon*; in the discussion they had adopted the hypothesis that Aischylos held certain primitive beliefs, and it seemed to the lawyer that it was an absurd waste of time to discuss such beliefs at all.

homosexual intercourse with a handsome boy anything but agreeable, and when old Philokleon in *Wasps* 568 includes as one of the pleasures of being a juryman 'looking at the genitals of the youths' who are undergoing their official young-citizen scrutiny he may be only expressing (see however, p. 125) the roguish side of the comic character. Right goes into more detail (972–980):

And at the gymnastics teacher's the boys had to sit with one thigh forward, so as not to show anything tormenting to the people outside. And then when a boy got up he had to brush the sand over and take care not to leave an imprint of his youth for his lovers. And no boy in those days would anoint himself with oil below the navel, so that moisture and down bloomed on his genitals as on quinces. And he wouldn't turn on an effeminate voice to catch his lover and pimp for himself with his eyes as he walked.

The pursuing lover is you or I, but the boy shocks us deeply if he actually tries to attract us, and everyone condemns him if he is too easily caught; this is the 'double standard' familiar in modern heterosexual societies and equally applicable to homosexual pursuit and capture in Athens, as is clear from a well-known passage of Plato's *Symposium* (182A ff.). We should not for a minute imagine that Aristophanes' audience listened to Right with straight faces. He dwells with romantic appetite upon a past densely populated with smooth, muscular, modest, shy, serious boys, and since he speaks from the point of view of the man, not of the boy, he is put in the absurd position of expressing in a tone of moral earnestness sentiments to which roguish jocularity is appropriate.

Even the end of the contest is ambivalent. Right having declared that to be *eurýprōktos* ('wide-arsed', a fairly common term of abuse in comedy) is the greatest of disgraces, Wrong compels his admission that tragic poets and politicians all come from the ranks of the wide-arsed, and (1094–1104):

WRONG: Don't you realize there's nothing in what you said? Now take a look at the audience and see which kind's in a majority.
RIGHT: I'm looking.
WRONG: Well, what do you see?
RIGHT: The wide-arsed are certainly in a big majority. I know *him*, for example, and him over there, and that one with the long hair.
WRONG: Well, what are you going to say?

RIGHT: I give in! Oh, you buggers! For God's sake, take my cloak—
I'm deserting to your side!

And there the contest ends. Having chosen not to pit Wrong against an
opponent worthy of him, Aristophanes submerges the issues, before
they have emerged in serious form, under an uproarious invocation of a
stock comic motif, gross vilification of the audience (cf. p. 53).

SOCRATES[10]

No individual in the whole history of Greek civilization is presented to
us so vividly and in such detail as Socrates. The majority of Plato's
philosophical works are dialogues in which Socrates takes a leading
part; Xenophon composed several works of the same type; so did minor
contemporaries and imitators of Plato; and from Aristotle onwards,
for the best part of five centuries, we encounter a stream of allusions
and anecdotes.

In certain very important respects this tradition is united against the
portrait which we find in *Clouds*. So far from teaching the tricks of
forensic oratory in return for fees, the Socrates of Plato and Xenophon
is outspokenly hostile both to oratorical techniques and to the principle
of teaching for money; his devotion to truth and justice is passionate
(though often expressed with urbane diffidence), and although he is
loyal to the letter of the democratic constitution his professed attitude
to political and forensic practice is one of bewildered innocence. The
only author to allege that he taught oratory is a certain Idomeneus,
who on quite other grounds is justly regarded as an irresponsible
gossip; he almost certainly treated *Clouds* itself as the grounds of his
allegation. A paragraph cited from a lost speech of Lysias, composed
for a case against a Socratic within twenty years (and perhaps much less)
of Socrates' death, is of special interest because its whole context is
unphilosophical:

> I thought that since he had been a pupil of Socrates and had engaged
> in so many impressive discussions of justice and virtue he would
> never attempt or venture what the worst and most dishonest of men
> attempt to do.

A second important respect in which the main tradition differs from
Aristophanes is in denying to Socrates those kinds of scientific and
philological interests which are one of the principal comic strands
throughout *Clouds*. Plato in the *Apology*, his version of the speeches

10   See Guthrie, op. cit. (n. 7 above), Part Two, especially chapter XII (5).

made by Socrates when prosecuted in 399,[11] represents Socrates as long beset by the general allegation that he 'investigates what lies beneath the earth and what is up in the sky, and makes wrong appear right and teaches others to do likewise' (*Ap.* 19B). The jury will themselves have seen 'Socrates' in *Clouds* 'saying that he was "treading the air" and talking a lot of drivel on subjects about which I know absolutely nothing' (19C). Told that he asserts the sun and the moon not to be gods but composed respectively of stone and earth, he replies 'Do you think it's Anaxagoras that you're accusing?' and goes on to point out that if he did claim these 'extraordinary' doctrines as his own the young men who learn from him would soon discover that they were drawn from the published works of Anaxagoras (26DE). Plato on another occasion represents Socrates as dependent on others for what little he knows about the technicalities of metre (*Republic* 400BC).

It therefore appears that in *Clouds* Aristophanes has foisted on to Socrates practices and beliefs which he could fairly have attributed to other intellectuals, but in so doing has ignored what the Socratic tradition in general treated as the differences which made Socrates unique. I do not think that we can plausibly accuse Plato and Xenophon of conspiracy to transmit a radically false picture of Socrates to posterity. Socrates had other pupils who wrote about him, sometimes in rivalry or hostility to Plato, and he had highly articulate philosophical adversaries, but from all the items of evidence which we can trace in the fourth century or later we cannot construct a Socrates who coincides with the Aristophanic Socrates.[12] There are only two ways of reconciling *Clouds* with the Socratic tradition: one is to postulate that Socrates

11 Socrates was prosecuted for injuring the community by 'corrupting the young' and evincing no belief in the community's traditional gods, introducing instead novel superhuman powers. The indictment, like nearly all Athenian prosecutions, was initiated and presented by private individuals, although the injury alleged was to the community as a whole. No laws explicitly forbade the offences with which Socrates was charged, but that was no obstacle to indictment. He was condemned to death. It is questionable whether he would have been condemned or even indicted but for his long and close association with Kritias and others responsible for the revolution of 404, and with Alkibiades (cf. Xenophon, *Memorabilia* i. 2.12–16). Fifty years later, Aiskhines (i 173) says to a jury, 'You' (i.e. your forebears) 'executed Socrates the sophist because he was shown to have taught Kritias'.

12 If the real Socrates had shown an interest in oratory, I would expect this to have come through to Aristotle and to have been mentioned by him in his work *The Sophist*, lost to us but used by late ancient writers interested in the history of philosophy.

at the time of the play (when he was in his mid-forties) had scientific and technical interests which he had abandoned by the time Plato's generation made his acquaintance; the other is to accept that Aristophanes failed to recognize, or chose not to recognize, differences which were (and are) of great importance to historians of philosophy. The first of these two hypotheses has sometimes been offered on the strength of a passage of 'intellectual autobiography' put into the mouth of Socrates by Plato in *Phaedo* 96A ff. Socrates says there that when he was young he was interested in the causes of things, and indulged in scientific speculation. Hearing that Anaxagoras argued for Mind as the ultimate cause, he read Anaxagoras, but was disappointed to find only mechanistic explanation where he had hoped for teleology; he therefore abandoned this line of enquiry. The attitude expressed in this passage conforms with the systematic 'myths' about the structure of the world and the underworld which Plato's Socrates propounds in some major works, always subordinate to an ethical purpose and alien in spirit to the scientific speculation of his predecessors and contemporaries. Given the dramatic context of the *Phaedo* passage, I doubt whether it need mean more than that Socrates rejected mechanistic theories of causation as soon as he came up against them. If we do try to make it mean more, we exchange a contradiction between Plato and Aristophanes for a contradiction within Plato's own work, for we have to reconcile *Phaedo* 96A ff. with *Apology* 19Bff.

To suppose, on the other hand, that Aristophanes decided to treat Socrates as the paradigm of the sophist and attached to him any attribute of the whole genus which lent itself to ridicule is not particularly difficult. Socrates was a close associate of some very wealthy and able young men, notably Alkibiades. The difference between his acceptance of their hospitality and friendship and (say) Protagoras's exaction of fees, in addition to hospitality and friendship, from his own wealthy and able pupils was not a difference which would have seemed significant to Aristophanes; Socrates and Protagoras were both, from the comic poet's standpoint, intellectual parasites dependent on patronage, and Socrates, unlike Protagoras, Prodikos and other eminent sophists, was an Athenian citizen, not a bird of passage. Moreover, even if Socrates rejected oratory as based on the dishonest exploitation of the irrational, Alkibiades and similar young men aspired to political power, not to the ascetic and contemplative life, and owed their achievement of this power in large part to their oratorical skill. It was probably Socrates' association with the prominent Alkibiades which made

Aristophanes choose him as representative of the genus. How well he himself knew Socrates is problematical; reference made by the guide-student in the play (137) to the 'miscarriage' of an idea has sometimes been related to the Platonic Socrates' statement (*Theaetetus* 150E) that he serves as 'midwife' to the philosophical thinking of others, some of whom have 'miscarried' because they left his company too soon. If, however, this concept was used by the real Socrates, it is surprising that it should not appear in Plato until a fairly late work; and certain other images with which the Aristophanic Socrates mystifies Strepsiades 'bring machinery to bear on you' (479f.) and 'snapping up' a problem, (489f.), are not known in the fourth-century Socratic tradition.

Even if a modern historian or philosopher could point out to Aristophanes the significance of the differences between Socrates and the general intellectual movements of his time, I am not sure that the poet would be abashed or impressed. People who are not interested in science or philosophy tend to regard as trivial differences which to the scientist or philosopher are momentous, just as those who care nothing for music or painting think in terms of the distinction between musician and non-musician or painter and non-painter but cannot focus their attention for long enough on the art itself to comprehend distinctions within it. If *Clouds* made life hard for Socrates, did Aristophanes care? If he entertained a genuine moral indignation against the subversion of custom and traditional beliefs, he would have welcomed such an out-come; if he was not so very indignant, but wanted to raise all the laughs he could and enlist the sympathies of the average member of his audience, I doubt whether he would have hesitated to buy success at the price of Socrates' security. One simple consideration suggests, at any rate, that the play is not good-natured fun which Socrates' friends could enjoy as much as anyone else: people really were prosecuted and outlawed or killed for alleged injury to the community, and this makes all the difference between the burning of Socrates' school and some modern fantasy depicting the boiling of a politician, for we no longer boil people (or even discommode them) for errors of political judg-ment.

We do not know why the play fared so badly at the Dionysia of 423, and since we possess neither its original version nor the plays which were placed above it speculation is, perhaps, idle. Socrates, according to Plato (*Laches* 181B), had acquitted himself very bravely at the battle of Delion the previous summer, and if Plato's account is true it is con-ceivable that the spring of 423 was just the wrong time to attack

Socrates; but we know that during his lifetime he was ridiculed in several comedies by at least three other poets, in terms similar to those of *Clouds*, and it would be unrealistic to suppose that his reputation must have stood high with his ordinary fellow-citizens.

IX

Wasps

Produced in 422, at the Lenaia, and placed second out of three.

SYNOPSIS

Wasps, like *Clouds*, portrays a father and son, but in quite a different
relationship. The old man Philokleon, in accordance with a common
Greek practice, has handed over the management of the family property to Bdelykleon, who is, of course, responsible for the maintenance
of his father. The two names are artificially constructed to suggest, for
the father, 'fond of Kleon' and, for the son, 'disgusted by Kleon'.
Philokleon suffers from what the whole household regards as a 'strange
illness' (71): he has a consuming passion for serving on juries all day
and every day. Bdelykleon is determined to keep him at home; with
his slaves, he has to keep watch on all possible ways of escape from the
house, in order to defeat the attempts of the energetic and ingenious old
man to run off to the lawcourts. Philokleon climbs up the chimney,
pretending to be smoke when he is seen emerging from it; he tries to
push the front door open against the slaves who push it shut; he clings
to the underside of a donkey, like Odysseus escaping from the cave of
the Cyclops by clinging to the underside of a great ram.

His friends, old men like himself with the same passion for jury-
service, call for him before dawn; they are the chorus of the play, dressed like wasps as a symbol of their angry and unforgiving character.
They are furious at finding their colleague imprisoned in his own house,
and with their encouragement he bites his way through the net which
has been fixed over the windows and starts to lower himself on a rope.
At this moment Bdelykleon and his slaves wake up, just in time to
stop Philokleon joining his old friends. Menaced by the chorus, they

beat it off with the help of all the slaves of the household—they use smoke and branches, as for wasps, and words, as for men. Bdelykleon eventually persuades the chorus to listen while he tries to persuade Philokleon to alter his way of life. So we embark on a formal contest, in which Philokleon first expatiates on the delights of the supreme irresponsible power enjoyed and harshly exercised by the jurors and Bdelykleon replies by demonstrating that this power is an illusion; the real power belongs to the politicians who play upon the jurors in order to revenge themselves upon their own enemies and in the meantime fill their own pockets with impunity. The chorus is convinced, and adds its pleas to Bdelykleon's. But the old man is not so easily moved, and to maintain his interest in life Bdelykleon arranges for him to play the juror at home. A domestic imitation of a lawcourt is set up; by a lucky chance one of the dogs steals some cheese, and is promptly brought to trial. His prosecutor is another dog, and the case is a transparent disguise of the prosecution of Lakhes by Kleon for alleged embezzlement while in command of a force in Sicily (*not* the famous 'Sicilian Expedition'). Philokleon is tricked into voting for acquittal, and faints with shame and horror at the realization that he has so betrayed his merciless principles.

The parabasis intervenes at this point, and after the parabasis we find Bdelykleon dressing his father up and preparing him for a more relaxed and self-indulgent life. The old man is still somewhat rebellious and seems likely to be an uncouth guest at the dinner-party to which he departs. But we soon hear that he has thrown himself into social life as immoderately as earlier into jury-service. Drunken and violent, in the highest of spirits, he arrives home with a slave-girl kidnapped from the party. Being as young as he feels, he talks to her rather as a lovesick youth with a stern father talks in much later comedies (1351–1359):

> If you'll be nice to me now, as soon as my son's dead I'll redeem you from your owner, piglet, and have you as a concubine. As it is, I don't have control over my own money; I'm young, you see, and hedged in pretty strictly. It's my son who keeps an eye on me, and he's a hard man and a real skinflint into the bargain. That's why he's so afraid I'll go the bad; I'm the only father he's got.

Bdelykleon deprives him of the girl, but is immediately faced with a ferocious bread-woman and a man, both of whom Philokleon has assaulted on his way home. Bread-women, like fishmongers (for some reason) and landladies, were commonly unsympathetic characters in Greek comedy, but the other victim of Philokleon's violence is a reasonable person. But both are treated alike; Philokleon makes matters worse by insulting them, and they go off threatening prosecutions for *hybris*, much to Bdelykleon's dismay. Philokleon is now seized by a desire to show off his skill in dancing, and issues a challenge which provides a spectacular ending to the play; three dancers (not speaking characters) enter in response to the challenge, and the four of them lead the chorus out.

PRODUCTION

Although there is no point at which it is demonstrable that four speaking characters are on stage together, any attempt to perform the play with three actors would involve some extraordinarily quick changes. Bdelykleon, who has been in sight, sleeping on the roof (67f.), since the beginning of the play and thus throughout the dialogue of the two slaves which continues down to 135, wakes up and calls out to them at 136. One of them is told to guard the door, the other to run round to the back of the house (138), and that gets rid of one slave. Philokleon starts to climb out of the chimney only five lines later, his first utterance being at 144. Bdelykleon is then on stage continuously, Philokleon almost continuously, until 1009. The slave has some lines to speak down to 502, and then at 835 a slave comes out of the house uttering curses at the dog inside; assuming that these two slave roles are played by the same actor, he has to enter the skene at some point between 502 and 835 without any indication of his movement in the text. At the trial of the dog the prosecuting dog is a human actor, because he has plenty to say, and the other dog is a dressed-up human, though the pleas in his defence are all uttered by Bdelykleon. Towards the end of the play the exits and entrances are as follows:

Slave: entrance 1292, exit 1325; entrance 1475, remains to the end.
Philokleon: entrance 1326, exit 1449; entrance 1482, remains to the end.
A man whom Philokleon has attacked: entrance (with mute characters, pursuing the old man) 1326, exit (with those same mutes) 1334.
Bdelykleon: entrance 1364, exit 1449.
Bread-woman: entrance (with a mute character who is identified at 1408 and 1412 as Khairephon) 1388, exit 1414.
Another man accusing Philokleon of assault: entrance 1415, exit 1441.

Since Bdelykleon's words at 1412–1414 are addressed to Khairephon, and Bdelykleon's two lines 1415f. say 'Here comes someone else . . .', the employment of four actors in 1388–1441 seems inescapable. If it is desired to restrict the work of the fourth actor to the minimum, it might just be possible to combine the role of the second slave at the beginning of the play with that of Philokleon, but the time available for the transformation is very short: hardly more than fifteen seconds, given the urgency and haste of the intervening lines, during which he must both change his costume and get up the 'chimney' from the inside.

The chorus is unusual in that it is accompanied on its arrival by some boys, who carry the lamps to guide the old men through the darkness before dawn. We have a passage of dialogue (248–258) between the chorus-leader and one of the boys, and a little later a lyric dialogue either between the chorus as a whole and the boys singing as a chorus or between the chorus-leader and the boy who has spoken before; a third possibility, that the sung dialogue is between the whole chorus and one boy, is at odds with the boy's use of the vocatives 'Father' (292, 303) and 'Dad' (296). The boys are sent running off at 408–414 to tell Kleon what is going on, and this provides a useful opportunity for the chorus to get rid of the outer garments which up to then have concealed their wasp-costume. It is curious that despite the advanced age of the chorus the boys are quite plainly meant to be their sons, not their grandsons; but, as we would have suspected from other evidence, late marriages and second marriages were so common that it was not difficult for Aristophanes to combine two elements which he wanted for separate theatrical reasons, a boy singer and a chorus representing old men. Boy singers appear in Euripides' *Suppliants*, which on stylistic grounds is datable close to *Wasps*, and they may have been popular in theatre of the 420s; cf. p. 134, on *Peace*.

No more than one door is required in the play, but for comic purposes it has to be a door which (unusually) opens outwards, or at least is envisaged in this way, in order that the slave may push madly against it to keep Philokleon in while the fierce old man pushes outwards (152–155); *pulling* on the door would not be easily represented in slapstick terms, and in any case is ruled out by the word 'push' at 152. After this incident we have twenty lines of dialogue between Bdelykleon and Philokleon before the former leads the donkey out of the house (cf. p. 62); where is Philokleon during these exchanges? It is hard to believe that he is shouting from behind the door, out of our sight, for all the parallels for such a procedure involve far shorter and less conversational utterances. The obvious answer is that he is at a window, and at 317 he sings to the chorus:

> Friends, I have long been pining,
> hearing you through the hole.

The word used here, *opé*, can mean any kind of aperture, hole or chink; Philokleon could indeed have heard the chorus without himself being in a position where we can see him, but the long dialogue in song and speech which begins at 317 is hardly conceivable with one of the participants indoors all the time, and the natural interpretation of *opé* is therefore 'window'. At 379 the chorus encourages Philokleon to lower himself on a rope from the window, denoted this time by the specific word *thyrís*. This he does; Bdelykleon wakes up in time to try to stop him, but not quite in time to succeed, and after a scene of comic uproar in which Bdelykleon, his slaves, Philokleon and the chorus are all engaged Philokleon ends up on ground-level, where we want him to be from now on. Plainly the *thyrís* is in an upper storey of the skene and, in accordance with the elaborate precautions described in the opening scene (125–132), it was covered with a net, which Philokleon, to the encouragement of the chorus, nibbles through during 367–371. The *opé* to which he refers in 318 could be the same window, and the conversation of 156–176 could be conducted through it.[1]

THE CHARACTER OF PHILOKLEON

It has already been observed (p. 37) that the principal character of an Aristophanic comedy sometimes behaves, with apparent impunity, in an uninhibited way which in real life would incur strong social disapproval or even severe legal penalties. The average member of the audience, identifying himself with such a character, may achieve a vicarious revenge on the social and political order within which he is compelled to live. Philokleon, as we have seen, is noteworthy for the readiness with which he inflicts on others drunken violence and insults to a degree which incurs threats of prosecution for *hýbris*. Recent commentators have remarked on the sympathy and affection which he evokes in the spectator and in the reader. I admit that he evokes mine; and yet I remain astonished at the hidden strength of antinomian

---

1   It does not have to be the actor playing Philokleon who is on the inside of the door; an extra could be pushing while Philokleon stands ready to speak through the upper window.

sentiment which that sympathy and affection imply. Aristophanes has invested Philokleon with such defects of character that beside him Dikaiopolis, Trygaios and Peisetairos are almost prigs. Let us list the charges.

1. What Philokleon likes about jury-service is not merely the opportunity to exercise arbitrary and irresponsible power but the opportunity to do *harm*. He expresses his spite in his declaration to the chorus (320–323) that he longs to escape and go with them to the court (literally) 'to do something bad', and (340) that his son

won't let me judge cases or do any wrong (*literally*, 'anything bad').

To some extent, what he says can be regarded as exemplifying that kind of dramatic inconsistency which is discussed on p. 59, but the emphasis conveyed by repetition is notable.

2. When the chorus suggests to him (354f.) that he should climb down from the window on a rope, it alludes specifically to an occasion when, as a soldier at the capture of Naxos, he stole some spits. Philokleon agrees wistfully (357),

Yes, I was young then, and able to steal.

The chorus-leader has earlier recalled to his fellows, as they lament their vanished youth (236–239):

. . . when you and I were on garrison duty at Byzantion, and as we made the rounds at night we pinched the baker's bowl and got away with it, and chopped it up and boiled some pimpernel.

Later in the play (1200f.) Philokleon boasts of 'stealing Ergasion's vine-props' as 'the most valiant deed' of his life.

3. In the context of his exploit at Naxos he also says (358f.):

And no one kept watch on me, but I could run away with impunity. But now soldiers arrayed in arms stand guard on the passes . . .

Whereas in his present circumstances he wants to 'run away' *through* the 'enemy' (i.e. Bdelykleon and the slaves) in order to do his public duty, the language he uses and the contrast he draws with his own soldiering days suggest that in those days he took whatever chance he had to run away out of danger; and cowardice is not to be found elsewhere among the characteristics of the 'comic hero'.

4. When boasting of the jurors' power, Philokleon tells us (583–586) that if a father dies and leaves his daughter (and a share of his property with her) to a husband whom he has named in his will, the jurymen do not worry in the least about the will and the seal which proves its validity, but award the daughter and the property to whoever petitions them persuasively enough. One cannot easily imagine Dikaiopolis behaving in this way, which is not only fundamentally contemptuous of law but has some affinity with a cowardly delinquency which earned very strong disapproval, injury (*kákōsis*) to widows, orphans and heiresses.

5. In 607–609 Philokleon relates with gusto how when he comes home from court, carrying his fee (in the usual Greek manner) in his mouth, his daughter makes a fuss of him and fishes it out of his mouth with her tongue. This kind of kiss was (naturally enough) known to the Greeks as highly erotic (e.g. *Thesm.* 130), and the passage is the only one in comedy which dares to hint at the enjoyment of incestuous contacts.

In short, Philokleon is not merely a comic character who does what the man in the street would really like to do; he seems to be the kind of man (fortunately, there are not many of them) who as a soldier loots from unarmed civilians but keeps clear of an armed enemy, and in old age spends his days in the infliction of pain on others and his evenings in running his hand up his daughter's skirt. If we still like him, why do we? Is it that Aristophanes, by some dramaturgical skill which resists analysis, has compelled us to like him? Or is it that we, through a deficiency of imagination which prevents us from reacting to fictitious creations as we do to the people and situations encountered in our own lives, have misunderstood Philokleon and his creator's intentions? Trygaios in *Peace* (54, 65) is regarded by his slave as 'insane' when he purposes to fly up to Olympos, but no one calls him that when he has brought back peace. Philokleon, on the other hand, is 'sick' (71, 87, cf. 119–124) so long as he is gripped by his obsessive desire for jury-service, and 'insane' (1486) at the end of the play when his insatiable aggressiveness turns in a different direction. Bdelykleon describes his 'sickness' as one 'inborn, from the beginning, in our city' (651); and this points to an interesting relationship between the personality of Philokleon as an individual and those aspects of the jury system which are also satirized in the play.

THE LAW COURTS

If Philokleon wishes to spend all day and every day serving on juries, why should anyone mind? In particular, why should his son wish to prevent him from performing with conscientious enthusiasm a public duty which gave him such pleasure and interest in life during his declining years? If it is *wrong* for Philokleon to serve on a jury, is it wrong because (a) it is a job for younger men, or (b) Philokleon brings the wrong attitude to the job, or (c) it is beneath the dignity of well-to-do citizens, or (d) trial by jury is itself wrong? If (c) is the case, the implication is that only the poor, glad of the three obols a day maintenance, should decide issues at law; if (d) is the case, the implication is that justice should be left to what Hesiod, moralizing indignantly three centuries earlier, called 'bribe-hungry nobles'.[2] There is no hint of (c) or (d) in *Wasps*, any more than *Knights* hints that the sovereignty of the people should be restricted. It is interesting to see that Aristophanes does not suggest a conflict between town-dwelling idlers who sit on juries and virtuous farmers who become the jurors' victims. Indeed, in *Peace* 349 the chorus which articulates the hopes of Attic farmers and identifies itself a few lines later (358) as belonging to the hoplite military class says that if only peace will come,

You won't find me a fierce, bad-tempered juror any more.

The idea that jury-service is better performed by younger men is not, taken by itself, an idea which Aristophanes is likely to have entertained, nor is it very practical; it is only reasonable that men who are past military service and have time on their hands because they have retired from day-to-day preoccupation with estate or craft or trade should spend some of that time on public service, and a mass of old men sitting as a jury is the democratic equivalent of an immemorial feature of human society, the elders of the community sitting as judges.

Why Philokleon's obsession is bad for the community is indicated to us at the end of the prologue, when his name and Bdelykleon's are revealed to us (133f.). It is by no means normal practice to tell us the names of the chief characters before they have appeared; Dikaiopolis's name is first revealed at *Ach.* 406, the Sausage-seller's ('Agorakritos') almost at the end of *Knights* (1257), Strepsiades' at *Clouds* 134 (after he has knocked on the door of the school), Trygaios's at *Peace* 190 (not in the expository prologue, but after his arrival on Olympos), and

2   In *Birds* 508–510 kings of the heroic age, such as Agamemnon and Menelaos, are jocularly associated with greed for bribes. From an anti-democratic standpoint, of course, it can be argued that a large jury which regards itself as representing the majority of the community is corrupt in so far as condemns a defendant in order to confiscate his property (*Knights* 1358–1360).

Peisetairos's not until *Birds* 644. When we hear that the old man is 'Philokleon' and his son 'Bdelykleon', immediately after we have been told that the old man is mentally sick with an obsession for jury-service and the younger man has done everything in his power to get him cured (just as he would have tried to cure him of severe arthritis or cancer), we cannot help relating the names to an aspect of political life which has been satirized in *Knights* and is in any case familiar to us; we are thus half prepared for the terms in which Bdelykleon will argue—and persuade the chorus, which, like the chorus of *Acharnians*, is ultimately amenable to reason—that his old father should stay at home.

Athenian juries were in a sense committees of the sovereign assembly, but committees of a rather special kind; they could not be called to account, nor was there any appeal against their verdicts, and to this extent they were themselves sovereign. Since prosecutions for administrative corruption, procedural irregularity, military failure and bad political advice were common, the juries had it in their power to make and break political careers, and the death penalty was inflicted quite readily. It is this irresponsible exercise of power which Philokleon and his aged friends find so congenial: to have distinguished men weeping, flattering them, begging them for mercy; to settle an inheritance lawsuit without regard for what the testator's will actually says; to be courted by Kleon and other politicians; to be welcomed home and made a fuss of, because of the extra three obols they bring. I, says Philokleon, enjoy the power of Zeus himself, and (626f.):

> When my lightning flashes,
> the rich and the proudest of men
> gasp and shit themselves.

Bdelykleon's argument is designed to prove that this power is illusory, and that the jurors are slaves (682, cf. 515–521); the real power lies with the politicians. This he 'proves' by arithmetic: the total income of the Athenian state is two thousand talents a year (twelve million drachmai), and how much of that is paid out at half a drachma a day to six thousand jurors? Where does the rest go? Not a difficult question, if we are permitted to do a little more arithmetic on the cost of fighting a major war and administering a large city, but we are not permitted; Bdelykleon successfully conveys the impression that somehow or other the money all goes to *them*, the politicians who manipulate in their own interests those very juries which they seem so to flatter and cherish. It is hinted that the ferocity of the old men and their unwillingness to forego the pleasure of convicting a defendant are a nasty kind of compensation for the inferior status which necessarily follows physical enfeeblement, an inferiority for which the outward forms of respect could not compensate enough. Their character is therefore well suited to exploitation by politicians, and to this extent *Wasps* satirizes an aspect of the same political style already satirized in *Knights*; the 'disease' of Philokleon is only an individual case of what Bdelykleon calls (651) 'a disease long endemic in our city'. Kleon appeals to the worst in people, and the loyalest of all his supporters will be a man devoid of shame, honesty, manliness, magnanimity and human kindness.

The Greeks did not rate the virtues of compassion and forgiveness as high as we do, but they did recognize them as virtues; this is clear not only from drama but also from fourth-century oratory, where juries are rarely criticized for harshness but often chided or complimented (according as the speaker is prosecutor or defendant) for habitual mildness. There is no room for doubt that the portrayal of Philokleon as flattered, but not moved, by appeals for pity is intended to be a portrayal of a disagreeable, un-Greek, un-Athenian way of behaving. Moreover, although Athenian law required indictments for offences against the community to be initiated by individuals, it is observable that the orators who initiate such indictments take some trouble to justify themselves—sometimes as personally wronged by the defendant, more often as moved to patriotic duty by the community's great peril —in a way which suggests that they are very anxious not to be thought busybodies. In the same way, too great an enthusiasm for spending one's time in jury-service might have incurred criticism as evidence of an insufficient inclination to mind one's own business. Aristophanes' 'heroes' do not refer to cases on which they have sat in judgment, and without *Wasps*—even making allowance for *Peace* 349, quoted above— we should not get the impression from comedy that the Athenian judicial system differed significantly from ours.

Philokleon's austere life as a juryman has something in common with the intellectuals' disregard of ordinary comfort in *Clouds*; both are deviations from a normal valuation of comfort and enjoyment and relaxation. But whereas Aristophanes would have answered the question, 'How is scientific research to be carried on? by saying 'Not at all', we can hardly imagine that he would have advocated the abolition of all prosecutions and lawsuits. If we assume that he is in no way suggesting that there should be any constitutional change in the recruitment, size and powers of juries, the general implication of *Wasps* is very close to that of *Knights*: it is moralizing, not politics, and it belongs —like most Greek comedy and much of the satirical literature of our own culture—within the tradition of didacticism directed not towards structural change but upon human attitudes and patterns of behaviour.

X

Peace

Produced in 421, at the City Dionysia, and awarded second prize. Aristophanes wrote another play of the same name, but we do not know when.

SYNOPSIS

Trygaios, like Dikaiopolis, is an Attic farmer, and filled with despair for the fate of the Greek world as the war continues through its tenth year. He plans to fly up to Olympos to talk Zeus into creating a state of peace, and for this purpose fattens up a dung-beetle to gigantic size.[1] On this creature he makes his flight; but Hermes, who answers his knock on the celestial door, tells him that the gods have moved house so as to be further away from the turmoil down below. War has moved in and has cast Peace into a deep cave, from which, perhaps, mankind will never see her emerge. A noise inside the house gives Hermes an excuse for moving off; Trygaios, apprehensive, withdraws to one side and sees War with his servant Tumult pounding in a mortar ingredients which symbolize the Greek states.

When War goes in again, Trygaios calls on all the Greeks to come with shovels and crowbars and ropes and rescue Peace from the cave in which she is imprisoned. We now have to forget that Trygaios is the only mortal who has ever flown up to Olympos, for the question of

1 The choice of a beetle rather than a bird is determined by (i) the comic extravagance of the idea, (ii) the opportunity so provided for jokes about excrement and (iii) a folktale—to which Trygaios refers, in a rather distorted form, in 129f.—about the beetle which revenged itself on the eagle by buzzing around the head of Zeus until Zeus let fall the eagle's eggs which he was guarding in his lap.

how the chorus gets there is not raised; nor will there be any reference to change of level on their part when later in the play the action moves back to earth. As soon as they address themselves to moving the rocks which block the mouth of the cave, Hermes reappears, proclaiming that Zeus has prescribed the death penalty for any attempt to rescue Peace (earlier he had said simply that the gods had left War to do as he pleased). The chorus pleads with him, reminding him of past sacrifices and promising more in future; Trygaios, prompt in invention, like other Aristophanic heroes, tells him that the Sun and the Moon are conspiring to betray the Greek world to the barbarians, who worship them and will not sacrifice to the Olympian gods. Overwhelming Hermes with extravagant promises that all the festivals at present held in honour of the other gods will in future be held in his honour, Trygaios clinches the matter with a bribe, a golden cup, such as might smooth the path of diplomacy on the human level. Hermes yields, and Peace is hauled out of her cave, together with her two beautiful attendants, Opora (*opóra*, the season at which fruit is gathered) and Theoria (*theōría*, attendance at festivals and games). After Peace has been joyfully saluted, the chorus puts a curious question to Hermes (601f.):

> Now tell us, kindliest of gods, wherever was she all this long time away from us?

This question is taken as meaning 'Why did the war start in the first place?', and Hermes embarks on a comic account (different from that given in *Ach.* 513ff.) of how Perikles, fearing exposure of his own involvement in some misdeed of the sculptor Pheidias, persuaded the Athenians to pass the Megarian Decree,[2] and the subject-allies of Athens bribed the leading men at Sparta to open hostilities. Then Trygaios returns to earth; Opora is to be his wife (whether or not the mother of his children is still alive, or what is to be done with her, we are not told),[3] and Theoria is to be given to the Council.

Back home, Trygaios answers questions from his admiring slave about his voyage into the sky, sets in motion preparation for his wedd-

---

2 Both this account (to which Trygaios and the chorus respond [615–618] with, 'Well, I never!') and the account given in *Acharnians* were taken seriously by historians in the fourth century B.C. and later.
3 Similarly in *Birds* Peisetairos asks for Basileia in marriage without enlightening us on whether he already has a wife and, if so, what he is proposing to do with her.

ing to Opora, hands over Theoria to the Council (an apparent case of 'audience participation', for the real Council had front seats in the theatre), and prepares for a ritual sacrifice to Peace. The sacrifice is in progress when the oracle-monger Hierokles arrives and tries to stop it; he is also hungry for a share of the sacrificial meat, and his importunity leads to his being stripped and driven away with blows by Trygaios and the slave. The second parabasis follows the Hierokles scene, and then the consequences of peace are exhibited in a pair of scenes: dealers in peaceful products bring Trygaios presents and are invited to the wedding, but dealers in arms are insulted and depart miserably.

Two boys, sons of guests at the wedding, come out to practise their songs. One, who sings resounding verses of heroic warfare, turns out to be the son of the bellicose Lamakhos (cf. p. 80, on *Ach.*); the other, who sings a poem of Archilokhos which deals jauntily with the loss of a shield, is the son of Kleonymos, against whom that same act of cowardice was alleged, and Trygaios, so far from crying 'That's the stuff!' deals more harshly with him than with the first boy. The play ends with the wedding procession of Trygaios and Opora, accompanied by a wedding song which uses the traditional refrain *hymḕn hyménai'* 5 and (unlike the elegant wedding song at the end of *Birds*) seems to be closely modelled on popular, sub-literary usage.[4] The naive, repeated question and answer of 1337–1340,

> What shall we do to her?
> What shall we do to her?
> We'll gather her in!
> We'll gather her in!

reminds us of a citation from a wedding song of Sappho (fr. 115 [Page]):

> To what, dear bridegroom, can I best liken you?
> To a slender young tree most of all do I liken you.

PRODUCTION

So far as doors in the skene are concerned, the surest datum in the play is that the door of the home of the gods, from which Hermes emerges at 179f. and which War uses for his entrance at 232–236 and exit at 288,

4 There was some textual variation in the song in antiquity, and perhaps ancient scholars shared the suspicion of modern scholars that Aristophanes cannot have written anything so crude and folksy. I do not profess to know why he did, but would feel no assurance in saying that he did not. The love-song in *Ass.* 952–968, though by no means an exactly similar case, is at least comparable.

cannot be the same as the cave of Peace, from which a barrier of rocks
has to be removed (224f., 361, 426f.) before she can be hauled out. The
distinction is plainest in 224f., where Hermes points to the cave:

> Into this cave, down below.[5] And you can see what a lot of stones
> he heaped up on top.

When Hermes hears a noise suggesting that War is about to 'come out'
—'out', that is, from the gods' house—he departs with the words 'I'll
go' (*eîmi*), not 'I'll go *in*', and he should therefore be envisaged as departing by the wings. That the cave is the central door of the skene
appears probable from the following considerations.

Although Opora and Theoria must be human extras, Peace herself
is a statue. According to a scholion on Plato (*Apology* 19c) Aristophanes'
rivals Eupolis and Plato Comicus made fun of him for 'raising up the
kolossikón statue of Peace'; the word *kolossós* in classical Greek does not
denote anything particularly large (it can even be used of a doll), and
the wording of the scholion may have its origin simply in the use of
kolossós, 'statue', by Eupolis and Plato Comicus with reference to
Aristophanes' play. When Trygaios wants to get back to earth, he
suddenly finds that his beetle has flown away (721)—at what point
after 181, the last reference to it, the text does not tell us—but Hermes
tells him that he can easily return (726):

> This way, past the goddess herself.

The most plausible explanation is that (i) the statue of Peace, with her
two attendants, is hauled out of the central door on a trolley (cf. p. 24),
(ii) the statue remains on its trolley in front of the door for the rest of
play, and (iii) at 726–728 Trygaios, Opora and Theoria enter the central
door. Thus the problem of returning to earth is turned into a joke about
the theatre, and Peace, like the chorus, is allowed to remain in situ, the
question of her movement from one level to another not being raised.

Trygaios's own house could conceivably be represented by the same
door as represents the gods' house, for there is no point in the play at
which both are in simultaneous use, but the representation of his flight
from earth to Olympos gains somewhat in clarity and symmetry if his
door is at one end of the skene and the gods' door at the other. This
third door will be the one used by the slaves and the children in the

5   The words 'down below' tell us that we are to imagine the cave as going
downwards. They do not imply that a hole had been dug in the theatre for the
occasion.

first scene. When we first see Trygaios on his beetle (80f.) he has been swung up into the air from behind the skene on the crane, then forward over the top of the skene, and finally deposited in front of the other end of the skene, close to the gods' door.[6]

It would be quite possible to act the play with three adult speaking actors, for the same person could play Hermes and Tumult (with twenty-one lines for a change of costume). The manuscript text appears to present us with a crowd of speakers in 1191–1264, for as soon as the dealer in agricultural implements accompanied by the (silent) cask-maker, goes into the wedding-feast (1207f.), an arms retailer, a spear-maker and a helmet-maker all arrive. The sigla not only indicate some lines as spoken by the second and third members of this trio, but also divide what I have called the retailer's lines between a 'crest-maker', a 'breastplate-maker' and a 'trumpet-maker'. If, however, we follow the indications of the dialogue itself, ignoring the sigla, we observe that the character to whom Trygaios refers quite explicitly as *hóplōn kápēlos*, 'retailer of arms' (1209) does not speak as if he himself manu-factured crests or breastplates, and when he speaks of trumpets he says (1240f.):

> What am I to do with this trumpet, then, which I *bought* for sixty minae?

The crest-maker, breastplate- and trumpet-maker are in fact figments of the imagination of ancient commentators who multiplied characters with insufficient regard for the words of the text (cf. p. 8). Equally, a careful reading of the dialogue shows that the spear-maker and the helmet-maker, of whose existence we know only because the retailer speaks of them (1213) and to them (1255, 1260), do not have to say any-thing themselves.

The boys of 1265–1302 are singing extras, and one of them will no doubt have taken the part of Trygaios's child in 111–149; cf. p. 124 on *Wasps*.

PEACE AND PANHELLENISM

Two apparently distinct questions, the political standpoint of the play and the constitution of the chorus, turn out to be different aspects of the same question, and to be related to a third question, the identity of the boys in 1265–1304.

The ending of the war is the theme common to *Acharnians* and *Peace*,

6 Cf. p. 198 on the advantage of having three doors in *Women in Assembly*.

but they differ both in the circumstances of their composition and in the characters of their heroes. *Acharnians* was composed in 426 and performed early in 425, when many of the most significant operations of the war lay still in the future. *Peace*, on the other hand, was performed only ten days before the formal conclusion of the peace-treaty of 421, and although Aristophanes may have conceived its central idea before the battle at Amphipolis (in the summer of 422), at which both Kleon and the Spartan Brasidas were killed, he had time to work it out in detail after general feeling had turned in the direction of peace. Thus Trygaios is not the mouthpiece of a far-sighted minority lamenting the continuation of an apparently unending war, but a man who performs on a level of comic fantasy a task to which the Athenian people had already addressed itself on the mundane level of negotiation. The progress of events made the play more of a celebration than a protest. Furthermore, whereas Dikaiopolis was determined to 'opt out' of the war for his own comfort and advantage, Trygaios talks the language of altruism, and that not only in the name of Athens but in the name of the whole Greek world (59, 63, 93.) When he summons the chorus to come and rescue Peace he addresses them as 'Greeks' (292), and they speak of themselves as *Panhéllēnes* (302). When they have begun to haul up Peace Trygaios exclaims (464):

Why, they're not all pulling alike!

and from then on he and Hermes upbraid those who are obstructing the operation or not taking their share of the work. The Boeotians are cursed for 'putting on airs' (465f.), words which reflect the resentment felt by the Boeotians in 422/1 at the progress of peace negotiations between Sparta and Athens. The Athenian general Lamakhos, whose enthusiasm for war we remember from *Acharnians*, is driven away (473f.); the Argives, neutral throughout the war, don't care (475–477, 493); the Megarians can't do much, because they are weak with hunger (481–483, a disagreeable joke about the toothy grimace of starving men), and they are angrily told to go away as displeasing to Peace, because they were the cause of the war (500–502; panhellenic affection for Megarians is too much to ask of Attic comedy). We might have expected that in the end only the Spartans and Athenians will be left, and Trygaios comments (478) that the Spartans are 'pulling manfully', but almost at once a reservation is added, and a little later the Athenians are accused of hindering the work (503–507). Thereupon the chorus-leader cries (508):

Come on, now, farmers only, let's put our hands to it ourselves!

At once everything goes right; as Trygaios says (511):

It's the farmers that are doing the job pulling, nobody else.

From here until the end of the play the chorus is a chorus not merely of farmers, but specifically of Athenian farmers; even when the pleasures to which they look forward and the sufferings they are glad to be rid of are applicable in general terms to farmers anywhere, they make many particular references to Athenian institutions and personalities, congratulating Trygaios on saving 'the sacred city' (1035; not 'the cities') and cursing the *taksíarkhoi* (1172; Athenian regimental commanders) for posting call-up lists at short notice by 'the statue of Pandion' (1183). This does not mean that the chorus at its first entry consisted of many more than the normal twenty-four and has been whittled down by driving away Boeotians, Argives, etc. If the chorus, divided between two or more ropes, has its backs to us when the hauling scene begins, we can think of it as the spearhead of a great host which includes us, the audience, and the world beyond us. The reproaches uttered against those individuals and nations which are treated as impeding the operation can be addressed in various directions, some of them over our heads as if into the distance, and when the chorus-leader at last calls on the farmers alone to pull he can gesture in a manner which suggests the separation of an élite from the rest of us.

It must also be observed that *before* the appeal to the farmers the chorus alternates between a Panhellenic character and a strictly Athenian character. Trygaios's original summons was (296–298):

Come here, farmers and merchants and craftsmen and workmen and aliens and visitors and islanders. . . .

The first four on the list are categories of population to be found in any state, and so far the appeal is international; but a resident alien (*métoikos*) or a visitor (*ksénos*) from another state can, of course, belong to any of those first four categories, and so can 'islanders' when they are at home on their own islands. Since 'islanders' is a term commonly used to denote the subject-allies of Athens, Trygaios's list is in fact a complete list of the categories of population one would expect to find at Athens, described from an Athenian standpoint; the audience would understand it as 'Athenian farmers and merchants and craftsmen and workmen, resident aliens at Athens, foreign visitors to Athens, and subject-allies of Athens from the Aegean islands'. And the chorus itself, *before* the reproaches against the Boeotians and others, sings in purely Athenian terms (346–356):

> Could I but live to see that day!
> All the troubles I've endured,
> sleeping rough, the lot of Phormion!
> No more will you find me
> a fierce, bad-tempered juryman,
> nor hard of heart as I used to be;
> you'll see me young again and easy,
> rid of all my troubles.
> For long enough we've been worn to a shadow,
> with spear, with shield,
> off to the Lykeion,
> back from the Lykeion.

Thus there is no really clear break at which the chorus is transformed from Greeks into Athenians. Trygaios's original concern was with all the Greek world; his summons to the chorus is half expressed in Greek terms, half in Athenian; the chorus itself is half regarded as Greek, half as Athenian, then as (unspecified) farmers, and finally as Athenian farmers; and as they settle down into this last role, Trygaios is treated more as a man who has brought peace to Athens than as a peacemaker for the Greek world.

What are Lamakhos and Kleonymos doing at his celebration of his wedding with Opora? The boys who come out and sing are their sons. Clearly Trygaios here is not to be imagined as a new Dikaiopolis who has gained something for himself but as a representative Athenian farmer in whose achievement all his fellow-citizens, whether he likes them or not, necessarily share. His wedding *is* the newly-won state of peace.

XI

Birds

Produced in 414, at the City Dionysia, and awarded second prize.

SYNOPSIS

Two Athenians—their names are given, when more than a third of the play has passed, as Peisetairos and Euelpides—are tired of living at Athens, and go searching for Tereus, a hero whose mythical transformation into a hoopoe had been the subject of a Sophoclean tragedy. They hope that he has somewhere seen from the air a city which will suit them. Guided by a crow and a jackdaw, they reach his home among lonely rocks and bushes. He cannot tell them anything to their liking, but Peisetairos is gripped by a wonderful idea: the birds can, if they will, rule mankind and starve the gods into submission. The hoopoe is persuaded at once, and agrees to summon all the birds and put the idea before them. He summons the nightingale to 'sing' with him—actually, to play the pipe, out of sight in the bushes, while he sings—and a splendid assortment of birds, the chorus of the play, gathers in answer to his call.

Men eat birds, and the Greeks like other Mediterranean people then and now, ate little birds as well as big ones. Birds therefore regard men as their natural enemies, and the chorus, loudly accusing the hoopoe of treason, prepares to destroy Peisetairos and Euelpides, who hastily arm themselves with all they have, cooking-pots and saucers and spits. Gradually the hoopoe persuades the birds that they really have something of great value to learn from the two humans. Their anger wanes, and the men cautiously lower their weapons; at length the birds swear a truce, and Peisetairos begins his detailed exposition. It is composed in the manner of a formal contest, each half being introduced by a choral stanza and exhortation (cf. p. 68); but instead of two opposed arguments, we find in the first half Peisetairos's 'proof' that the birds were the original rulers of the universe, and in the second half his advice on the building of a bird-city midway between gods and men. The birds are convinced and delighted, and the hoopoe takes the men into his house, promising that he has a magic root which will make them sprout the necessary wings.

The parabasis comes at this point, and after it we see the two men winged, and rather self-conscious about it. With the hoopoe they choose a name for the bird-city, 'Cloudcuckooland' (*Nephelokokkȳgía*, from *nephélē*, 'cloud', and *kókkȳks*, 'cuckoo'). Peisetairos issues businesslike orders for the building, and we do not see Euelpides or the hoopoe any more.

No less than eighteen new characters (or seventeen, if we identify the last messenger with an earlier one) appear between now and the end of the play. The first group is of people concerned in different ways with the founding of the city: a priest who officiates at the sacrifice of foundation, reeling off an interminable (but rudely terminated) list of bird-deities; a lyric poet who seeks patronage[1] and is charitably given a shirt before being dismissed; an oracle-monger, like Hierokles in *Peace*, who is chased away; the mathematician and astronomer Meton, whose ideas on symmetrical city-planning earn him a beating; and finally an 'inspector' and a 'decree-seller' from Athens, who are also beaten despite their threats of vengeance at law (cf. p. 37). After this group comes the second parabasis. Then two messengers arrive: the first describes the miraculous speed with which the walls of the city are rising, thanks to the great flocks of birds and ingenuity with which they use their beaks and feet; the second brings the alarming news that a divine spy has penetrated the city's defences. The alarm is given, and Iris, the personification of the rainbow and in tradition one of Zeus's messengers, glides in to land, no doubt by means of the theatrical crane. Peisetairos mocks and bullies the poor goddess into a helpless rage and shoos her away as one would a bird.

Now the herald who had been sent to mankind returns with the news that all men have rushed headlong into ornithomania, and it is to

---

1 The great lyric poets of the late archaic and early classical periods, Simonides, Pindar and Bacchylides, had profited from the patronage of the Sicilian tyrants and aristocratic families in Greece. The stock comic picture of a lyric poet therefore represents him as a parasite dependent for his living on eloquent flattery of the rich and powerful.

be expected that thousands will come to Cloudcuckooland to be fitted
with wings. Peisetairos has a stock of wings brought out in readiness,
and three immigrants from earth arrive in succession. The first is a
young man attracted by the lack of inhibition with which birds
assault their own fathers (the same point is made in the context of
'nature vs. convention' by Pheidippides in *Clouds* 1427–1431);
Peisetairos tells him the situation is not quite as simple as he thinks, arms
him, and sends him off to war to work off his aggression in a more
acceptable manner. The dithyrambic poet Kinesias skips on declaiming
phrases about winds and birds and the sky, such as are associated in
comedy with this genre of poetry;[2] what Peisetairos does to get rid of
him is not entirely clear from the text. The third character of the group
reveals himself as a *sȳkophántēs* (a combination of 'informer' and
'blackmailer', not 'sycophant') who specialises in victimizing citizens
of the subject-allies and realises how he could speed up his work if he
had wings. He is impervious to Peisetairos's reproaches and is driven
away by whipping. The store of wings is abruptly taken indoors.

   The siege of the gods has done its work, and Prometheus, traditionally
the friend of man and enemy of Zeus,[3] comes hiding under a parasol
to tell Peisetairos how bad things are in heaven, and to advise him on
the demands he should make when a divine embassy comes to treat for
peace. The embassy consists of Poseidon, Herakles and a 'barbarian'
god of the Triballians, a people who lived in the centre of the Balkans.
Peisetairos has quickly organized the cooking of some birds 'condemned', he says (1583f.) 'for revolting against the democratic birds',
and he affects to be much more interested in culinary details than in
what the gods have to say. But he is magnanimous (1596–1602):

   Well, we didn't ever start the war against you, and now, if it's agreed,
   we're willing, if you're at last prepared to do what is just, to make
   peace. Our just demand is that Zeus should render his sceptre back to

---

2   Cf. especially *Clouds* 331–339 and *Peace* 827–831.
3   The legends about Prometheus represent him as punished by Zeus for
advancing the self-sufficiency of man. Since he was worshipped at Athens in
Aristophanes' time, it was emotionally necessary for the Athenians *either* to
refrain from asking themselves whether Zeus and Prometheus were still
enemies *or* to believe that Prometheus had been released from his bondage and
was reconciled to Zeus. Aiskhylos's play *Prometheus Bound* is one of a pair; it
portrays the punishment of Prometheus, who at that time is understandably
hostile to Zeus, but the other (lost) play, *Prometheus Unbound*, portrayed the final
reconciliation.

the birds. If we can reach a settlement on this basis, I invite the embassy to lunch.

'Lunch' is enough for the gluttonous Herakles, who agrees and bullies the Triballian into agreeing. When Peisetairos goes on to demand the divine housekeeper, Basileia, as his wife (she looks after Zeus's thunder-bolts), Poseidon threatens to break off negotiations, but Peisetairos again brings round Herakles by some fast talking, and the Triballian falls into line (cf. p. 6). Peisetairos has won. The final scene, intro-duced by a messenger proclaiming a splendid hotch-potch of poetic hyperboles, is the wedding-procession of Peisetairos and Basileia.

PRODUCTION

Despite the large number of characters in the play (most of whom appear only after the parabasis), only three actors would be needed until the arrival of the embassy of the gods, in which we need a fourth for the Triballian—who, like the King's Eye in *Acharnians*, has only some gibberish to utter. A certain mystery, not yet fully resolved to every-one's satisfaction, surrounds the two mute slaves who are addressed by the hoopoe in 433–435:

> Come on, now, you and you, take back this panoply (*panhoplíā, a full set of arms and armour*) and hang it up (and good fortune attend!) over the hearth indoors, next to the stand.

The only 'arms' are the improvised defences of Peisetairos and Euel-pides, and it is extraordinary that the hoopoe should order their removal without a word to the two men whose lives depend on them and before a truce has been sworn (the truce comes in 438–447, after this passage). The birds have used only their beaks and wings as weapons (cf. the order 'level beaks!' in 364), and the only reference to their having more conventional arms comes in a parody of orders given to human infantry (448–450). There has been no occasion for the hoopoe to arm himself. Therefore it would seem that the order is given not by the hoopoe but by Peisetairos, and either (i) it originally stood after 447, and has been misplaced, or (ii) for some reason, Aristophanes wants the cooking-pot, saucers, etc., out of the way at this moment and does not mind that jokes about the making of a truce are still to come. But in either case, whose are the slaves? We might have expected that Peise-tairos and Euelpides would have had slaves with them, to carry their luggage; but in that case, why did they put up with the discomfort (for at least the first sixty lines) of carrying each a bird on his own wrist, and why do they give no orders to their slaves to help them when they are about to be attacked by the chorus? Bdelykleon, after all, makes good use of his slaves in fighting off the 'wasps'. The answer, I believe, is that the two men addressed as 'you and you' are slaves of indeterminate status, like the 'attendants' of *Peace* 729f., who appear when required—summoned more probably by the hoopoe than by Peisetairos—to carry the properties into the skene; we are not to imagine Peisetairos's implements as going into the hoopoe's house, but simply stage properties going into the property store, and Aristophanes' purpose in having them removed now is to extract humour from the situation by using language appropriate to the returning of arms and armour to their usual place in a real household. Somewhat later the hoopoe again addresses two slaves—this time, giving them the common slave names 'Xanthias' and 'Manodoros'—and tells them to take in the main baggage of the two Athenians.

Even more of a puzzle, since there are no other passages in Aristophanes which offer us any help, are the two birds, a crow and a jackdaw, which the Athenians are carrying at the beginning of the play, evidently in such a way that their fingers are in constant danger of being pecked (8, 25f.). Are these models or real birds? Models would be hard to get rid of when they are no longer wanted, i.e. after line 60. Real birds, on the other hand, could be held by a short cord in the hand as long as they are wanted and released when the hoopoe's slave opens the door and the two men collapse with fright at his appearance; indeed, it is clear from the dialogue in 86–91 that the crow and the jackdaw are supposed to have been inadvertently released through that fright.

The men are frightened of the hoopoe's slave because of his great gaping beak (61), which gives us an indication that bird-characters are at least in part dressed as birds. Accordingly we see from the dialogue (93–106) that the hoopoe has a beak (99) and a crest (94), but not, apparently, wings (103–106), which were perhaps felt likely to be an encumbrance to acting—rather as Prometheus says to Peisetairos (1507f.):

> But so that I can tell you everything that's going on up above, take this parasol and hold it over me.

(Greeks need their hands to express themselves). Evidently the nightingale-piper who plays in accompaniment to the chorus has a beak too, for a reference is made to her beaked mask when Euelpides thinks of kissing her (670–674).

The entry of the chorus must have been spectacularly staged. When the hoopoe has issued his call to all the birds, for a disappointing moment nothing happens. Then comes a flamingo (268–273), a *Mêdos* (274–278), a second hoopoe (279–286) and a *katōphagâs* (287–290); each of these four, as it arrives, is a subject of jokes and questions put to the hoopoe. In 294 Peisetairos exclaims on the great throng of birds in the wings, and as they enter each one is named as a different bird-species (297–305). There are twenty-four names in this list, and if we add the first four we have twenty-eight birds altogether, four more than the normal number of the comic chorus. And there is something special about those first four; what is said of them in 279 and 292f. makes it clear that they have 'occupied crests', and a joke on the double sense of *lóphos* ('crest' on a helmet and also 'hilltop', as in English) is not enough to obscure this. If, as has been suggested, the four birds are simply gorgeously-dressed extras who parade in front of us and go off again, what are these 'crests' which they occupy, and would it not be remarkably confusing to see them going away when the purpose of the hoopoe's call was to summon all birds to a meeting? It seems to me clear that these first four birds, certainly gorgeously costumed but not members of the chorus, arrive where one would expect birds to arrive, on the roof of the skene, from which they can withdraw once the chorus has assembled and our attention is engaged by what is happening in the orchestra.

COMIC AND TRAGIC POETRY

All the five extant Aristophanic plays from the period 425–421 implicitly recommend modifications of political or social behaviour; this is not to say that any such recommendation was necessarily intended by the poet, but that it is there, whether we like it or not. *Birds* differs from those five plays in that it does not even by subtle implication direct the attention of the community towards any desirable policy-decision or any reform of its political habits. At the time of the play the Athenian expedition sent to Sicily in the summer of 415 was just moving from its winter station at Katane to resume the offensive against Syracuse. All that had gone wrong so far was that Alkibiades, one of the three generals in command of the expedition, had deserted to the Peloponnese rather than face charges of blasphemy incurred before he had sailed to Sicily; Sparta had not yet shown signs of giving effective help to Syracuse by reviving the war on the Greek mainland, no one in Sicily had given evidence of a capacity to inflict serious damage on the

Athenian expedition, and Athens had sufficient reserves of men, ships and money to meet any trouble that might blow up in the Aegean. We know that by the autumn of 413 both the expedition and the reinforcements sent out in that year had been utterly destroyed, and Attica was being systematically ravaged by a Peloponnesian force in permanent occupation of Dekeleia; but at the time of writing *Birds* Aristophanes could not know that all that was going to happen. He may have had forebodings, and he may have agreed with those who had argued in 415 that it was better to use Athenian resources on recovery of rebellious areas of the empire in the North Aegean than on an enterprise as far afield as Sicily, but there is no justification for the belief that *Birds* is an 'escapist' play appropriate to a time of national anxiety. If the expedition succeeded it would bring Athens renown as well as increased power and wealth, and Aristophanes may well have been gratified by this prospect (cf. the imperialistic language of *Knights* 1329–1334).

Peisetairos and Euelpides have left Athens because they want a quiet life free from the constant litigation which at Athens (they say) costs so much in fines and damages. This is the stock joke which the Athenians expected to hear against themselves (cf. *Clouds* 207f.), and throughout the Classical period they paid lip-service to *aprāgmosýnē*, not interfering in other people's business and not becoming involved in litigation, as a virtue, however inadequately they may have pursued it. It seems that Aristophanes needs some dramatic motivation, however perfunctory, for bringing his characters into contact with the world of the birds. Similarly in Pherekrates' *Savages*, produced in 420, the plot seems (Plato, *Protagoras* 327C) to have required two or more misanthropes to go off in search of primitive simplicity; misanthropy also appears as an attribute of well-known characters in Athenian folklore (e.g. Timon).

Aristophanes extracts all the humour he can from the assimilation of bird life to human life (Krates' *Beasts*, a much earlier play, which certainly had a chorus of animals, may have relied on similar methods for much of its humour) but he also seems to speak *for* birds. No doubt he enjoyed eating them, and his attitude to their trapping, killing and caging might chill the blood of a modern bird-lover, but at the same time he can imagine and express what they would say to us and about us if they could speak. The parabasis of *Birds*, unlike the parabases of earlier plays, does not drop the thread of the story in order to deal with topicalities or the poet's own virtues, but pursues the same line as Peisetairos's exposition of the antiquity of the birds and the potentiality of bird life. Much of this is jocular, as when they produce a comic version (favourable to themselves) of myths about the origin of the world or explain the advantages of having wings. But some is serious; the ode and antode use the vocabulary and imagery of tragic and lyric poetry to bring the birds, as part of the order of nature, into a relation with the gods which is independent of man. The antode (769–784) runs thus:

> Thus did swans
> (*tiotiotiotiotiotiotiotink*!) [4]
> blending their cries together
> with beating wings proclaim Apollo
> (*tiotiotiotiotink*!),
> sitting on the bank along the river Hebros
> (*tiotiotiotiotink*!),
> and through the clouds far above went the cry;
> and every busy race of beasts went to ground,
> and the clear sky, windless, allayed the wave
> (*totototototototototink*!)
> and all Olympos echoed it,
> and wonderment came upon the lords;
> and the Graces of Olympos, and the Muses,
> shrilled a responding song
> (*tiotiotiotiotink*!)

It is interesting to find some of the same terminology in the mouth of Agathon's slave in *Thesm.* 43–51, where it is treated by an irreverent eavesdropper as tragic bombast:

> SLAVE: And let the sky, windless, hold the breezes in check, and let the grey wave of the sea make no sound.
> OLD MAN: Wooooo!
> EURIPIDES (*to old man*): Quiet!
> OLD MAN (*to Euripides*): What does he *mean*?
> SLAVE: And let the races of winged ones be laid to sleep and the feet of wild beasts that roam the forest stir not.
> OLD MAN: Wooo-woooooo!!!
> SLAVE: For Agathon, poet of beauteous verse, our overlord, will in a moment—

4 In Greek the representations of bird-song end in *-tinks*, not *-tink*, but *-ks* seems to have been a spelling-convention in many onomatopoeic words to which it is inappropriate, e.g. *pappaks* for an explosive fart and (absurdly) *brekekekeks koaks* for the croaking of frogs.

OLD MAN: What? Get fucked?
SLAVE: Who was it that uttered?
OLD MAN: Windless sky!

Of course the slave invites ridicule, because he is using of a human poet language inappropriate to mere humanity, but that does nothing to alter the fact of coincidence between the tragic language parodied in one play but used in the other to create a majestic picture of whooper swans gathering and uttering their splendid cry on a winter's day in the Balkans.

The song in which the hoopoe summons the birds is one of the most exciting things in Greek poetry in respect of the sequence of different rhythms, the relation between each rhythm and the next, and the relation between rhythm and phrasing—little of which can be reproduced in a language such as English, which depends for its rhythmic effects on stress, not quantity. The song is preceded by a shorter appeal to the nightingale to start singing, and there is an interesting relationship between part of this passage and a choral passage of Euripides' *Helen*, produced two years after *Birds*. *Birds* 209–216:

> Come, my partner, cease from sleeping,
> let your holy music rise free,
> the lament your divine voice utters
> for Itys, yours and mine, mourned with many tears,
> trilling with liquid songs of vibrant[5] throat.
> Pure goes the sound through the dense bryony leaves
> to the throne of Zeus . . .

Helen 1107–1113:

> On you who dwell in halls of the Muses
> in the dense cover of the trees,
> on you will I cry,
> most melodious singing bird,
> the tearful nightingale;
> come, trilling through vibrant throat
> to join with me in lamentation,
> as I sing of the sufferings of Helen . . .

When two poets both describe the singing of the nightingale and refer

5 I have taken this translation of the much-disputed word *ksouthós* from the late Professor A. M. Dale's commentary on *Helen*.

to the myth that she is the heroine Prokne, mourning for her son Itys, they are likely to exhibit some coincidence of language, but the coincidence in these two passages is rather large, particularly since the verb *elelísdesthai*, 'trill' is not found elsewhere in extant Greek poetry.[6] It would seem that at the same time as comedy plundered tragedy for parodic purposes, a tragic poet was not above borrowing from a comedian.

We may compare the fact that a rare type of choriambic dimeter, $-\cup\cup\cup-\cup\cup-$, used in the parody of Agathon's lyrics in *Thesm.* 106, 119,125, is re-used by Aristophanes later in the same play (316) for his own chorus's invocation of Apollo. Sometimes the interplay of tragic and comic lyrics can be detected in unexpected places. In *Frogs* 1099 the chorus says:

Great the matter, strong the quarrel, violent comes the war,

in a form which exactly echoes a passage of Euripides' *Phaethon* (fr. 773.56f.) on a completely different topic:

The god gave, time brought about a marriage for my rulers.

Frogs:

$\cup\ \cup\ \cup\ -\ \cup\quad\cup\ \cup\quad\cup\ -\ \cup\quad\cup\ \cup\quad\cup\ \cup\ \cup\quad-\ \cup\ -$

méga tò prâgma,   polỳ   tò neîkos,   hadròs ho pólemos érkhetai.

Phaethon:

$\cup\ \cup\ \cup\ -\ \cup\qquad\cup\quad\cup\ \cup\ -\ \cup\qquad\cup\ \cup\ \cup\ -\ \cup\qquad-\ \cup\ -$

theòs édōke,   khrónos ékrāne,   lékhos emôisin   arkhétais.

6 It occurs in other senses, e.g. 'be shaken', 'be twisted', and *elelísdēn* in the sense 'raise a warcry' is also attested.

XII

Lysistrata

Produced in 411, probably (cf. p. 169) at the Lenaia; with what success, is not known.

SYNOPSIS

Lysistrata, an Athenian woman, organizes a secret conference at which she tries to persuade not only the other wives of Athens but representatives from the wives of the other belligerent cities to swear an oath that they will deny sexual intercourse to their husbands or lovers[1] until the men agree to end the war. She succeeds with difficulty in persuading them. The foreign wives depart to their own countries, and Lysistrata, with the other Athenian wives, occupies the Akropolis, which has already been seized by a determined band of old women (cf. p. 43); the state's reserve of money, without which the war would come to a standstill on the Athenian side, was kept there.

There are two choruses in this play, each presumably of twelve members. The first chorus, of old men, arrives at the Propylaia (the gateway to the Akropolis) laden with fire-pots and wood; having heard of the seizure of the Akropolis, they have come to burn down the door, if the women will not open it, and smoke the women out. Before they can put this plan into effect, a chorus of old women arrives from the opposite direction, carrying water. After an altercation between the two choruses, the men threaten the women with their torches and the women lower the men's spirits by throwing the contents of their water-jars over them. Further strife is averted by the arrival of an unnamed 'proboulos', one of a commission of elderly and

[1] Adultery is meant, not pre-marital intercourse. All the women who have any part in *Lysistrata* are assumed to be married.

distinguished citizens appointed in the autumn of 413, in the aftermath
of the Sicilian disaster, to keep a tight hand on the economy. He is full
of indignation—not at the sex-strike, the existence of which is not yet
realized by the men—but at the occupation of the Akropolis, and he
blames the increasing delinquency of women on the complacent
permissiveness of modern husbands. Lysistrata, with other women in
support, comes out to confront him. He orders his policemen to arrest
them, but the police (as so often in farce, though more rarely in reality)
are routed by these Amazons, and Lysistrata and the proboulos are left
to fight out the issue in a verbal contest, the former backed by the
women's chorus and the latter by the men's. Lysistrata contends that
women have come to realize that they have more sense than men and
will set everything to rights if they are given the chance. The proboulos, bursting with indignation, unwisely says (588) that war is
'nothing to do with women', and Lysistrata retorts (588–597):

LYSISTRATA: Why, you damned fool, we have to endure it in double
quantity, in the first place because we've borne sons and sent them
out as soldiers.
PROBOULOS: Quiet! Don't bear malice!
LYSISTRATA: Secondly, when we ought to be enjoying life and getting
the best out of our youth, we sleep alone, because of all the expeditions. And it doesn't matter so much about *us*—it's the girls growing
old indoors that I'm worried about.
PROBOULOS: Don't men grow old too?
LYSISTRATA: Why, it's not the same thing! Anyone who comes back,
even if his hair's grey, is married to a girl in no time; but a woman
doesn't have her chance for long, and if she hasn't managed to grasp
it no one wants to marry her, and she sits at home watching for
omens.

The women mockingly thrust on the proboulos articles of their dress
and spinning implements and send him packing with the suggestion
that it's high time he was dead and buried.

Where we should expect a parabasis, we have an elaborate exchange
of incivilities between the two choruses, the men exhorting one another
to action which the threats from the women's side prevent them from
taking. Then we see Lysistrata in trouble; abstinence is proving too
much for her fellow-conspirators, and they are inventing excuses to
slip away. She rallies them by producing an oracle, an ornithological
enigma (cf. p. 76) seasoned with obscenities. The women being thus

confirmed in their resolve, the first tormented man appears—Kinesias,[2] husband of Lysistrata's friend Myrrhine.[3] Myrrhine comes down from the Akropolis as if willing to have intercourse with him, but repeatedly, as he comes within seconds of penetration, she puts him off by running in to bring out a mattress, a pillow, scent, another kind of scent, none of which seems to him required; and when she has exhausted the possibilities of delay, she slips back into the Akropolis for good and leaves him in the frenzy which she has so artfully aroused.

Now we learn that the women's conspiracy is successful at Sparta, for a Spartan herald, walking in as dignified a manner as his permanent erection will allow, arrives to announce his country's intention to treat for peace. Before the Spartan embassy comes, the two choruses become reconciled, the old women taking the initiative in a sentimental way and the old men grumbling (1038f.):

> And how right the old saying is: '(*sc. we can live*) neither with you— damn you!—nor without you—damn you!'

The Spartan envoys and their Athenian counterparts appeal to Lysistrata to bring them together, which she does with a typical Aristophanic personification (1114–1121):

> Where's Reconciliation? (*A beautiful young woman comes out of the skene. Lysistrata addresses her*). Go and bring the Spartans across first of all; and not with harsh and violent hand, or boorishly, as our husbands did, but as women should, with true affection. If he won't[4]

2   There is no reason to suppose that we are meant to regard this man as Kinesias the dithyrambic poet, who appears in *Birds* and is mentioned elsewhere in comedy. The name and demotic (cf. p. 89), *Kīnēsíās Paionídēs*, are chosen to remind us of *kīnên*, 'move', and *páiên*, 'strike', both common slang words for sexual intercourse.

3   It is curious that in 411 the priestess of Athena Nike was named Myrrhine and the priestess of Athena Polias was almost certainly named Lysimakhe; cf. D. M. Lewis, 'Who was Lysistrata?', *Annual of the British School of Athens* (1955), 1–12. If we dismantle *lȳsimákhē* and Lysistrata's name in Greek, *lȳsistrátē*, the former means 'ending battle' and the latter 'ending army'. It seems hard to believe that Aristophanes means us to think of Lysistrata as the priestess Lysimakhe and of Myrrhine as the priestess Myrrhine; it is more likely that (*a*) wanting a name which would mean 'ending war' Aristophanes deliberately avoided Lysimakhe and constructed 'Lysistrata' as the nearest he could go, and (*b*) since Myrrhine was an exceedingly common name at Athens, the fact that the priestess of Athena Nike bore that name was not important.

4   Literally *oikéiōs* is 'as if a member of the same family'; to speak to someone, or act towards him, *oikéiōs* is to speak or act as if recognizing that his happiness and interests have a superior claim.

offer you his hand, lead him by the prick. And now bring the Athenians—take hold of them by whatever they offer.

Lysistrata castigates both sides for their betrayal of their common religious and cultural heritage and for their forgetfulness of ancient favours conferred by Athens and Sparta on one other. Their eyes dwelling on the anatomy of Reconciliation, they make concessions with a minimum of resistance, and peace is assured.

While the chorus sings, Athenians and Spartans go into the Akropolis to feast and drink, their more obvious physical need now entirely forgotten, since its immediate satisfaction would be irreconcilable with the way Aristophanes wants the play to end.[5] When they come out from the feast, a Spartan does a spectacular solo dance and song to a piper's accompaniment, and it is he, not the chorus, who utters the last words of the play[6] (1320f.):

> Hymn the goddess,
> mightiest, invincible
> goddess of the House of Bronze.

Athena, the patron goddess of Athens, was worshipped at Sparta with the cult-title 'of the House of Bronze'.

THE LYRICS

Lysistrata is one of the Aristophanic plays most often staged or broadcast at the present time, partly because people who know nothing else about Aristophanes may have a vague recollection of seeing translations of *Lysistrata* in pornographic bookshops, or because the scene in which Kinesias repeatedly comes within a few seconds of penetrating Myrrhine soon gets the audience sitting (as Aristophanes would put it [*Ach.* 638]) on arse-tip. But anyone who goes to the play in the expectation that continuous bawdy jokes will keep him laughing from the first line to the last is likely to find that the choral lyrics, after the first vigorous encounter between the old men and the old women, fall rather flat.

---

5 We must not imagine that the men and women have intercourse on the Akropolis before dinner, for intercourse on sacred ground would be a gross violation of a religious rule shared by all Greek communities.
6 There is room for doubt about this. In 1279–1294 the chorus sings a song which ends with exultant cries and a reference to victory. This looks so like a typical ending to a comedy that it has been persuasively argued that 1273–1294 was the ending Aristophanes intended but was misplaced in the course of the transmission of the text.

Even the professional student of Aristophanes, however interested he may be in the formal aspects of the lyrics, is bound to admit that their content represents tediously unsophisticated aspects of Greek comedy (by contrast with the lyrics of *Acharnians* or *Birds*). While the two choruses are at odds, their abusive words and threats of violence go on longer than (to our taste) humorous invention can be sustained, and when they are united they devote no less than four whole stanzas to the primitive joke 'if anyone wants to borrow anything from me, let him come to my house at once—and he'll get nothing'. Thus:

1049-1057: ... If anyone needs a bit of cash, it's at home, and we've got purses. And if peace ever comes, whoever has borrowed anything from us now needn't pay back what he's received (*implying he won't have received anything*).

1058-1071: We're preparing a dinner-party for some visitors. ... So come to my house today ... come straight in, just as if it were your own house—because the door will be shut.

1189-1202: I don't begrudge the loan of dresses or ornaments. ... Anyone can come and take anything he likes. ... But he won't see anything in the house, unless any of you have sharper eyesight than I have.

1203-1215: If any of you don't have enough food. ... Bring a sack ... and my slave will put wheat in it. But I do warn you, don't come to the door—you've got to be very careful of my dog.

Enough's enough, one feels, but no doubt there were plenty of people in the audience who liked it. The same joke is central to the final scene of *Women in Assembly*, where the slave who brings news of the great communal dinner extends the invitation to the spectators and judges (1141f.), and Blepyros steps up the tone of the invitation in order to bring it to a resounding anticlimax (1145-1148):

... and mind you don't leave anybody out, but freely invite old man, young man and boy, for the dinner's prepared for every single one of them—if they'll go home!

Greekless spectators who have found a good deal to make them laugh in *Lysistrata* are inclined to watch and hear the final scene of the play with stony faces; a song and dance in praise of Sparta and its deities seem a let-down after so many good jokes about erections. The trouble is that if a modern audience is told that a Greek play is funny they will count every painful minute of the intervals between laughs, whereas if they are told that it is serious they may be somewhat more inclined to blame themselves than to blame the poet if the play does not hold their attention all the time. This fundamental difficulty in the presentation of Aristophanes to modern audiences is accentuated by the difference between ancient and modern opinion on what constitutes a climax. We can accept the ending of (e.g.) *Women at the Thesmophoria* as swift and tidy, despite a certain element of artificiality in the introduction of the final scene, but we are brought up in a theatrical tradition which makes it hard for us to adjust ourselves to the principle of ending (*Lysistrata*) on the note 'now that that's settled, let's have a song and dance' or (*Wasps*) 'since that isn't settled, let's have a song and dance instead'.

CHARACTERS

Certain passages of *Lysistrata* are among our clearest examples of dialogue involving four speakers; one has already been discussed (p. 26), and there are two others in which a prima facie case for *five* actors can only be resolved by attributing the words of the putative fifth speaker to one of those who have already spoken. In 430–449 the proboulos tries to arrest Lysistrata and the women who accompany her. Lysistrata speaks 430–432, and in 433f. the proboulos tells a policeman to seize her. Lysistrata threatens the policeman (435f.: 'if you lay a finger on me . . .'), who shrinks back. Then:

WOMAN A: If you so much as dare to lay a hand on her, I swear, I'll jump on you till you shit yourself (*The policeman runs away*)[7].
PROBOULOS: (*Scornfully*) Pah! 'Shit yourself', indeed! Where's another policeman? (*To this second policeman*) *She's* got a lot to say—tie up *her* first!
WOMAN B: If you lay a finger on her, I swear, you'll be nursing a black eye! (*The second policeman runs away*).
PROBOULOS: What's going on here? Where's a policeman? (*To a third policeman*) Get hold of *her*! (*To the women*) I'll put a stop to this sally[8] of yours!

7   The policemen must, I think, run off through the wings, and not merely shrink away from the women; we need the proboulos to be defenceless in the scene which follows. Cf. p. 82 on what may be a similar case in *Acharnians*.
8   *Éksodos*, literally, 'road out', does not refer to the women's emergence from the gates of the Akropolis but metaphorically to their capture of it, for the word is used of the purposeful departure of a military force.

WOMAN C: If you come near her, I'll pull your hair out by the roots and that'll hurt you! (*The third policeman runs away*).
PROBOULOS: Oh, my God! The Force has given out!

A fragment of an ancient text (fourth century A.D.) indicates the women speakers only by dashes. Are they all different women? If so, there are five speakers altogether in this scene; the number could be reduced by identifying Lysistrata herself with Woman B and Woman A with Woman C, or simply by identifying Lysistrata with Woman C; or again, Woman C could be the bellicose chorus-leader of the women, who in 471f. says:[9]

Well, you ought not to lay hands on your neighbour just as you please. If you do so, you're bound to get a black eye.

The other passage which raises the question of the number of women speakers is 728–761. Lysistrata has just complained to the chorus about the ways in which the women are trying to slip away from the Akropolis and resume their sex-life. At 728 'Woman A' demands to go home in order to rescue her wool from clothes-moths; at 735, 'Woman B', in order to treat some untreated linen; and in 742, 'Woman C' claims to be on the point of giving birth, which would defile the sacred ground of the Akropolis. Lysistrata exposes Woman C as a fraud who has put under her dress the helmet off the statue of Athena, whereupon Woman C says (758f.):

But I can't even *sleep* on the Akropolis, ever since I saw the snake that looks after it.[10]

And someone else adds (760f.):

And *I*—I'm just *dying* of insomnia, because of the owls that keep hooting all the time.

If this last speaker is 'Woman D' we again have five speakers, but here there is no good reason why we should not give the lines to Woman B.

A curious problem of identification is raised by the arrival of the Spartan herald. Kinesias, tormented and deserted by Myrrhine, has cried despairingly (956–958):

---

9 It has been suggested that the women other than Lysistrata who speak in this passage are individual old women of the chorus.
10 *The* snake which guarded the Akropolis was presumably imaginary, but no doubt many people were convinced that they had seen it.

> How can I get the baby fed?
> Where's the Dog-fox?
> Hire me your nurse![11]

We might have imagined that at this point he runs out of the theatre, waving his arms, but a few lines later we find he is still there, for when the chorus of old men reviles Myrrhine for 'what she has done to you' he cries (970):

> No, I *love* her! She's a *honey*!

So nothing in the text has indicated the departure of Kinesias before a Spartan herald arrives with the words (980f.):

> Where is the council of Athens and the prytanes? I have something to tell them.

At once someone replies, and this person is not the chorus-leader, for later in the conversation he points to his own erect penis (the old men of the chorus are too decrepit for that)[12] and goes off to inform the council. One ancient textual tradition, recorded by the scholia, attributed 1014f., a generalization about the shamelessness of women, to Kinesias; there is little doubt that this generalization is in fact spoken by the men's chorus-leader, since it initiates the dialogue between the two choruses leading to their reconciliation, but the ancient commentator who gave it to Kinesias presumably believed that Kinesias had been on stage all the time and could therefore be the interlocutor of the Spartan herald. This interlocutor is PRO, i.e. proboulos, in the sigla. That is not convincing; for one thing, the proboulos whom we encountered earlier in the play was decrepit (598–607); and for another, the herald addresses his interlocutor as *kyrsánios*, a Spartan word explained by the scholia and by ancient lexicographers as a patronising and derogatory term for a youth. We seem to be left with two alternatives, neither of which is completely satisfactory: *either* Kinesias remains on stage but adjusts his mood very considerably from

---

11 'Dog-fox' was a brothel-keeper; ostensibly Kinesias wants a nurse for the baby, but we are allowed to imagine that he might put her to other uses too. This passage is the only reference in the play to prostitution; cf. p. 160.

12 Old men in Aristophanic comedy are either ferocious and well-preserved (e.g. Dikaiopolis and the Acharnians) or very old and feeble; the old men of Lysistrata look back to events (274ff., 664f.), firmly established in Athenian tradition, which—if we cared to do the arithmetic—would make them about 120 at the time of the play!

the tempestuous emotion created by his scene with Myrrhine to the confidence and self-control shown in the conversation with the herald, *or* Kinesias departs at some time between 970 and 980 and a prytanis materializes promptly in response to the herald's question, 'where are the prytanes?' The word *kyrsánios* does not help us very much; since Athenians often married late and could be much older than their wives, the fact that Kinesias and Myrrhine have a baby does not tell us that Kinesias is a young man, and since the council was constituted by sortition a prytanis might be no more than thirty years old. In any case, use of the word may only satirize a (real or alleged) patronizing attitude on the part of Spartan emissaries.

The problems of identification and staging raised by 1216ff. have been discussed already (p. 11).

WOMEN AND WAR

The sentiments which inspire Lysistrata bring her closer to Trygaios of *Peace* than to Dikaiopolis of *Acharnians*; she thinks about the predicament of the women of the belligerent cities in general, not merely about herself. The situation at the time of the play, however, was rather different from that of 421; in consequence of the destruction of the Sicilian expedition in 413, a large part of the Athenian empire was in revolt, the Peloponnesians had taken heart at the prospect of a decisive victory, they had made an alliance with the Persians, and a Syracusan fleet had come to join them in the Aegean. Yet, although the scales were weighted in favour of the Peloponnesians, Athens had made a remarkable recovery from the collapse of 413; it was possible to argue (and the history of the next few years seemed to justify the argument) that with every month that passed Athenian chances of at least establishing a stalemate and a compromise peace improved, and this is the kind of peace that Lysistrata achieves. She is no more concerned than any other Athenian to renounce war at the price of putting Athens into real danger.[13]

As in the case of *Acharnians* and *Peace*, reservations and complications

13 Perikles, as represented by Thucydides, would have contended in 411, as he did up to his death in 429, that anything short of decisive victory and absolute rejection of Peloponnesian demands was dangerous to the future of Athens. Thucydides, however, represents Perikles not as voicing a determination shared by all Athenians but as arguing against a substantial current of opinion which regarded the Peloponnesian war (or sequence of wars) as similar in essence to other wars. In any case, the precedent of a negotiated peace in 421 must have affected many people's views in 411.

beset any statement to the effect that *Lysistrata* positively advocates peace by showing us war through women's eyes. Not the least of these complications is the need to enquire into the possibility that to the Athenians of Aristophanes' time the presentation of women conferring, conspiring and forcing a change of policy on the city is as great a flight of imaginative humour as the presentation of birds building a city and forcing the gods to surrender, or of the attainment and preservation of a private peace by magical means. Aristophanes has the gift, shared also with Homer and the tragic poets,[14] of making his characters put the arguments which those characters really would put, without revealing his own standpoint. Certainly there is no lack in *Lysistrata* of mockery directed against women themselves; they are, as always in comedy, bibulous (*Lys.* 114, 194–208, 233–239, *Thesm.* 347f., 626–633, 74–761) and adulterous; the indignant speech of the proboulos on this subject (403–419) belongs together with the comic confessions of the disguised old man in *Thesm.* 469–501. It must also be remembered that the Greeks (by contrast with Europeans in the nineteenth and early twentieth centuries) tended to believe that women enjoyed sexual intercourse more than men [15] and had a lower resistance to sexual temptation. This belief was closely related to their high valuation of the adult male warrior's ability to endure privation and their correspondingly low valuation of feminine softness; Xenophon in his encomium on the Spartan King Agesilaos speaks (5.4) of the king's noteworthy chastity in the same context as his endurance of heat and cold and his resistance to fatigue and sleep. It is in accordance with these assumptions that when Lysistrata first propounds her scheme to the women they reject it ('Anything but that! Let the war go on!') until the Spartan woman, coming as she does from a culture which permitted women to take physical exercise and made them, by Greek standards, masculine women, agrees that she will try it. Lysistrata's acclaim (145),

My dearest friend, the only *woman* among the lot of them!

is a humorous adaptation of an idiom seen, for example, in Xenophon, *Hellenica* vii 1.24:

14 We may compare the fluency and cogency with which Euripides can express opposing arguments, e.g. in *Suppliants* 399–512 on oligarchy and democracy.
15 There was a legend that Zeus and Hera once argued about this. They referred the question to Teiresias, who was in the unusual position of having been both male and female, and his verdict was that the woman received nine-tenths of the pleasure of intercourse, the man one-tenth.

The Arkadians were filled with pride and delighted with Lykomedes and thought him the only *man*.

In these circumstances it is not surprising that the women show signs of cracking under the strain of the strike before the men do.

A curious feature of the plot of the play, commonly unnoticed in modern discussions of it, is that the strike is not in fact a strike of all women but a strike of the wives of citizens. Slave-prostitutes, slave-concubines, hetairai, all the women who made extra-marital sex easily accessible at Athens, are never mentioned in the play, and the deserted husband goes around miserably with a continuous erection as if they did not exist. Apparently, men cannot even masturbate—though women can, for Lysistrata refers (108–110) to the difficulty of buying a six-inch artificial penis since Miletos (which manufactured and exported this common article) defected. We have been allowed to hear in *Thesm.* 491f. of the readiness with which married women will console themselves with lusty slaves and muleteers, in a context entirely devoted to humorous exaggeration of the wicked ways of women, but not a word of this in *Lysistrata*. Again, homosexual relations among males were so much taken for granted at Athens (cf. p. 114) that a man denied his wife would not have needed to spend much trouble or money (it was, after all, a slave-owning society) in search of a youth on whom to exercise himself. It is possible that we have here an example of the readiness with which Aristophanes selects from real life certain ingredients required to make a plot and simply ignores the other elements and causal sequences which, if taken into account, would spoil the plot (cf. p. 42). On the other hand, it is possible (and may be thought more likely) that in *Lysistrata* Aristophanes is looking at real life from a standpoint different from the standpoint adopted in some other plays. The impression we get in *Acharnians*, *Wasps*, *Peace* or *Birds* that a healthy man's sexual life is essentially the seizure of fleeting opportunities and that there is not much more to marriage than the first few months in bed with a pretty girl, may result from the exaggerated roguishness and uninhibited fantasy characteristic of comedy but not necessarily so conspicuously characteristic of Athenian life.[16]

16   It is easy to go wrong about what was normal in Greek society, and salutary to remember what Homer (*Odyssey* i 428–433) says of Odysseus's old nurse, Eurykleia: 'Laertes bought her with his wealth when she was in the flower of youth ... and honoured her on a par with his own wife ... but never slept with her, *for he wished to avoid his wife's anger*'. For polemic against the assumption that a Greek woman was no more than an instrument of pleasure

Lysistrata is about marital love and sexual loyalty; Kinesias's declaration of his love for Myrrhine *after* she has cheated him, a declaration in opposition to the vilification of her by the chorus of old men (cf. p. 157), is drawn from life.

When Lysistrata is asked by the proboulos what she would do to bring Athens safe out of its perils, her recipe, closely modelled on how women deal with a tangle of wool and in the end make a cloak out of it, begins with 'embassies hither and thither' (570) but insensibly passes into what is a recipe not so much for peace as for strength (574–586, in many respects comparable with *Frogs* 686–705), implying that from a position of strength one can get a peace which is to one's own advantage. When the play has finally come to the point of negotiations, the issues which were actually important to the belligerents in 411—notably what the Peloponnesians, ever since 431, called 'the freedom of the Greeks' from Athenian rule—are not raised. Lysistrata appeals to sentimental tradition (1145–1148):

LYSISTRATA: When that is what the Athenians have done for you, you ravage the land which has been your benefactor?
ATHENIAN: Yes, they're in the wrong, Lysistrata!
SPARTAN: (*Perfunctorily*) We're in the wrong. (*Gazing at Reconcilation*) But what a glorious arse!

Peace is not achieved without concessions, but the concessions extracted from each side are chosen for their potentiality as sexual puns; Lysistrata persuades the Athenians to give up Pylos in Lakonia (not a pre-war Athenian possession, but acquired as part of an operation of war) and the Spartans to withdraw from three places, about which their protest is lightly turned aside.

The ending of the play with a Spartan singer invoking and praising deities who are also (particularly Athena, of course) deities in Athenian eyes is a more powerful reminder than the negotiation scene that not only sexual love, but also international festivals and poetry and dancing are much more enjoyable than war. But did Aristophanes or anyone else really believe that peace, however desirable, was to be had in 411 without concessions which would weaken and impoverish the Athenians more than they would tolerate?

see A. W. Gomme, *Essays in Greek History and Literature* (Oxford, 1937), chapter V.

XIII

Women at the Thesmophoria

Produced in 411, probably (cf. p. 169) at the City Dionysia; with what success, is not known.

The date is not preserved in the hypothesis, but is inferred from (i) lines 1059–1061, which speak of Euripides' *Andromeda* as having been performed 'last year', and (ii) lines 808f., which refer to 'last year's council' (i.e. of 413/2) as surrendering its powers to the commission of probouloi. Statements made by the scholia on lines 190 and 841 also show that ancient commentators dated the play to 411.

The Greek title is *Thesmophorásdōsai*, commonly Latinized as *Thesmophoriazusae*. Aristophanes produced another play with the same title, from which we have a number of citations, but we do not know its plot.

SYNOPSIS

Euripides has learned that at a women's festival, the Thesmophoria, the women of Athens intend to discuss how they can secure his destruction, since his portrayal of legendary wicked women in his tragedies has given all women a bad name. Taking an old kinsman along with him, he goes to the house of Agathon, a young tragic poet whose appearance is effeminate, in the hope of persuading Agathon to attend the Thesmophoria disguised as a woman and put the case for the defence. Euripides and the old man stand aside as a slave of Agathon comes out and, in tragic language, calls upon all nature to be silent, since his master is about to compose; the old man interrupts the recitation from time to time with vulgar noises and words (cf. p. 147). Then Agathon is wheeled out on the theatrical trolley and recites a passage of choral lyric which (we have to presume, since no plays of Agathon have survived) is a parody of his style. The old man makes coarse fun of his effeminate appearance, partly in terms parodying the tragedy in which Aiskhylos represented Lykurgos as upbraiding Dionysos, but Agathon keeps his temper, and Euripides explains what he wants of him. Agathon absolutely refuses, and now we see the dramatic necessity for the old man's presence; he offers to go instead, Euripides accepts his offer, and the old man is duly shaved, singed down below,[1] and dressed up in woman's clothes freely lent by Agathon. Agathon is wheeled in; and the old man extracts from Euripides, before they part, an oath that Euripides will do everything possible to rescue him if he gets into trouble.

We now have to envisage the scene as changed to the Thesmophoreion. The chorus of women enters, plus women who will have speaking roles, and the old man mingles with them. A series of prayers and formal curses is uttered, modelled on the customary procedure of the Athenian assembly but distorted to bring in references to Euripides and to the secret vices of women; the chorus responds in lyric stanzas. The 'assembly' thus constituted, the first speaker begins with a formulaic disclaimer which we meet again in the fourth-century orators (383–387):

> I assure you, ladies, that it is not through any desire to thrust myself forward that I have risen to speak; but I really cannot endure to see us insulted as we have been for so long by Euripides . . .

A second woman speaks more briefly, and then it is the old man's turn. He argues that Euripides has not revealed more than a fraction of the tricks that women play; I myself, he says (478–481):

> . . . had only been married three days, and my husband was asleep beside me; and I had a friend who had laid me when I was seven. He was so eager for me that he came and tapped on the door. . . .

The women are outraged by his catalogue of delinquencies, and fall upon him furiously as a traitor to their sex (but not, we notice, as a liar). Suddenly there arrives Kleisthenes, a contemporary Athenian whose sparseness of beard caused him to be regarded as effeminate—and so, for the purpose of this play, an 'honorary woman'. He tells them that

---

1 This singeing serves no logical purpose, for so long as his dress covers him it does not matter how hairy he is, and when his dress is lifted his male organs give him away; but it serves a dramatic purpose, providing the occasion for some noisy slapstick.

there is a rumour² of the presence of a disguised kinsman of Euripides among them. The old man cannot now escape; he is apprehended, his dress is lifted and his sex revealed. Kleisthenes goes off to tell the prytanes, for the intrusion of a disguised man into a women's festival is a serious offence. The old man seizes a baby from one of the women and takes refuge at the altar (the motif is the familiar one from Euripides' *Telephos*, as in *Ach.* 335ff.). The 'baby' proves to be a wineskin, and when the old man 'kills' it he pours out the wine; but there is no avenue of escape open to him.

After the parabasis the old man, hoping that Euripides will keep his promise, recites verses from Euripides' *Helen*. Euripides arrives pretending to be Menelaos, and the dialogue between them, at times interrupted scornfully and indignantly by the woman who is guarding the old man, is adapted from the recognition of Helen by Menelaos in the tragedy, combined with some passages from the prologue; this is the only sustained parody in Aristophanes for which we possess the original intact³ and can study the technique of parody in detail. The scene is interrupted by the arrival of a prytanis, and Euripides departs. The prytanis tells the policeman who accompanies him to take the old man indoors and fasten him to the 'board', the cumbrous and painful ancient equivalent of handcuffs. While they are inside the chorus sings a long invocation to a series of deities.

The policeman comes out with the old man and almost at once goes in again to get himself a mat. The old man spots Euripides in the distance in the guise of Perseus, and he himself sings a long monody which parodies Euripides' *Andromeda*. When Euripides appears, however, it is first as the Echo which in the tragedy responded to Andromeda's lament; this provides an opportunity for him to mock the returning policeman by echoing all his words. Then Euripides declares himself to be Perseus and to be in love with 'Andromeda'; the policeman, though mystified by this perverted passion for an old man, tolerantly suggests boring a hole in the back of the board, but soon

2   One should not enquire too closely *how* Kleisthenes could have heard such a thing, but it must be remembered that the ubiquity of slaves made the keeping of secrets hard; in *Frogs* 752f. Xanthias and the slave of Pluto talk in gleeful terms of divulging the overheard conversations of their masters, as a slave's way of getting his own back. This element in the structure of Athenian society would have ensured that Kleisthenes' words did not sound as strange to the original audience as they do to us.

3   In fact, the closeness of the parody makes it possible for us to restore line 561 of *Helen*, accidentally omitted in our surviving manuscripts of Euripides.

turns nasty when Euripides makes as if to release the prisoner, and Euripides flees.

While the policeman snoozes on his mat the chorus sings an invocation to Athena, Demeter and Persephone, and Euripides reappears in the guise of an old woman, with a dancing-girl and a girl piper. He promises that if they will let him secure the release of his kinsman he will not slander them again, and they agree. The policeman is roused from sleep by the sound of the pipe and roused sexually by the dancer, whom Euripides, after a perfunctory show of reluctance, allows him to take indoors. At once Euripides releases the old man, and they make their escape. The policeman, returning satisfied (after less than one minute) from his encounter with the girl, is frantic on finding what has happened; the chorus deliberately gives him confusing information, and he rushes off in pursuit in the wrong direction.

CHARACTERS

In the Ravennas, the only manuscript to preserve this play, the sigla and scholia alike call the old man 'Mnesilokhos', but he is never named in the text; that he is a relation of Euripides by marriage is all that we are told. A fragment dating from the second century A.D. exhibits at line 279 the siglum *ho kēde*, i.e. 'the relation-by-marriage (*kēdestḗs*)', and it is probable that his identification as Euripides' father-in-law, Mnesilokhos, is a theory (not necessarily wrong, but not demonstrably right) put forward by a commentator in late Roman times. His readiness to undertake a dangerous mission on Euripides' behalf and the casualness with which Euripides accepts the offer suggest that we may be meant to think of him as a 'poor relation' rather like Aziz's uncle in *A Passage to India*, whose functions are to fetch and carry and entertain the guests by buffoonery. This kind of relation cannot have been common in the Greek world, since primogeniture played no part in inheritance, but there must have been occasions on which a man had to assume responsibility for his wife's surviving relations, impoverished by war or the loss of a ship or the enormous fines which Athenians sometimes incurred.[4]

The play needs four actors, since at 929 a conversation involving the old man, Euripides and one of the women is interrupted by the arrival

4 Thucydides ii 53.1 (on the plague) is interesting in this connection: 'they saw how sudden were the changes of fortune of those who were prosperous but suddenly died and those who *previously had nothing* but straightway got the property of the dead'.

of the prytanis, whose first words are separated from Euripides' parting words by only one line. Allocation of parts to the different women characters is not just a matter of constructing the kind of jigsaw puzzle with which the reader will by now be familiar, but raises a new question, the functions of the chorus-leader, and is relevant to the question of exits (like that of Kinesias in *Lys*. 971–979?) of which no indication is given in the words spoken. When the women assemble, a female herald[5] introduces the proceedings by uttering the formal prayers, reciting the 'motion before the house' and putting the question (379), as in the real assembly, 'Who wishes to speak?' Two women speak, of whom the second says at the end of her speech (457f.) that she must leave at once to make up an order for garlands. The actor who plays the second woman is thus free to play Kleisthenes, who is on stage from 574 to 654 (an explicitly motivated exit). The woman whose 'baby' the old man seizes—her name is revealed as 'Mika'[6] in 760—can be the first woman speaker and the only woman to speak throughout the scene in which the old man's disguise is revealed. So far, then, we can allocate parts as follows:

> Actor I: the old man.
> Actor II: Euripides; Mika (Mika has a motivated departure at 764).
> Actor III: Agathon's slave; Agathon; the Herald.
> Actor IV: The second woman speaker; Kleisthenes.

The only way in which the play down to this point could be performed by three actors would be by taking the herald off once the assembly has got down to business and by making the second speaker arrive after that point, thus permitting the same person to play both the herald and the second woman. Neither an exit by the herald nor a late entrance by the second woman is indicated by the text. But if the herald does not go off, what does happen to her? She seems to have nothing more to do or say in the whole play after line 380. *Either* we give her more to do, by taking away from Mika some of the dialogue of 533–654, which still leaves us with the problem of an unmotivated exit for her at some point thereafter; *or* we give her nearly nine hundred lines of silent presence;

5   It is clear both from the orators and from documentary inscriptions that at the opening of an assembly it was a herald, not a priest, who pronounced the prayers and curses, and naturally a herald put the formal question, 'Who wishes to speak?' (cf. *Ach.* 45).
6   'Mika' is attested as an ordinary Athenian woman's name on several epitaphs of the fourth century B.C.; emendation to 'Mikka', often favoured on etymological grounds, is wrong.

or we identify her with the chorus-leader. This last solution would be attractive but for one passage, 377–383:

> HERALD: . . . and that the first item of business should be: Euripides: what penalty should be imposed upon him, inasmuch as we are all agreed that he has committed an injury. Who wishes to speak?
> MIKA: I do!
> HERALD: Then put on this crown first, before speaking.
> [:] Quiet! Silence! Pay attention! She's clearing her throat now as the speakers do. It looks as if she's going to make a long speech.
> MIKA: I assure you, ladies. . . .

Who says 'Quiet! . . .'? The Ravennas indicates no change of speaker; but if the herald says it, it represents an odd change of standpoint from procedural control to the passive role of the audience. We may compare Theokritos 15.96–99, portraying two women spectators at a festival in Alexandria:

> Quiet, Praxinoa! She's going to sing the Adonis-song . . . I'm sure she'll give us a lovely performance. She's clearing out her throat now.

For the same reason, if the chorus-leader says 'Quiet! . . .', the chorus-leader and the herald should not be the same person; and it would be equally odd, from a formal point of view, if the whole chorus, minus the chorus-leader, sang a pair of lines in a dialogue metre. These considerations incline me to believe that the herald does go off, without comment, at an early stage after the initial proceedings are completed, and that for a time we have four actors in view together—the old man, the herald, Mika and the second woman.

A similarly unmarked exit, plus an entrance not obviously motivated, seems to occur later in the play. When the old man has exposed the 'baby' as a wineskin and has drained the wine out of it, the following dialogue occurs (758–764):

> OLD MAN: The skin here goes to the priestess!
> [:] What goes to the priestess?
> [OLD MAN:] This! Catch!
> WOMAN: Oh, poor Mika, who's cleaned you out?[7] Who's drained your only daughter dry?

7 The verb *ekkorên*, literally 'sweep out', is also meant to suggest 'deprive of a daughter (*kórē*)'; a slightly different verb, *ekkorísdēn*, can have a sexual sense in slang, but that is not wanted here.

MIKA: This swine! Anyway—now that you're here, guard him, so that I can go and get Kleisthenes and tell the prytanes what the old man has done.

The old man is parodying a common rule of sacrificial procedure that the animal's skin should be a perquisite of the officiating priest or priestess. Here, as before, the Ravennas indicates no change of speaker for 'What goes . . .', but it is clear from what Mika says that the priestess arrives just in time to hear the old man's words—and at once pricks up her ears at the prospect of personal gain, as we would expect of a religious official in Aristophanic comedy (cf. the priest in *Wealth* 1171f. and Hierokles in *Peace* 1052ff.). Mika is now free to go, and the priestess (whose name is given at 898 as 'Kritylla') stays with the old man. But when does she go? Her last utterance is 934f. In this case her function perhaps explains both her entrance and her exit. In the earlier part of the play the women constitute an 'assembly', but in the latter part the idea of the assembly is dropped and they regard themselves as celebrating the festival; their songs of invocation in 954–1000 are introduced by the chorus-leader (947f.) with the words:

> Come now, let us sing and dance as it is customary for the women to do here when we celebrate on the sacred appointed days the solemn rites of the two goddesses. . . .

The priestess arrives after the language appropriate to an assembly has ceased and before that appropriate to a festival has begun. If, as seems likely from 'here' in 947, we are to remember that we are at the Thesmophoreion, her entry into the skene at 946 can be effected without causing any of us to wonder what she is doing.

It is noteworthy that the parabasis, 785–845, is not delivered, as it was in earlier plays, with all actors off-stage; the old man and the priestess Kritylla must be there all the time.

TOPICALITY

It is not difficult to say what the play is about: major parodies of *Helen*, *Andromeda* (both of which were first performed in the previous year) and at least one play of Agathon, plus minor parodies of some other Euripidean plays and a parody of the proceedings of the assembly, are combined with slapstick, vulgar buffoonery, jokes about adultery and the ways of women, and a foreign policeman's pidgin-Greek, to present something for all tastes, and the happy ending (happy for everyone except the policeman) leaves us with nothing difficult to think about. The parabasis is largely concerned with one of the central motifs of *Lysistrata*, the superiority of women to men, but it has nothing to say about making peace; by playing on the etymology of women's names it suggests rather more the women of the tribe shaming the men into valour and virtue.

The situation inside Athens in the early months of 411 was one of unusual danger and difficulty. The generals in command of the Athenian forces at Samos were in touch with Alkibiades, who had been in exile since 415 and was now suggesting that he could secure from the Persians in Asia Minor a large financial subsidy for Athens—if she would agree to suspend the democratic constitution and entrust the government to a 'reliable' oligarchy. These plans were well advanced among the generals by the middle of January, and by February their emissary to Athens had set an anti-democratic conspiracy in motion. The efficient organization of this conspiracy and its programme of selective assassination intimidated the Athenians, and towards the middle of the summer, when it was put to the assembly that there was no hope of victory without acceptance of Persian money on Alkibiades' terms, the democratic constitution was suspended. The chronology of the early months of the conspiracy depends on the narrative of Thucydides, in which the winter solstice is a firm datum, but there are unfortunately some uncertainties in the details. The dramatic festivals took place in the Athenian months Gamelion (Lenaia) and Elaphebolion (City Dionysia); if it were possible to establish the relation between these months and the winter solstice in 412/1 and also to discover whether *Lysistrata* was performed at the Lenaia and *Thesm.* at the City Dionysia or vice-versa, something interesting about the relation between comedy and political issues might emerge. Since the structure of the Athenian calendar differed from ours, and we are short of calendar-equations, there is no question of simply identifying Gamelion with January. Examination of all the relevant data from the period 415–411 suggests to me (but some details are highly controversial) that in 411 the Lenaia fell at the beginning of February and the City Dionysia at the beginning of April; which is to say that the development of the oligarchic conspiracy can hardly have been appreciated at the time of the Lenaia but cannot have failed to arouse widespread apprehensions by the time of the City Dionysia.

One very small consideration tells in favour of assigning *Lysistrata* to the Lenaia. When Lysistrata reproaches both sides for fighting each other instead of maintaining the religious and cultural unity of the Greek world, she says (*Lys.* 1133f.):

> Enemies are to hand with a barbarian army, but you destroy Greeks and Greek cities.

(The first clause sounds obscure, but I adhere closely to the original.)[8] Now, until about the end of January the Peloponnesians were known to be receiving Persian support, whereas the Athenians had for at least three years been giving active support to a native rebellion against Persian rule in Asia Minor; then the situation changed when Alkibiades opened his secret negotiations with the Athenian generals at Samos, and in February it was widely known at Athens that there was a possibility of Persian money for the Athenians. Hence if *Lysistrata* was performed at the Lenaia the reference to barbarian enemies is one about which the Athenians could feel self-righteous.

Aristophanes can hardly have waited until a month before the City Dionysia before writing *Thesm.*, and the plot may well have begun to take shape in his mind immediately after the performance of *Helen* and *Andromeda* at the beginning of 412. It would have been possible for him to refashion individual passages up to the last minute,[9] and there are in fact two passages of *Thesm.* which look very much as if they allude to the unhappy situation at the time of performance.

The first is line 361, which comes in the sung response of the chorus to the curses pronounced by the herald. These curses are a blend of those pronounced in the real assembly (for example, against anyone who plots against the city) with comic curses fitted to the dramatic situation. The response names categories of people who would in reality be cursed as enemies of Athens (356–360),

> ...those who deceive (*sc. the people*) and transgress the oaths sanctioned by tradition, for their own gain, to the detriment (*sc. of the people*),

and the chorus continues (361f.):

8 Literally, 'barbarian enemies being present with an army' (*bárbaros*, as usual, means 'non-Greek', not 'barbaric'); emendation of one letter in the Greek gives a more normal phraseological and rhythmic balance, 'enemies being present with a barbarian army'; the verb *parênai*, 'be present', I take to be used here in the sense 'be available', comparing Aiskhylos, *Eumenides* 864, literally, 'let there be war abroad, being present in no small quantity, i.e. 'fight your wars (*sc. not within the city, but*) abroad—there is no shortage of them'.
9 This can be done even at the dress rehearsal of a comedy; I have seen it done.

... or seek to replace decrees by law and law by decrees.

The word used for 'substitute ... for each other' is *antimethistánai*; neither the word itself nor any other example of the double prefix *anti-met(a)*- occurs in Attic Greek before Aristotle, but since he uses it to mean 'replace ... by each other', and that is what we would expect to be the force of the prefixes, we have little choice but to take it that way in Aristophanes. Since the oligarchs' proposal later in the year was that the Athenians should by an act of the assembly, i.e. a decree, annul the inherited democratic constitution (*nómos*, 'law'; cf. p. 111) [10] and thereafter treat as *nómos* the oligarchic structure authorized by decree, the words of *Thesm.* point at the conspiracy.

The second passage occurs in the last choral song, 1136–1159, in which Athena and Demeter and Persephone are invoked in a pattern especially familiar in the ode and antode of a parabasis. [11] The invocation of Athena ends (1143–1147):

> Appear, you who detest tyrants, as is right. The assembly of women calls upon you. May you come to me and bring with you peace which delights in festivals!

It is natural enough that a comic chorus in 411 should pray for 'peace which delights in festivals', and such a prayer does not commit itself to the terms of peace. But the reminder to Athena that she 'detests tyrants' strikes an unusual note (contrast the invocation of Athena in *Knights* 581–594, which also invites her to 'appear'). The expression 'as is right' (or 'just', 'reasonable', 'expected'), which occurs twice elsewhere in the play (722, 974), seems here to be a declaration of faith that Athena *must* hate tyrants—rather as a Greek politician is not deterred from calling an opponent 'hateful to the gods' by the difficulty of ascertaining the gods' views. The words which follow, literally 'the assembly calls upon you, (*sc. the assembly*) of the women', are artfully arranged. For a moment it sounds as if the chorus is discarding its role and speaking for the Athenian people; then 'of the women' pulls them back into their role as women; yet their return to this role is by no means smooth, for since the parabasis the humorous exploitation

10 The plural *nómoi* usually corresponds to the English expression 'the Law', but the singular *nómos* in a collective or personified sense is attested in both poetry and prose.
11 The parabasis of *Thesm.* contains no ode and antode; the matter appropriate to them is postponed until 947–1000 and 1136–1159 and so treated much more extensively.

of the gathering of women as a quasi-political assembly has been discarded, and the song and dance of 947ff. have reminded us most explicitly of the Thesmophoria as a women's festival (cf. p. 168). The terms in which Athena is invoked cannot be explained by reference to the characteristics of comic choral invocations in general, or as arising out of the dramatic situation, or as a natural and necessary part of the portrayal of women celebrating the Thesmophoria. It is also remarkable that the invocation from 'appear . . .' to '. . . right' is cast in four units of bacchiac rhythm ($\smile — —$), which is so characteristic of tragedy that it is normally employed in comedy only for parodic effect; but there can be no question of parody in the present case. It seems that we should regard lines 1143–1147 as dictated by the political context of the production and as expressing a hope that the democratic constitution will not be overthrown.

The expression of sentiment is guarded, and no doubt the conspirators themselves would have echoed it, arguing that they were not really overthrowing *nómos* and that what they envisaged was not 'tyranny'— rather as both parties to a dispute can declare themselves fervently in favour of 'justice' and 'moderation' while retaining irreconcilable objectives. It should not surprise us that Aristophanes takes the side of the 'establishment', i.e. of the democracy (cf. p. 33). We do not know how he himself fared in the course of 411; we can only observe that he survived, apparently with reputation unimpaired, both the oligarchic revolution and the democratic backlash which succeeded it (cf. p. 53, on the parabasis of *Frogs*).

XIV

Frogs

Produced in 405, at the Lenaia, and awarded first prize.

SYNOPSIS

Two strange figures enter at the beginning of the play; one is recognizable, by his combination of long yellow dress and youthful mask with lionskin and club, as Dionysos disguised—imperfectly—as Herakles, and the other is his slave (Xanthias, a common slave's name at Athens), mounted on a donkey but also carrying the luggage on a stick over his own shoulder. They call at the house of Herakles, to whom Dionysos explains that he sadly misses Euripides, who has recently died; as the god of the dramatic festivals, Dionysos is especially affected by the loss of a man whose career as a tragic dramatist had lasted for nearly fifty years. So Dionysos is going to the underworld to bring him back, and has disguised himself as Herakles to fortify himself against the dangers of the journey. The real Herakles once went down to the underworld to bring up the monstrous dog which guarded its door, and Dionysos wants advice from him on how to get there. Herakles makes fun of him and does his best to frighten him, but at least promises him that when he hears the companies of initiates[1] he will be close by the palace of Pluto, the god of the underworld.

Dionysos encounters a corpse on its way to burial and tries to engage it to carry the luggage, but the corpse wants too high a price, and

[1] The cult of Demeter and Persephone at Eleusis, with which certain other deities (e.g. Iakkhos) were associated, offered the prospect of preferential treatment in the afterlife to those who went through a process of initiation into 'mysteries'. There were mystery-cults, some of them associated with Dionysos, in other parts of the Greek world.

Xanthias agrees to carry it all himself. They reach the lake which borders the underworld, and while Xanthias runs round it (for Kharon, the ferryman of souls, will not let slaves on to the boat) Dionysos is ferried across, to the accompaniment of a chorus of frogs, from which the play takes its title. Dionysos, who is required to do some of the rowing himself, engages in a lyric duel with the frogs. He meets Xanthias on the other side and they make their way through darkness, imagining unpleasant monsters on the way, until they hear singing, and the chorus of initiates (the main chorus of the play) enters.

The chorus has almost the whole of 316–459 to itself, and much is included here which in a play of more traditional pattern would have appeared in the parabasis; in particular, a recitation by the chorus-leader (354–371) which is ostensibly a proclamation to the impure and uninitiated to stand aside from the procession of initiates, is turned into praise of comedy and denigration of various disagreeable individuals and types, using language which hovers all the time between mystery-ritual and the theatre, e.g. 354–357:

> Let there be silence! Out of the way of our choruses ('*khorós*' *can be used of singers and dancers in any religious observance*), whoever is unacquainted with utterance of this kind ('*lógoi*' *could be used equally of the chorus-leader's recitation or of what is said in an initiation-rite*), or is not pure in thought, or has not seen or danced in the rites of the noble Muses ('*Muses*' *is not applicable to initiation*), or has not been initiated in the Dionysiacs of the tongue of Kratinos the bull-devourer (*this suits the picture of Kratinos as a kind of Falstaff, but also suits certain Dionysiac mysteries*). . . .

Dionysos and Xanthias eventually accost the chorus and are told that they have arrived at the palace of Pluto.

But they are not welcome. The man who answers the door (cf. p. 8) regards Herakles as a dog-thief, because of the seizure of Kerberos, and after denouncing the disguised Dionysos in ferocious tragic language goes off with threats of vengeance. Dionysos, terrified, persuades Xanthias to take over the Herakles-disguise, while he himself pretends to be a slave. Xanthias fancies himself as Herakles, but is embarrassed when the next person to appear is a servant of Persephone, Pluto's consort, with a pressing invitation to dinner. In the end he accepts, but Dionysos stops him and insists on a reversal of disguises. We can guess what is likely to happen next. Two indignant landladies, to whom the real Herakles owes money for enormous meals, beset

Dionysos. When they are finally disposed of, Dionysos coaxes Xanthias into assuming the guise of Herakles once more.

The humour of alternating good and ill is now dropped, for the doorkeeper returns with policemen, who seize Xanthias-Herakles. Xanthias swears that he is innocent of the theft of Kerberos, and, availing himself of Athenian judicial procedure, in which a slave could be examined under torture, waves a hand airily towards his baggage-carrier Dionysos (616f.):

> Take my slave here and put him to the torture. And if in the end you convict me of a crime, take me off to execution.

Dionysos declares his identity as an immortal, and they are beaten in turn to discover which of them, as a god, is immune to pain. Each of them exclaims in pain, but contrives to explain away his exclamations, and in the end the doorkeeper invites them in so that Pluto and Persephone can tell which is which.

The parabasis follows; there are no 'anapaests', because we have had them already.[2] The epirrhema and antepirrhema (cf. pp. 50f.) are of an unusually serious character, because unusually specific in the advice which they offer, the former recommending genuine amnesty for citizens who were involved in the short-lived oligarchic revolution of 411; the antepirrhema, characteristically employing a comic conceit which lightens the mood to a small degree, compares the politicians of the moment to the recently introduced bronze coinage and the class of potential leaders now spurned to the good old silver coinage which was respected throughout the world (cf. pp. 95f.).

After the parabasis comes a conversation between Xanthias and a slave of Pluto. The plot is about to take a completely new turn, and this conversation serves as a kind of explanatory prologue.[3] Euripides, on arrival in the world of the dead, laid claim to the seat next to Pluto's which belonged as a right to the supreme poet and was at the present time occupied by Aiskhylos. Aiskhylos resisted the claim, and Dionysos, a uniquely qualified judge who has arrived so opportunely, is to be asked to judge between them. Pluto has ruled that the issue is to be decided by a careful weighing and measuring of the art of the two poets.

---

2 It is an interesting peculiarity of *Frogs* that the parabasis is *preceded* by a succession of short scenes such as in earlier plays follow the parabasis and illustrate the resolution of the crisis (cf. p. 66).

3 The fact that the two characters are slaves increases the resemblance of this scene to a prologue; on the importance of Xanthias, cf. pp. 204ff.

The detailed scrutiny which we are thus led to expect does not in fact begin until 1119, and the 'weighing' of tragic verses, transformed into a physical weighing on scales, not until 1365. Before any of this we have a full-dress contest between the two poets, adhering closely to the formal pattern of contest as we see it in *Clouds*, with the addition of Dionysos in the combined roles of moderator and buffoon. Euripides claims that Aiskhylos used to stupefy his audiences with theatrical effects and portentous language, while he himself, having put Tragedy on a diet and slimmed her down, has introduced matter which falls within the everyday experience of the audience; thus he exposes himself to their informed criticism and at the same time sharpens their critical capacity in their ordinary lives. Aiskhylos, having secured Euripides' agreement that poets should be judged by the teaching which they impart—and considering the point to which the previous stage of the argument had been led, Euripides is not in a position to disagree— Aiskhylos claims that his plays set heroic examples of warlike courage, while Euripides' have by their example encouraged women in adultery and men in undisciplined idleness.

Now comes the detailed scrutiny. First, the opening words of plays: Euripides criticizes Aiskhylos for ambiguity and obscurity, while Aiskhylos enjoys himself in tacking on ' . . . lost his oil-flask'[4] to every prologue whose opening words Euripides recites. Secondly, lyrics: Euripides parodies Aiskhylean lyrics as empty and incoherent verbal noise, while Aiskhylos produces a long and skilful parody of the style of Euripidean lyrics. Thirdly, the weighing of individual verses in the scales: this is treated in such a way that the real weight of the subject-matter, e.g. a river or a pile of corpses, not the metaphorical weight of the language, decides the issue.

Aiskhylos wins this test, but Dionysos still cannot make up his mind. Some one says (1414):

Then you won't accomplish the purpose for which you came.[5]

This must be Pluto himself, for he goes on to give permission—permission which only the ruler of the underworld could give—for the return to earth of whichever of the two Dionysos does in the end choose, and

---

4 The joke probably depends not merely on the incongruity of a domestic mishap in a heroic genealogy but also on a slang usage; the words *might* mean 'wore out his cock'.

5 Classical Greek script had no question-mark, and this line is sometimes interpreted as a question.

Pluto is certainly present by 1479, for he there invites Dionysos and Aiskhylos to dinner. How long he has been on stage we do not know for sure: a silent background figure since 830,[6] or an unannounced arrival immediately before he speaks, or an arrival announced in lines now missing from the text? Dionysos decides to pose two questions on politics, but the two poets' answers still do not enable him to decide; we expect a third question (cf. p. 91), but it takes the unusual form of Dionysos's consultation of his own heart (*psȳkhḗ*), in consequence of which he chooses Aiskhylos. Euripides' anguish and indignation are of no avail; Aiskhylos and Dionysos are entertained by Pluto, and Aiskhylos is escorted in triumph on his way up to our world.

THE CHORUSES

Do we see the frogs or only hear them? The predominant opinion, ever since antiquity, has been that they are an invisible chorus, and certain considerations tell in favour of this. One is that the principal chorus of the play has yet to appear, and the economic burden of costuming two choruses might be thought to press too heavily on the manager at a time when the cost of the war, in terms of loss and damage and taxation, was exceptionally high. Moreover, Kharon tells Dionysos (205f.) that he will 'hear' the songs of 'frog-swans', not that he will see anything of them, and the lyric dialogue between Dionysos and the frogs refers consistently to their noise, not to their colour or their jumping. Kharon's words are, however, natural, since frogs are more often heard than seen, and there is one rather important consideration which points to a visible chorus. The *principal* chorus of the play is dressed in rags. This is put beyond doubt by what they sing in 404–413, addressing Iakkhos, the Eleusinian deity whose worshippers they represent, and saying in effect that since the wearing of rags is customary in the actual worship of Iakkhos the costuming of a chorus representing his worshippers is unusually cheap:

> It was you who had us tear,
> for laughter and economy,
> these rags and this old sandal.
> You thought of how to hold a festive dance
> without expense.

---

6 In favour of this is the statement (784–786) that 'Pluto is preparing to hold a contest straight away . . .'; but 'hold' (*poên*, lit., 'make') is used also in *Wealth* 583 of Zeus's relation to the Olympic games held in his honour.

Iakkhos, friend of the dancers,
lead on the way I go.

I stole a sideways glance
just now, and saw a girl—
oh, what a pretty face!—
dancing among us, blouse torn down the side:
out peeped a tit.

Iakkhos, friend, etc.

Now, if the principal chorus is dressed 'without expense' and the subsidiary chorus does not appear at all, the manager is getting away with something rather unusual. The dramatic festivals are, after all, festive occasions on which the gods are conciliated, and the morale of the population raised, by the artistic splendour of processions, dancing, singing and drama. I suspect that the Athenians would have thought economy in this sphere a false economy, and the measure taken in 406/5 to divide managerial responsibility between two men for each play, like the similar division of responsibility for the equipment and maintenance of warships in the closing years of the war, was not intended so much to relieve those liable to this form of taxation as to ensure that standards were kept up. But if the chorus of frogs actually appeared, dressed in skin-tight costumes of green and yellow, crouching and leaping in all directions round the orchestra like frogs in a marsh, after such an agreeable and ingenious spectacle Aristophanes could not only have the chorus of initiates dressed in rags but could even put into their mouths a pert joke about the economy of that part of the proceedings; what was expected of the manager had been fulfilled by the frog-chorus. Perhaps we should also wonder whether an unseen chorus could ever have furnished the play with its title in (presumably) the official records and (certainly) the written text put into circulation; granted that titles indicating animal-, bird- or insect-choruses were common and traditional, the tradition hardly had the force of obligation.

At certain points in the succession of recitations and songs which we have from the chorus of initiates and their leader on their first appearance it was suggested by the ancient scholar Aristarkhos that Aristophanes intended a division between two half-choruses, and the sigla in many manuscripts conform to this suggestion. Aristarkhos may have been wrong. A division between the chorus-leader and the chorus as a whole is clear enough, the latter responding to the commands of the former, e.g. 370 ~ 372ff., 384f. ~ 386ff.; this is a phenomenon demonstrable in both comedy and tragedy. But the theory of a division into half-choruses perhaps originated in 440–447:

> (CHORUS-LEADER): Go (khɔ̄rête) now to the sacred enclosure of the goddess, to the flowery glen, with song and dance, all you who take part in the festival to the gods. I will go with the girls and women, where they pay all-night honour to the goddess, and I will carry the sacred torch.
>
> (CHORUS): Let us go (khɔ̄rɔ̂men) to the flowery fields full of roses. . . .

It is very difficult to take the prima facie indications of the text literally; it would mean the exit of the chorus-leader, either alone (seeking the girls and women somewhere out of our sight) or with some part of the chorus which so far has represented the girls and women; and once our chorus-leader has gone, how do we get him back? Another theoretical possibility is that in addition to a chorus-leader we have a 'torch-bearer', who departs now; there was such a person officiating in the rites of initiation at Eleusis, but what we are witnessing in *Frogs* is most certainly not rites of initiation.[7] Difficulties are avoided if we suppose simply that in 440–446 the chorus divides into two halves, the 'female' half (plus the chorus-leader) moving to one side of the orchestra and the 'male' half to the other; the entire chorus sings 447–459, and the two halves are joined again at 674, when the parabasis begins. The words in 440–447 are recited and sung *as if* initiates in the underworld were parting in two directions (cf. p. 138, on *Peace*), and there is a touch of roguishness in the chorus-leader's announcement that he is going with the more attractive section.

PROPERTIES AND MACHINERY

Frogs is unique among extant plays in providing us with the spectacle of a moving vehicle, Kharon's boat, which has to arrive, take on Dionysos, put him off, and disappear again with Kharon. No one can pretend to know just how this was done, but equally no one can pretend that it is difficult; difficulties arise only when we postulate for a Greek play something which would have been prohibitively expensive or technologically beyond the capacity of the Greeks. The boat could have been

---

7 The actual process of initiation at Eleusis was secret and could not be divulged to any non-initiate; we can take it for granted that nothing said or sung in *Frogs* is an adaptation or parody of any part of the initiation-rite itself.

on wheels (hidden under an apron) and hauled with a long rope out of one wing and away through the other, by men out of sight; or it could have been pushed along by men hidden inside it.

A more interesting problem is posed by the donkey on which Xanthias is mounted at the beginning of the play; nothing is said about it when Dionysos and Xanthias depart from the house of Herakles, and it is clear from the following scenes that it is no longer with us. As in the case of the crow and jackdaw at the beginning of *Birds*, it is possible to pick up from the text a hint of what was done. After Dionysos has knocked on Herakles' door, he evidently steps some way back from it, for he exchanges with Xanthias a brief conversation (40f.) which Herakles is not meant to hear; a moment later he says to Herakles (44):

Come over here, I want to ask you something.

This is unlike normal life, in which Dionysos, stopping in the course of a journey to call on his half-brother, would naturally be asked indoors; but normality has to be distorted for theatrical purposes, and the distortion allows for a naturalistic way of getting rid of the donkey. A visitor's horse or donkey would commonly be led off by one of the host's slaves for feeding and watering, and I suggest that when Herakles moves forward in response to Dionysos's request, unblocking the doorway and focusing the audience's interest well forward of the skene, a slave comes out and leads the donkey away. It has served a limited humorous purpose, and Aristophanes does not want to be encumbered with it.

PROBLEMS OF COMPOSITION

The fact that *Frogs* was performed at the Lenaia may mean that its composition was well advanced by the time the archons took office in the summer of 406 (cf. p. 15); and even if that is not a fair inference, at least the essential scheme of (a) a descent into the underworld by Dionysos to bring back Euripides and (b) a contest between Aiskhylos and Euripides, in the light of which Dionysos alters his intention, must already have been formulated when Sophokles died at some date between the summer and the Lenaia. Sophokles' career as a tragic dramatist had begun sixty-four years earlier, and he had distinguished himself by a large number of first prizes. So long as he was alive, it would have been nonsensical for Dionysos to say, as he does in his dialogue with Herakles, that there are no good poets left at Athens; on the other hand, once Sophokles was dead, it was impossible to evade the questions, 'Why not bring back Sophokles?' and 'Where does Sophokles come in the rivalry for the throne of poetry in the underworld?' The play in fact answers both questions briefly, the former mainly by saying (76–82) that Sophokles is not the kind of man who can be persuaded to 'run away', and the latter by representing Sophokles (786–794, cf. 1515–1519) as admitting the supremacy of Aiskhylos but ready to take on Euripides should Aiskhylos lose the contest. These two passages, together with most of the wider context of the former, 71–107, must obviously have been composed after Sophokles' death, possibly with little time to spare before the festival, but there is no real justification for supposing that if Sophokles had died earlier Aristophanes would have sent Dionysos to the underworld in search of *him* or that he would have left Aiskhylos out of the play and represented Sophokles and Euripides as rivals for a throne. The chronological relation between Aiskhylos and Euripides and the nature of the artistic differences between them provided the opportunity for the kind of contrasts which Aristophanes liked to portray; neither the technique of Sophokles' poetry nor the character with which he was credited afforded a satirist any firm hold, as is apparent from the rarity, not only in Aristophanes but in our citations from other comic poets, of jokes about or against Sophokles.[8]

At three points in the last three hundred lines of the play alternative versions of the same passage appear to have been superimposed. One is the choral song introducing Euripides' parody of Aiskhylos's lyrics: 1257–1260, 'For I wonder in what way he will criticize . . .', repeat the sense of 1252–1256, 'For I am full of curiosity about what criticism he will bring to bear . . .'. The second is 1431f., where the Ravennas has:

AISKHYLOS: It is not right to rear a lion-cub in a city. It is preferable not to rear a lion in a city; but if one is reared, accommodate to its ways,

but the second line, repeating the sense of the first, is omitted in the Venetus. The third passage occurs in 1436–1466: Dionysos asks the two poets a highly general question about what Athens should do to ensure her survival, and each of them gives an answer in general terms, but another answer by Euripides, a fantastic and comic idea for naval warfare, is superimposed on his general answer in a way which it is very hard to produce convincingly on stage, thus:

8 Phrynikhos fr. 31 (from *Muses*, produced on the same occasion as *Frogs*) is a moving epitaph on Sophokles.

1435f. DIONYSOS: I want each of you to give me one further opinion:
        how do you suggest the city should surmount its troubles?

1437– EURIPIDES: If someone fitted Kleainetos with Kinesias as
1441   wings . . . and they had vinegar-bottles and sprinkled it into
       the eyes of the enemy.

1442   I know, and I'd like to explain.
       DIONYSOS: Go on.

1443– EURIPIDES: When we regard as trustworthy . . . if we did the
1450   opposite of what we done before, things cannot fail to turn
       out right.

1451f. DIONYSOS: Well done, Palamedes! (*The legends of Palamedes
       portrayed him essentially as an inventor, not as a fount of political
       wisdom*) You have a brilliant mind. Was it all your own idea
       or Kephisophon's? (*Kephisophon was believed to have col-
       laborated in the writing of Euripides' plays*)

1453f. EURIPIDES: All my own—but the vinegar-bottles were
       Kephisophon's.
       DIONYSOS: (*Turning to Aiskhylos*) Well, now, what do *you*
       say?

It is natural to wonder whether apparent superimpositions of this kind
result from conflation of a version of the play composed before the
death of Sophokles with a version revised in a hurry after that event;
but no connection with Sophokles is apparent, and each of the three
passages exhibits features calling for an explanation not applicable to
the other two. The lyric passage 1252–1256 exhibits a metrical oddity
(three 'catalectic' verses in succession)[9] and a clumsiness of style
(calling Aiskhylos 'the Bacchanalian lord', a title appropriate to
Dionysos himself, 'Bacchanalian master' in *Thesm.* 988) which suggests
that it is not Aristophanic at all, but an interpolation by someone
of a later period trying his hand at choral lyrics. The alternative versions
of the line about the lion-cub may indeed be Aristophanes' own[10] but
cannot conceivably have anything to do with the death of Sophokles.
The superimposition of Euripides' two answers has been defended as
Aristophanes' deliberate intention, and in calling it 'hard' to produce I

9 There are, however, some parallels for a run of catalectic verses: *Peace*
785–787 ~ 807–809, Pherekrates fr. 79, Eupolis fr. 163.
10 My own opinion is that *Clouds* 653f. are a similar conflation of two different
versions of the same joke; and a recently published papyrus (*Zeitschrift für
Papyrologie und Epigraphik* i 117–120) seems to have conflated both a compressed
and a full version of *Lysistrata* 187–198.

did not mean 'impossible'; a theory that the text has been dislocated in transmission would also account for the facts.

It so happens that there is another item of evidence, unconnected with the death of Sophokles, which has been cited in support of the belief that two slightly different versions of the play were put into circulation by Aristophanes himself. The ancient hypothesis tells us that *Frogs* was so greatly admired that it was performed a second time; the hypothesis gives Dikaiarkhos, a pupil of Aristotle (d. 322), as its source, but it does not say whether the second performance was at the Lenaia of 405, or at the City Dionysia two months afterwards, or (despite the topicalities built into the parabasis and the last scene) some years later, nor do we know whether Dikaiarkhos's statement rested on the festival records or on a tradition lacking documentary control. In short, the number of unknowns relevant to the question, 'In what ways, and for what reasons, did written versions of *Frogs* in circulation late in Aristophanes' life differ from one another?' is large, and the scope for discussion and exercise of individual judgment is wide; which would be a very bad reason for ceasing to discuss the question.

CRITICISM OF TRAGEDY

When *Frogs* was produced, Aiskhylos had been dead for just over fifty years; Aristophanes—unless our biographical evidence (cf. p. 13) is badly misleading—cannot have set eyes on him, and only men in their seventies or over were in a position actually to remember the first production of *Persians* or *Seven against Thebes*. Since Euripides' first competition in a dramatic festival was in 455, there was a neat dividing line between the careers of the two poets. Looked at from the standpoint of Aristophanes' time, Aiskhylos was the poet of the generation which fought off the Persians and created the Athenian empire, Euripides the poet of their own more precarious days. This makes it possible for Aristophanes to assimilate the contest between Aiskhylos and Euripides to the familiar antithesis between the valour, virtue and security of the past, sustained by what seemed from a distance to be unanimity in the maintenance of traditional usage and belief, and the insecurity of the present, beset by doubts, 'unhealthy' curiosity and 'irresponsible' artistic innovations. We find in the contest some echoes of the similar contest between Right and Wrong in *Clouds*, e.g. *Frogs* 1069–1071:

AISKHYLOS: (*To Euripides*) And secondly, you taught them (*i.e. your audiences*) to cultivate mere talk and nattering, which has emptied the wrestling-schools and worn down the backsides of the young men who natter all the time. . . .

Clouds 1015–1018:

RIGHT: . . . But if you cultivate what they do now, you'll have a pale skin, small shoulders, a narrow chest, a big tongue, a small haunch. . . .

Clouds 1052–1054:

RIGHT: (*Bitterly and indignantly*) That's it! That's the kind of stuff that makes the baths crowded with young men who talk all day, every day, and makes the wrestling-schools empty.

The issue between Aiskhylos and Euripides is expressed very largely in terms of the moral effect of tragedy on its audiences. This treatment is not confined to that section of the contest which begins (1007–1010) with agreement on the propriety of assessing a poet by the moral effect he has, but underlies the argument of the previous section and even intrudes (1325–1328) into the parodying of lyrics. But neither poet is talking, as some modern readers of Greek tragedy might have expected them to talk, of the ethical and religious sentiments so often expressed in the choral lyrics of tragedy or of the moral insights which can emerge from reflection on the plot of a tragedy and on the manner in which the characters are presented. It is interesting to see that these aspects of tragedy are also ignored by Plato, who discusses the moral effects of tragedy in *Republic* II, and by Aristotle's *Poetics*, which analyses the technical means by which tragedy achieves its theatrical purpose. It will hardly do to explain this silence on the part of writers so different in standpoint by saying that (*a*) Aristophanes is playing to the gallery, (*b*) Plato following the logic of his argument in despite of his own sympathies, and (*c*) Aristotle intellectually and temperamentally incapable of seeing 'what tragedy is all about'; a case could be made for (*a*) and (*b*), but (*c*) is a perverse and superficial view. A much simpler explanation is provided by observing, first, that nearly all moral or religious generalizations uttered by tragic choruses, however colourful their language, are banalities which few Greeks ever questioned anyway, and secondly, that such generalization had been a well-established tradition of serious Greek poetry, including non-dramatic choral lyric, long before tragedy was invented, so that it was in no way a distinguishing feature of tragedy.

The moral effect of tragedy, as discussed in *Frogs*, can be manifested in two ways: in the imitation of behaviour presented on stage, and in the adoption of reasoned opinions and doubts voiced or implied by characters on stage. The idea that presentation of a coward or an adulteress in fiction increases the incidence of cowardice or adultery in real life is certainly widely held in our own time, especially by people whose perception of literary and theatrical technique is undeveloped and by people whose intellect and emotions are very strongly engaged by aspects of life to which the arts have no obvious relevance. It is likely that the same belief was held in antiquity by the same categories of people. Yet it is not immediately clear why, if Euripidean characters such as Stheneboia and Phaidra[11] could be held to induce respectable women to commit adultery, an Aiskhylean character such as Klytaimestra should not have been regarded as inspiring them to murder their husbands; indeed, in Antiphon i 17 a young man prosecuting his step-mother for poisoning his father calls her 'this Klytaimestra', and Plato's examples (*Republic* ii 379E–380A, 382D) of bad moral teaching in tragedy are drawn from Aiskhylos. Moreover, there is no shortage in Euripides of heroines of ostentatious virtue (an intensely patriotic speech by one of them is quoted approvingly by Lykourgos, *Prosecution of Leokrates* 100). The answer is partly, I think, that it was easy to treat Klytaimestra, 'a woman with a man's heart' (*Agamemnon* 11) as a person who could not readily or naturally be imitated, whereas Greek belief that women were by nature feeble in resistance to sexual temptation (cf. p. 159) led to quite a different estimation of Stheneboia. Hence Aiskhylos is made by Aristophanes to boast (1044) that he 'never portrayed a woman in love'. The answer may also be sought in the possibility that in some plays Euripides presented weakness in a way which captured the reluctant sympathy of the audience, as it captures ours. Equally, he made characters say things which were often, perhaps, felt but rarely said; Medea's declaration (Eur., *Medea* 250f.),

> So let me stand three times in line of battle
> rather than once give birth,

devalues the male virtues and may have been thought an insubordinate sentiment in keeping with Medea's character as a wicked sorceress.

11 It must be remembered that the *Hippolytus* which we possess is the second of two plays which Euripides wrote on the legend of Phaidra and Hippolytos, and there is good reason to believe that in the earlier play Phaidra was not, as she is in our *Hippolytos*, a helpless victim of Aphrodite.

This leads us to the second aspect of tragedy which plays so large a part in *Frogs*, its intellectualization by Euripides, as opposed to the theatrical effect sought by Aiskhylos. Unless (as is always possible) we are being led astray by our own attitudes and predilections, we can best see what Aristophanes means by looking at evidence which is not mentioned in *Frogs* at all, Euripides' *Elektra*, where the story of Orestes' vengeance on his mother, in which he is helped by his relentlessly unforgiving sister Elektra, is translated out of the supernatural and heroic terms in which Aiskhylos presented it into something much closer to life as we know it, with the result that we see the vengeance as a crime paranoid in motivation and squalid in execution. Aristophanes, devoted as he was to the theatre and acutely sensitive to dramatic effect, probably believed that the intrusion of intellectual scrutiny and neatly-organized arguments into tragedy was inimical to drama. This much is implied by what the chorus sings in congratulating Aiskhylos on his victory (1491–1495):

> What wins admiration, then,
> is not to sit by Socrates and talk,
> discarding song and poetry
> and leaving out what matters
> in the art of tragedy.

I have little doubt that in an after-dinner conversation Aristophanes would have expounded his views on this subject judiciously,[12] but when one is trying to make thousands of people laugh and applaud there is a limit to judiciousness, and one of the most striking things about *Frogs* is the degree of compromise Aristophanes achieves between presentation of the technical issues which he himself understood very well and comic exploitation of what were believed to be the issues by people who understood less. It is to be observed first of all that Aiskhylos does not have a walkover victory. As a person he is proud, irascible and violent, and if we did not possess some of his plays we might well bring away from our reading of *Frogs* the impression that the chief characteristics of his work were unintelligible and bombastic language (uttered largely by warriors doing verbal war-dances) and a straining after spectacle. When Dionysos is asked to adjudicate between Aiskhylos and Euripides, he does not at once repent of the passion for Euripides which led him in the first place to undertake a journey to the underworld; on the contrary, he continues in a state of

12   These views might not have differed in essentials from Aristotle's.

indecision even at points where the advantage of the moment seems to us to lie with Aiskhylos, e.g.;

1411–1413:   They are both dear to me, and I won't decide between them; I don't want to be on bad terms with either. One of them I regard as *sophós*, and the other I enjoy.

1433f.:   Well, I must say, I honestly can't decide. One of them spoke *sophôs* and the other one plainly.

The word *sophós* (adverb *sophôs*, abstract noun *sophíā*) was most commonly used in the archaic and early classical periods to denote artistic, technical or scientific skill; less often, but increasingly in the later classical period, it denoted practical, moral or political insight, and thus began to approximate to our word 'wise'. Like any complimentary term (e.g. 'honest', 'beautiful'), it can be used sarcastically, but it is rarely used, and never by Aristophanes, in a derogatory sense (as e.g. our 'subtle' can be used). In Aiskhylos's valediction to the underworld, *sophíā* is the quality which he claims for himself (1515–1519):

> And you meanwhile
> give my throne to Sophokles
> to guard and keep. (One day, perhaps,
> I shall return). For him I judge
> second in *sophíā* to myself.

In 1433f. *sophôs*, 'like a true poet', refers to Aiskhylos's image of the lion-cub, and *saphôs*, 'plainly', to Euripides' 'I hate a citizen...'.[13] Accordingly the judgment expressed in 1413 acknowledges Aiskhylos to be the greater poet, but Euripides to be enjoyable; to represent Dionysos, the god of the dramatic festivals, as enjoying Euripides is a way of recognizing the popularity and success which Euripides had in fact achieved.

One of Aiskhylos's claims to greatness is the wide scope of his theatrical imagination and his readiness to experiment; in *Prometheus* the fettered Titan, the arrival of the daughters of Okeanos through the air, their father's winged beast, the earthquake which engulfs them at the end; in *Eumenides* the chorus of Furies sniffing round the orchestra like hounds; examples can be multiplied from the few plays which

13 Interpretations which reverse the reference overlook 1413 and 1434 and the fact that imagery and enigmatic allusion, which the hearer must 'solve', are characteristic of early fifth-century poetry.

survive and from our information about the lost plays. But this aspect of Aiskhylos, apparent to a modern historian of literature, could not be easily appreciated in the late fifth century B.C.; because conservative people, idealizing the first half of the century, admired Aiskhylos more than living poets, they tended to think of Aiskhylos himself as conservative, which is a common but dangerous type of *non-sequitur*. And since idealization of the past was not counteracted by significant progress in techniques affecting the standard of living, or by any conspicuous grounds for thinking the past crueller or less honest than the present there must have been a great many people whose reaction to Aiskhylos was, 'that's the sort of stuff that made them the men they were in the good old days'. The tradition of didacticism in poetry (cf. p. 52) will have reinforced the tendency to think in those terms, and Aristophanes exploits it very fully.

The parody of Aiskhylean lyrics, designed to suggest that they are concatenations of big words in which sound-effects and fragmentary, elusive associations matter more than sense, may not have been wide of the mark from the average man's point of view. It was part of a poet's job to be allusive and enigmatic, and I greatly doubt whether any two members of the original audience of the *Oresteia* would have agreed in the paraphrase which they could have offered of any one lyric stanza in it; but they did agree, I think, that listening to those lyrics was a linguistic experience appropriate to a dramatic festival. The parody of Euripidean lyrics in 1309–1363 is more subtle, and can afford to be, because Aristophanes could draw upon those passages of recent plays which he knew to be fresh in people's minds; the monody uttered by the woman who awakes from a nightmare and finds that her cockerel has been stolen is reminiscent in its general character, with its repetitions of words and its overwrought emotional tone, of the monody of the Phrygian slave in Eur., *Orestes* 1369–1502.

Since tragedies were written for mass audiences, tragedy as a whole could be used as material for humour in the same way as agriculture and sex and war could be used; it was part of the life of the community, not like chamber music or Shakespeare—the cultural interest of a minority. How accurately the man in the street recalled the individual tragedies which he had seen, how minutely he discussed them with others, and how keenly he appreciated the details of parody, are questions which are not adequately answered simply by studying what Aristophanes parodies and how he does it. For one thing, it is observable nowadays that a majority in an audience can be surprisingly tolerant of parody which only a minority can really appreciate;[14] each individual seems to feel that everyone else must have seen the point and that he *ought* to see it himself. But what is more important is a factor which we can divine but cannot assess accurately: the extent to which Aristophanes chose for parody and quotation only those scenes, passages, lines and stylistic tricks which he already knew to be the most familiar. In some cases a tragedy might become better remembered through repeated parody than in its own right, so that an allusion to Telephos in *Women at the Thesmophoria* might be appreciated not through immediate recollection of the tragedy *Telephos*, performed sixteen years earlier, but through recollection of parodies of it in *Acharnians* and perhaps other plays which we do not have. We must remember, too, that when Aristophanes makes clever and amusing use of a tragic line he is not setting the audience an examination, as if saying 'Give the context of . . .', but using something which may well have passed into quasi-proverbial use. The famous line from Euripides' *Hippolytus* 612,

My tongue is under oath, my heart unsworn,

is paraphrased by Dionysos (101f.) as an instance of memorable tragic invention, and a spectator does not have to be very highly educated to appreciate 1469–1471:

EURIPIDES: Mindful of the gods by whom you swore that you would take me back,[15] choose those who are dear to you.
DIONYSOS: My tongue is under oath—but I'll choose Aiskhylos!

14   I have watched a close parody of *Citizen Kane* (in a television show designed for a mass audience) in the company of a friend who gave every appearance of finding it very funny but turned out to have no idea of what was being parodied.
15   We are not told elsewhere that Dionysos swore to take Euripides back, but that is not important; when A considers that he has been led to expect something from B he is likely, in a moment of emotion to say 'You *promised* . . .!' and Euripides is simply being rhetorical. Cf. also p. 133 on Zeus's threat of punishment in *Peace*.

XV

Women in Assembly

The hypothesis is defective, but the play was probably produced in 392. This is an inference from the scholion on line 193, which says that 'two years before, there was an alliance of the Spartans and Boeotians'. This scholion is only explicable as a corrupt abbreviation of a historical statement, which would be correct, that Athens made an alliance *with* the Boeotians *against* the Spartans in 395/4. The dramatic festivals of 393/2 fell, of course, in the early months of the year which we call 392. The historical allusions in the play in any case indicate the late 390s.

The Greek name of the play is *Ekklēsiásdōsai*, commonly Latinized as *Ecclesiazusae*; the verb *ekklēsiásdēn* means 'attend the assembly'.

SYNOPSIS

The theme of the play has something in common with *Lysistrata* and *Women at the Thesmophoria*, particularly with the former, since it has a female character, Praxagora, who dominates and organizes the women of Athens. They have agreed (at an earlier festival, the Skira [59]) to disguise themselves as men, pack the assembly at first light, and vote for transference of political power from men to women. Praxagora checks their disguises and rehearses them sternly in the part they are to play; her demonstration of how the motion should be proposed includes a swift—and to us, somewhat enigmatic—survey of the current internal and external political situation. When all is in order, they move off.

In order to disguise themselves as men they have taken their husband's clothes, and a certain Blepyros, getting up in the night to relieve his overloaded bowels, has to come out wearing his wife's dress and women's shoes. A neighbour who spots him in the dark remarks that his own wife has treated him in the same way. This neighbour goes off to the assembly, and Blepyros squats and strains to no effect until his efforts are cut short by another friend, Khremes, who is on his way back from the assembly. Khremes tells him how a great crowd in the assembly, pale-faced 'like shoemakers', has voted (455f.):

> ... to hand the city over to the women. After all, they thought this was the only thing they hadn't yet tried.

Blepyros and Khremes go into their houses, and the women return triumphant, taking care now to remove their disguises and return their menfolk's clothes. Praxagora does not quite make it before her husband indignantly accosts her, suspicious that she has been visiting a lover. She allays his suspicion by claiming that she had to go out in a hurry to a friend who was in labour, and she affects surprised innocence on hearing from him the decision of the assembly to hand over power to the women. But, she says, this will be greatly to the city's advantage, and she expounds her reasons in what formally resembles one side of the typical fifth-century 'contest'.

Up to now we have been given very little idea of the political reforms which the women have in mind, and their original insistence on 'the old ways' (216) has perhaps led us to think of reaction rather than revolution. More recently, Khremes' account of the argument used in the assembly, that women are accustomed to be more open-handed and more honest in the lending and returning of property (446–450), has given us an important hint, and so has Blepyros's foreboding that it will be hard for old men if women assume the sexual initiative (465–470). Now Praxagora unfolds her programme, answering her husband's succession of questions and objections. All property and money are to belong to the community. Any man may have intercourse with any woman and beget children by her; the interests of the ugly, men and women alike, will be protected by legislation which will give them first go. All children will regard all men as their fathers. There being no private property, there will be no lawsuits, and assault will be punished by exclusion from the communal meals. The work of the fields will be done by slaves. Praxagora returns at the end to the sexual aspect of the reforms, and this secures her husband's approval, since it offers him protection against the competition of the young and handsome.

We now see a law-abiding citizen preparing to hand in all his

property, harassed by another man, an incorrigible cynic, on these
lines (762–772):

A: Why, ought one not to obey the law?
B: What law, you silly man?
A: The law that's been passed.
B: Passed? You *are* stupid!
A: Stupid?
B: Why, yes, the biggest bloody fool ever.
A: Because I'm doing what I'm told?
B: Why, ought a man with any sense [1] to do what he's told?
A: More than anyone!
B: No, only a clod.
A: Aren't *you* going to hand in your stuff?
B: I'll take care not to until I've seen what most people think about it.
A: But of course they're ready to bring in all their property.
B: Seeing is believing!

When a woman herald proclaims that everyone should go to the
general's office (Praxagora is the 'general') to draw lots for places at
dinner, the cynic cheerfully goes off to do so, trusting to luck that he
will also manage to keep his own property.

The next scene, which is long and complex, illustrates some sexual
consequences of the revolution. A girl and an old woman are waiting
for a lover, mocking each other and singing love-songs in rivalry; the
reforms being now in force, we should not think of them as prostitutes,
but as members of humble citizen families, the girl probably fourteen
or fifteen years old (she is sorry that her 'friend' has not come, because
her mother is out [911–913]). The youth for whom the girl is longing
comes to visit her, but before he can enter her house he is seized by the
old woman, who demands her rights. The girl comes out and manages
to drag him away, but is put to flight in her turn by a second old
woman, who wants him for herself. The poor youth is being taken off
by this old woman (who has the law on her side) when a third woman,
even older and more hideous, stakes her claim to him, and still clings
to him when he is finally forced into the second old woman's house.
An interesting feature of this portion of the play is the duet of love-

---

1 The adjective used, *sōphrōn*, commonly means 'law-abiding', and that gives
B a splendidly paradoxical utterance, but the adjective can on occasion have the
same point as the verb *sōphronēn* in the common expression *ei sōphronēte*, 'if you
are wise', 'if you are sensible'.

songs sung by the youth and the girl; one pair is in the same metrical form as some Athenian drinking-songs, while the other pair has an extensive refrain and (if correctly transmitted in the manuscript text) a certain metrical uncouthness, both features which may point to its 'popular' character.[2]

The play ends in something of a rush. A servant comes looking for her mistress's husband, who alone of the citizen population has not yet arrived for dinner.[3] She comes across him, hands over to him the girls whom she has brought with her,[4] and they all go off to dinner to the accompaniment of a choral song about food (cf. pp. 72, 154).

THE CHORUS

A remarkable structural feature of this play is that the chorus assembles silent during lines 30–56, a few at a time, and has nothing to say until 285; and at that point it starts to go *out* of the theatre, on its way to the assembly, disappearing from our sight at 310 and returning at 478. It has a song to accompany its departure (285–310), another to accompany its return (478–503), and a long stanza introducing the contest (571–582) between Praxagora and Blepyros, but thereafter the chorus-leader does not speak until 1127, and there is no choral song until the close of the play. There is no parabasis; the only lyric passages in the course of the second half of the play are the songs of the old woman, the girl and the youth. At two points, however, 729 (just before the virtuous citizen appears packing up his goods) and 876 (just before the old woman and the girl appear), the Ravennas presents us with the word *khorô*, literally 'of (the) chorus', as if choral songs not transmitted in the text of the play had once stood there or were believed by an ancient commentator likely to have stood there.

2   It is not easy to tell whether Aristophanes is simply choosing to write in 'popular' style (cf. p. 134, on *Peace*) or parodying a genre for which he did not have a high regard; cf. C. M. Bowra, 'A Love-duet', *American Journal of Philology* lxxix (1958), 377–391.
3   On the assumptions that he is Blepyros, the husband of Praxagora (cf. p. 196), and that the servant is Praxagora's, it is hard to see why he is late for dinner, since Praxagora's husband said (725–727) that he would stay close behind her; hard to see, that is, *if* we respond to a joke by at once perceiving its incompatibility with a different joke four hundred and sixty lines earlier.
4   'These girls', as she calls them, seem to be merely an ornament for the final scene (cf. pp. 27f.); it is not quite impossible that the expression is a humorous reference to the women of the chorus, but, if it is, the chorus-leader is dissociating himself from the rest of the chorus in an unusual way by saying 'take *these* with you' in 1151f.

This bare indication of a choral song becomes more familiar to us in *Wealth*, where the total number of lines sung by the chorus is only a dozen and of those spoken by the chorus-leader only thirty, while one or more manuscripts present *khorô* no less than seven times. We may—indeed, we must—make allowance for some erroneous insertion of *khorô* in late antiquity, but even when such allowance has been made it is clear that *Ass.* and *Wealth* show a rapid progress in the direction of the 'uninvolved' chorus.[5] In New Comedy at the end of the fourth century a choral interlude, marked in the text simply as *khorô*, occurs four times in the course of a play, dividing it into five 'acts' (cf. p. 223). The first of the interludes is introduced by one of the characters with some such words as (*Dyskolos* 230–232):

> I see some worshippers of Pan coming this way, and they've had a bit too much to drink. I think it would be a good idea not to get in their way.

The second, third and fourth interludes occur without any such allusion in the dialogue, and it seems a fair inference that the comic poet no longer regarded it as part of his own job to write the songs which served simply as entertainment during breaks in the action.[6] It should not be supposed that the elimination of the chorus from the action and of the writing of choral lyrics from the responsibilities of the dramatist proceeded in a straight line from *Wealth* in 388 to *Dyskolos* in 316, and some citations from plays of the mid-fourth century suggest that adoption of more or less old-fashioned forms was always open to a poet, but it is remarkable to find the process beginning as early as *Ass.* (especially in view of the theme and title of the play) and developing so rapidly in a few years in Aristophanes' own hands. No one, after all, could accuse Aristophanes of incapacity in the composition of choral lyrics. If he fell in with a fashion which others had begun, it can only have been because the public approved of this fashion and he would have imperilled his chances of first prize if he had gone against it; or again, if he himself led the fashion, some reason

5   Cf. E. W. Handley, '*ΧΟΡΟΥ* in the *Plutus*', *Classical Quarterly* N.S. iii (1953), 55–61.
6   It appears from Aristophanes' reference to Kratinos in *Knights* 529f. that lyrics from comedies could go into circulation as popular songs divorced from their original contexts, and lyrics of this kind may often have provided the interludes in fourth-century comedy. On the whole question see K. J. Maidment, 'The Later Comic Chorus', *Classical Quarterly* xxix (1935), 1–24.

other than incapacity has to be sought.[7] It is significant that of the two Aristophanic plays produced (by his son) later than 388, *Aiolosikon* and *Kokalos*, the former is described as 'having no choral songs' and the latter as anticipating the type of plot common in New Comedy. It almost looks as if Aristophanes himself was forcing the pace; and, if so, this is likely to be a product of three distinct tendencies: a positive liking on the part of the audience for the revival of old songs, regardless of their irrelevance to their new context; an intensification of Aristophanes' own positive interest in social satire and realistic characterization; and an awareness on his part that comedy could expect much wider popularity in the Greek world—such as tragedy was coming to enjoy—if the element of Athenian topicality, associated especially with the parabasis, were greatly reduced.

CHARACTERS

Apart from the scene in which the youth is involved with the old women and the girl, there are prima facie eight men in the play, and the reader has to work out for himself the extent to which this appearance may be illusory. The eight roles are:

(A) Blepyros, who is on stage 311–477 and is addressed by name in 327.

(B) A neighbour of Blepyros, on his way to the assembly, 327–356.

(C) Khremes, who returns from the assembly in 371 and departs ('Well, I'll be going') at 477, where he is addressed by name.

(D) Praxagora's husband, 520–727; he departs with her, saying (725–727):

> I'll follow close behind you, so that everyone will look round at me and say, 'Look at the general's husband! Isn't he marvellous?'

(E) A man who suddenly interrupts Praxagora's argument with her husband by saying (564):

> For heaven's sake, man, give your wife a chance to speak![8]

7 There is no getting away from the fact that *Wealth* is not merely deficient in the kind of sparkle that we like in the earlier plays (I have in mind the rather ponderous moralizing of 159f. and the unsophisticated humour of 1095f. and 1204–1207) but also clumsy in detail (cf. p. 196 on 'Man E'). The possibility that Aristophanes had had a stroke cannot be absolutely excluded; but then one might have expected him to go on trying to write the kind of play he was used to, rather than write a new kind.

8 It is possible that the new arrival speaks 562f., protesting at what Praxagora has just said, and D speaks 564. In any case D and E are both there.

This man is also the probable speaker of an aside (568) and must be there throughout the formal argument, because Praxagora says at the end (710):

Well now, tell me, are *you both* satisfied?

And after Praxagora's husband has decided to follow the 'general', this man says (728f.):

And I—I'll go through my property and get it ready so that I can take my things to the city-centre.

(F) A man packing up his things for surrender to the community (730–871), contrasted with—

(G) A man who has no intention of surrendering anything, but does not propose to miss the free communal feast; 746–876.

(H) The husband of the woman who owns the female slave who enters at 1112 looking for him. This man is the only one who has not yet found his way to the feast; he enters at 1128, and goes off in the general exodos.

It is reasonable to identify Blepyros with D and H, especially since Blepyros's wife left him her dress while taking his cloak (315–318) and this is just what Praxagora's husband complains about. It is also natural to identify E and F, since F's actions accord with E's declared intention, and this man may well be Khremes, who accepted the revolutionary decisions of the assembly with complete equanimity. B and G *could* be the same man, but whether Aristophanes intended them to be could only be known if we knew—as we do not—whether they wore the same mask; dress would be irrelevant, since B, like Blepyros, has had his cloak taken by his wife, whereas by the time that G arrives on the scene the women have all returned and shed their disguises, and such men as lost their cloaks have them back. We must, I think, be content not to know precisely how many different men there are in the play; it does not matter. What matters more, from the point of view of drama-tic technique, is the entirely unannounced entry of E=Khremes at some point before he speaks 564. He seems to be a vestigial relic of the type of character who interposes jokes and asides during a contest (Dionysos in *Frogs* 905–1098 is a good example), handled as if the dramatist did not know how to handle him; we must, however, con-sider the possibility that he had a larger share in the contest than is in-dicated by the manuscripts, e.g, in 646–648.

Four actors are required from 938 onwards, for (i) the first old woman runs on at 1044 while the youth and the girl are both on stage, and the second old woman appears at 1049, whereupon the girl flees, and (ii) when the slave of Praxagora enters at 1112 the young man is being pulled indoors by both the second old woman and the third old woman (who appeared at 1065). It seems that in the opening scene of the play three women speak as well as Praxagora, but one of them can be the chorus-leader.

STAGING

The scene of conflict over the youth constitutes strong evidence for more than one door in the skene. The old woman is described by the girl as 'peeping out' (884, 924, 930), the words used being the same as those used in *Peace* (78, 982, 985) of peeping through a door. Since they cannot be peeping in rivalry through the same door at the same time they either have a door each or they are looking out of windows (cf. p. 125, on *Wasps*; it has been suggested that they are on the flat roof, but the language of the scene seems to me incompatible with that). Since the young man calls on the girl to 'run *down* and open the door' (961f.) we may be meant to see that they are looking out of windows, but even if that were so it would still not enable us to manage with one door. In 974–990 the dialogue goes:

> YOUTH: . . . open, take me in your arms!
> For you I suffer torment!
> OLD WOMAN: You—why are you knocking? Is it me you're looking for?
> YOUTH: No, of course not!
> OLD WOMAN: Well, you bashed at the door!
> YOUTH: I'm damned if I did!
>
> .   .   .
>
> YOUTH: I don't know what you're talking about. (*Literally:*) I've got to knock this one.
> OLD WOMAN: Yes, when you've knocked at my door first!

After or while singing 'For you . . .' the youth knocks at a door; that much is plain. If there is only one door, that is the one from which the old woman appears, to his horror, in answer to his knock; if there are two, the old woman emerges from the door at which he has not knocked, pretending that she thought the knock had been at her door (not an unusual misunderstanding in real life when two small houses are adjacent). The youth's replies sound appropriate to the latter situation, not to the former. The last lines quoted involve a pun, facilitated by the feminine demonstrative *tēndedī*, which could apply equally to a door or a woman. 'Knock' is a slang term for sexual intercourse; it would be contrary to comic usage if the youth used it first in this slang sense and then the old woman took it up with coy and sinister innuendo; we want the youth to use the word with reference to the girl's door (as distinct from the old woman's door), and the old woman to exploit the double meaning of which the youth was unconscious.

The old woman insists that the youth come into her house (1037 *ēságō*, 'I am taking *in* . . .'). When the second old woman appears ('popping *out*', 1052) the girl runs away, one would have thought, through the door from which she herself had emerged, not into the second old woman's door. The third old woman does not seem to have a door of her own; the second and third old women quarrel over the youth, pulling him in different directions, but he comes nearer and nearer to the second old woman's door, as he shows by his words, 'near the door', in 1093, to which the third old woman replies (1094f.)

That won't help you at all, because I shall get pulled in with you!

This is what seems to happen; in his last despairing speech he cries that he will be 'shut up with monsters' (1104) and that he is being 'borne in here' by the *two* of them (1106). Thus we seem to have a strong case for a *three*-door skene in this scene of *Ass.* (cf. p. 135, on *Peace*), and that has many advantages for the earlier parts of the play also. The second woman to speak (35) after the prologue is Praxagora's neighbour, at whose door she taps (33f.). If, as seems to be the case, Blepyros is Praxagora's husband, we want one door for Blepyros and Praxagora and another for the neighbour. The first man who observes Blepyros squatting in the dark speaks of 'my neighbour Blepyros' (327); we can imagine him as the husband of the second woman. Then Khremes will be the occupant of the third house; this will account for his unobtrusive arrival shortly before 564, drawn by the noise of dispute between Blepyros and Praxagora, and it both supports and is supported by the identification of the virtuous citizen of 730ff. as Khremes.

WOMEN AND PROPERTY

The Greeks did not regard the state as a mechanism for the special protection of those who wish to acquire and transmit private wealth, and they would not have denied the appellation 'free' to a man who, although subject to nothing and no one but the law made and enforced by the majority of his fellow-citizens, was at the same time forbidden by that law to own property. A state is free if no other state can tell it what to do, and an individual is free if no other individual can control him in defiance of a law which applies to all alike. There is no limit to what the state can demand of the individual in the interests of its own security; which does not mean that no one hoped and tried to escape his obligations, or that rich men smilingly acquiesced in every measure which had the effect of diminishing their wealth to the advantage of the poor, but does mean that there was a shortage of theoretical arguments against the abolition of private property, always provided that the abolition was decided on constitutionally and put into practice without favour. Plato, who was no democrat, envisaged the ruling class of his ideal state as absolutely precluded from acquisition of private property of any kind (*Republic* 416D–417A).[9] Aristotle (*Politics* ii 5) subjected this proposal to a series of criticisms based on his estimate of the damage which society would suffer from suppression of man's natural drives to ownership and generosity and from a special category of conflicts which community of property can observably generate. To Aristotle, as to Plato, alternative economic structures are means to an end and must be judged by the qualities of the whole society which they serve.[10] The orators contemporary with Plato and Aristotle, however different in detail, reveal a similar scale of values when they have occasion to touch in general terms on the relation between the state and the individual; it would clearly have been difficult for them to examine publicly, and it may have been difficult for them even to contemplate, the possibility that the state itself can be wrong or unjust in its treatment of the individual. It must be remembered also that the very slow pace of technological progress, the small scale of commerce and manufacture, the predominant concern of the citizen-body with land, crafts or retail, and the exclusion of resident alien traders and manufacturers from political rights all prevented the growth of a political philosophy in which the spectacular rewards of competitive business would take an important place.

9   The workers who support his ruling class are allowed private property.
10   The idea of abolishing private property does not seem to have aroused in the Greeks the same tempest of emotion as it arouses in some of our contemporaries. Several modern interpreters of *Women in Assembly* have taken the finale, which contains an elaboration of the traditional joke (cf. p. 154) 'You're all invited to dinner—in your own homes!', as designed by Aristophanes to show that communism is a swindle.

There are two reasons why Aristophanes should represent community of property as a reform introduced by women. One is that women were not themselves concerned with the acquisition or disposal of property. A woman could not make a will or enter into a contract involving more than a trivial sum; a bride brought a dowry with her, but she was essentially the medium through which her father transmitted that portion of his estate to his grandchildren. Her function as a housewife was to manage the household, but she could not easily feel, as she did a job which could have been done by a slave-steward or slave-housekeeper, that the property was hers. When Khremes reports to Blepyros the reasons given by the 'pale-faced young man' in the assembly for entrusting the state to women, these include (446–450):

> And then he said that women lend one another clothes, gold, money, vessels, just between themselves, not before witnesses, and they give all this back and don't try to make away with it—but most of *us*, he said, do try to.

A much more important reason is that since marriage within the citizen-body was not a consequence of falling in love but a mechanism for the transmission of property (it was the girl's father who decided whom she should marry), two issues which seem to us separate, community of women and community of property, were regarded by the Greeks as cognate issues and are so treated by Plato in the *Republic*.[11] Since one 'has' a wife and 'has' an acre of land, the simple Greek ways of expressing notions like 'common ownership' or 'common property' are naturally taken to include sexual communism unless that is explicitly excluded.

The affinities between Praxagora's reforms and the ideal state constructed by Plato have naturally provoked inquiry into the possibility that Aristophanes is satirizing Plato. On chronological grounds this is impossible unless we postulate an early edition of part of the *Republic* later subsumed in the *Republic* as we know it;[12] and it is in any case doubtful whether Aristophanes would have chosen to satirize a purely philosophical idea without making its association with philosophers clear in the play. Different ingredients of Platonic communism may

11   Aristotle treats them together because Plato did; *Politics* ii 2–6 are a systematic critique of Plato's ideal state.
12   Cf. James Adam's edition of Plato's *Republic* (Cambridge, repr. 1962), vol. i 345–355.

have been anticipated by fifth-century intellectuals[13] and may have filtered into less specialized media (a character in Euripides' *Protesilaos* [fr. 653] appears to have expressed the sentiment that women should be common to all men), but the theme of *Women in Assembly* is more than anything a confluence of two comic traditions: the assumption of some degree of social and political initiative by women (*Lysistrata, Women at the Thesmophoria*), and a golden age, far-distant land or underworld in which the normal order is reversed and no one needs to work, since everything comes of its own accord (e.g. Krates' *Animals*, Pherekrates' *Miners*).

13   The statement of Aristoxenos (fr. 67) that 'almost the whole' of Plato's ideal state was taken from Protagoras is not reconcilable with Aristotle's statement (*Politics* ii 7.1) that no one, whether philosopher or statesman, apart from Plato, has ever proposed community of women and children. This statement, incidentally, does not permit us to infer that Aristotle was unaware of *Women in Assembly*: he would naturally not take account of comic fantasies in evaluating political and philosophical theories.

XVI

Wealth

Produced in 388; at what festival and with what success, we do not know.

Aristophanes had produced another play of the same name in 408. Some allusions in the scholia on our play show that an ancient commentator believed himself to be commenting on the play of 408; but he was wrong, as historical references in the play itself demonstrate beyond doubt.

SYNOPSIS

Khremylos, accompanied by his slave, Karion, has been to consult the Delphic oracle on whether his son ought, if he is to succeed in life, to try to be a good man or a bad. Apollo told Khremylos to take home with him the first man he met on going out of the sanctuary. The first man was old and blind; pestered by Khremylos and Karion to tell them who he is, he reveals that he is Wealth, blinded by Zeus in order that he might not recognize good men from bad and so reward only the former.[1] He has fallen into cynicism and despair (which is not surprising), but Khremylos and Karion eventually persuade him to come home, overwhelming him with excited protestations. Zeus, they argue, is not to be feared, for he rules 'through money', with which Wealth 'provides' him (130–132); men sacrifice to Zeus only in the hope of money (133f.) and could not sacrifice unless Wealth 'gave' them the money with which to buy sacrificial victims (135–143). Wealth, in fact, is both the final cause and the prerequisite of all activities. Khremylos is

[1] The assumption that Zeus deliberately makes things difficult and unpleasant for mankind is not uncommon; it is a translation of the observation that life is hard from empirical into theological language.

encouraged, by the way the oracle has turned out so far, to believe that he will be able to restore the sight of Wealth. When it is restored, Wealth will go only to honest men; the implication, not made altogether clear, is that thereafter no one will have any motive to be dishonest.

Karion summons Khremylos's friends, hard-working old men who consider themselves poorer than they should be. He teases them at first, sending them into a peevish rage, but finally reveals the good news. They dance for joy, singing with Karion, in alternating stanzas, a jocular song deriving its inspiration from the Odyssey. Meanwhile, Khremylos has sent for his friend Blepsidemos, who suspects that Khremylos has made money in some dishonest way. Khremylos finally persuades him of the truth, and tells him of his intention to take Wealth to the sanctuary of Asklepios for a miraculous cure. Their conversation is interrupted by the arrival of a menacing old woman who proclaims herself to be Poverty. Khremylos, with some backing from Blepsidemos, argues with Poverty in a contest which is formally a rather degenerate descendant of the contests which appear in the fifth-century plays; there are no choral introductions or comments, only one choral exhortation (to Khremylos, at the beginning), and no clear division into two halves. Poverty asserts that without the fear which she inspires no one would produce or import anything, so that if everyone had money there would be nothing for him to buy with it. She rejects Khremylos's denigration of poverty as 'beggary', and draws a distinction between the two; but as the distinction does not appeal to Khremylos and Blepsidemos, she is doomed to lose the argument, and she flees with the threat (608f.):

> The day will come, I can tell you, when you'll send for me to come back here.

Khremylos and Karion now go off to the sanctuary of Asklepios with Wealth, and immediately (that is, after a choral interlude? Cf. p. 193) Karion returns and gives Khremylos's wife the good news that the cure has been successful. He describes the whole process in a long and colourful narrative, which includes the unpleasant fate of the politician Neokleides (who was trying to get his eye-disease cured), the greed of the priest who gathered up all edible offerings made to the god, and (of course) the fearful fart released by Karion on the approach of Asklepios, much to the embarrassment of the female deities accompanying the god. Wealth himself now returns, saluting Attica in tragic style, and Khremylos follows close behind.

Khremylos's house is now miraculously wealthy, with a cistern full of olive oil and all the crockery turned to gold and silver. The rest of the play illustrates the consequences of Wealth's recovery of his sight, but Aristophanes does not adhere consistently to one or the other of two concepts: that everyone is now wealthy, or that the good are now wealthy and the bad impoverished. The first two men to arrive illustrate the second concept: a good man, suddenly finding himself rich, comes to pay his respects to Wealth, while an informer comes lamenting his poverty. The second pair is an old woman and a youth whom she has retained as her lover by lavish presents. Suddenly enriched, he no longer needs to conceal his contempt for the wrinkles that lie under her layer of make-up. He does not sound to us like a *just* man, but perhaps to the Athenians his ingratitude to a randy old woman raises no moral issue at all; he goes into the house to make a dedication to Wealth, and Khremylos, whose admonition of him is almost diffident compared with the harsh treatment given to the informer, jollies the old woman into coming in too. The next arrival is Hermes, who comes threatening divine vengeance on the household of Khremylos, since no one now troubles to sacrifice to the gods. But Karion, who opens the door to him, is in no way impressed by threats, and Hermes, desperately hungry, is reduced to begging for a job. Eventually he is admitted on condition he helps in the kitchen. The last to come is a priest, and he too is hungry, because he has relied in the past on the perquisites from sacrifices. He thinks it would be a good idea to forget about Zeus and stay with Wealth; but Khremylos identifies the two, and suggests that they instal Wealth on the Akropolis (1192f.):

... where he used to be installed, always looking after the treasure-room of the goddess.[2]

A procession for the installation is organized and moves off.

SLAVES IN COMEDY

Karion is a very important character in *Wealth*. In the first scene he pesters his master to explain the point of following the blind old man, and will not yield to commands or threats; so Khremylos explains the

2 After the Peloponnesian War Athens lost her empire and with it the tribute which she extorted from her subject-allies. The fourth-century Athenian therefore looked back to the fifth as to an age of great national wealth. This does not mean, however, that the *average* Athenian was poorer by 388 than his counterpart in 438.

situation, justifying his indulgence with a compliment that is given a comic twist (26f.):

> Well, I won't keep it from you; for of all my slaves I regard you as the most faithful—and the biggest thief!

In their efforts to persuade the old man to come home with them, Karion and Khremylos act more like a pair of friends than slave and master; and it is Karion who summons the chorus and (metaphorically and literally) leads them a dance. Karion comes back ahead of Khremylos from the sanctuary of Asklepios, congratulates the old men of the chorus on their good fortune, and relates to Khremylos's wife the whole story of the cure. It is Karion, again, who interviews the unhappy Hermes and gives him a job in the kitchen; there is no room for doubt about this, since Hermes addresses him by name (1109f.). In the preceding scenes with the honest man, the informer, the old woman and the youth, the manuscript tradition is divided on the identification of the representative of the household to which these characters come, and the scholia in the Ravennas and Venetus show that this division represents alternative interpretations in antiquity. There seems little doubt that Karion is the interlocutor of the honest man and in the informer, because in 874–876 the informer threatens to have him put to the torture to extract a confession of his misdeeds, and even the most outrageous informer could not easily utter so empty a threat against a citizen. There is equally little doubt that Khremylos is the interlocutor of the old woman and the youth, for the youth calls him an 'old man' (1066) and later (1077) professes to feel 'respect for your age', a respect which he could not have shown to a slave without a heavy sarcasm which would be quite inappropriate to the drift of the humour at that point. In the very last scene of the play the interlocutor of the priest is Khremylos, as is shown by his exercise of authority (e.g. 1193, 'give me, someone, . . .'). Thus we have: Karion 802–958, Khremylos 959–1096, Karion 1097–1170, Khremylos 1171–1207; an almost even balance in the last third of the play, but up to that point Karion's has been the heavier role, and his self-confidence in dealing with the honest man and the informer is what we should expect of a citizen rather than a slave.

This is plainly a different kind of slave-role from anything that we find in the early plays. *Knights, Wasps* and *Peace* all begin with dialogue between slaves, but in *Knights* the slaves are 'phased out' and in *Wasps* and *Peace* they appear at a late stage in the play only in subordinate roles.

In *Wasps* 1292–1325, where Bdelykleon's slave laments the blows which Philokleon has rained on him, Aristophanes has recourse to a cheap and brutal humour which a year later (*Peace* 742–747) he repudiates as unsophisticated. He was not finished, however, with the extraction of humour from the maltreatment of slaves; it is almost certainly the mainstay of *Lys.* 1216–1224 (cf. p. 11), and in *Birds* 1313–1336, where Peisetairos's store of wings is being brought out of doors, a human slave, desperately running to and fro, is mocked, shouted at, hit, and (I think) pecked in the bottom by the birds' sharp beaks. One surprising feature of the treatment of slaves in comedy—and this applies not only to Aristophanes, but also to New Comedy—is that they are not portrayed as speaking incorrect Greek. Scythian policemen, who are public slaves, speak the barbarous Greek of foreigners, but domestic slaves do not produce any of the malapropisms and near-misses which characterize the speech of uneducated people in our own culture, nor is it possible to discern any syntactical differences between the language of slaves and that of free men. To this extent a shift of dramatic weight from free men to slaves is facilitated.

Xanthias in *Frogs* is the true forerunner of Karion, for once he and Dionysos have left the house of Herakles he establishes a remarkable ascendancy over his vain and cowardly owner. He is tough, courageous and resourceful, and we are not surprised to find that before long that Dionysos is reduced from the status of a master to that of a suppliant; after the encounter with the landladies he wants Xanthias to take on the Herakles-disguise once more (579–589):

DIONYSOS: I love my Xanthias, I'm damned if I don't!

XANTHIAS: I know—I know what you're thinking! Stop it—not another word! I will *not* become Herakles.

DIONYSOS: Oh, *please*—my dear old Xanthias!

XANTHIAS: (*Sarcastically*) How could I—a slave, a mortal—become the son of Alkmene (*i.e. Herakles*)?

DIONYSOS: I know, I know you're angry, and you're quite right to be. Even if you hit me, I couldn't say that you shouldn't. But if I ever, from now on, take the disguise away from you, may I perish root and branch—myself, my wife, my children—and bleary Arkhedemos![3]

XANTHIAS: I accept your oath, and on those conditions I take the disguise.

3 Arkhedemos was a politician prominent at the time of *Frogs*; his inclusion in the curse is a characteristic 'side-step' out of the dramatic situation.

As Xanthias paves the way for Karion, so does Karion—over a much greater interval of time, during which the development of comedy is known to us almost exclusively from a mass of disconnected citations—pave the way for the dominating and resourceful slaves whom we meet in New Comedy. In Menander's *Dyskolos* 181–184 Sostratos, unable to see how to achieve his end, declares his intention of consulting his father's slave Getas, who is 'red-hot' and 'experienced in every sort of business'. Since the fortunate outcome of events turns out not to depend on Getas, it seems that Menander is making use of a motif, the young master's dependance on the wily slave, which had already become established in comedy, and perhaps some other dramatists had taken this dependance further than Menander does. Slaves are certainly much more important in the comedy of the late fourth century than in that of the fifth; in *Dyskolos* it is Getas who sets up the last scene of the play, the song-and-dance and knockabout element which follows the resolution of the issues involving Sostratos and Gorgias and Myrrhine, and Getas who utters the closing words of the play to the audience.

How far the increasing prominence of slave-characters in fourth-century comedy can or should be linked with social and cultural changes is uncertain. One of the most important categories of evidence for such changes is the scale of values assumed by a forensic speaker who is commending his own character to a jury and denigrating his adversary's; but since we have so much oratory from the fourth century and so very little from the fifth, we are always in danger of drawing an exaggerated contrast between the 'hard' virtues of the fifth century and the 'soft' virtues of the fourth. It is a fact, however, that fourth century comedy was progressively 'softened' by reduction of the elements of violence, vulgarity and sexuality in the characters to whose happiness and success the plot leads, and in so far as elements of this kind were still welcome in comedy it was natural to transfer them, in the form of earthy, cunning, self-regarding roguishness, to slave-characters. The institution of slavery, like every other institution, came under intellectual scrutiny from the late fifth century onwards, and sentiments to the effect that a slave can be a better man than his master, or that no one is by nature a slave, find expression as early as Euripides (fr. 511).[4] To acknowledge the validity of these sentiments, even to applaud them in the theatre with a murmur of 'Ah! How true!', did no more to make people dis-

4   On various aspects of Greek slavery see (ed.) M. I. Finley, *Slavery in Classical Antiquity: Views and Controversies* (Cambridge, 1960), particularly chapters I, IV and V.

pense with their slaves than acknowledgement that the flesh is weak makes the flesh stronger, but it may well have helped to create between the audience and slave-characters in comedy a relationship of which the dramatist could make good use.

WEALTH AND MORALITY

It has been remarked (p. 199) that compared with farming, crafts and retail trade the part played by Athenian citizens in manufacture and overseas trade based on Athens was of minor importance, and also that technological progress in manufacture was by modern standards very slow indeed. For these reasons the Greeks tended to associate wealth and poverty much more with luck than with management or enterprise. People became poor through bad weather, plant and animal diseases, enemy action or the loss of a cargo at sea; through the crippling fines sometimes imposed for political and administrative offences, or through the strong moral and social obligation to help out relatives and friends who had to pay such a fine; or through being outwitted, in matters of inheritance, loans or other contractual obligations, by people who were on the wrong side of the law but ingenious in putting off the day of reckoning. Since documentary evidence played only a small part in legal proceedings and the sworn statements of witnesses a very large part, the organization of perjured evidence (in return for a consideration) was more practicable than it would be nowadays; hence the fundamental idea of *Wealth* that a man becomes rich by dishonesty and will stay poor if he is honest. A manufacturer was a man who owned skilled slaves, not a man who employed citizen craftsmen for wages; indeed, very few citizens were employed by other citizens, so that questions of wealth, poverty and economic justice were not conceived in terms of the distribution of profits between capital and labour.

The idea that the gods punish perjury is already accepted in the world which Homer depicts, and since the taking of oaths was an essential part of rival claims made in allegation or rebuttal of an injustice the punishment of perjury and the punishment of dishonesty and injustice in general were not clearly distinguished. Hesiod presents a positive side of this doctrine in saying (*Works and Days* 225–285) that while Zeus inflicts war, famine and plague on those who give 'crooked' judgments, he also blesses men of 'straight' judgment with peace and fertility. Common observation makes it hard to believe that virtue and vice are so efficiently rewarded and punished, and in the later archaic period people were more inclined to think that divine punishment fell on the children or descendants of the offender; this had the advantage that when disaster befell a good man it could be postulated that one of his ancestors must have sinned. Such a belief, however, began to go out of favour during the classical period, when increasing moral sophistication attached more importance to individual responsibility and tolerated less readily the infliction of suffering on the innocent in retaliation for the sins of others. In response to this moral demand a belief in judgment after death came into greater prominence than the traditional belief in judgment deferred to posterity. Herakles in *Frogs* 145–151 makes use of the idea that people who had violated the rules which commanded respect for strangers and parents lie in the underworld in 'eternal filth',[5] and in the course of the fourth century a certain coalescence of the concepts of 'justice' (or 'honesty') and 'piety' becomes apparent from praise of the dead in epitaphs, from attitudes implied in oratory and from moralizing sentiments in comedy. It is difficult to assess how far the audience of *Wealth* still retained any expectation that virtue would be divinely rewarded in this life and vice divinely punished. It is possible to collect utterances which seem logically to presuppose such an expectation, but they need not mean much more than 'Oh, my God!' on the lips of an agnostic. The mutability and unpredictability of fortune impress the fourth-century Greek much more than the rewards of virtue. The relation between virtue and prosperity assumed at the beginning of *Wealth* is inverse, and the only way to create a direct relation is as discordant with reality as the means by which Trygaios obtained peace. The play is less about economics and sociology than about magic, fantasy and the supernatural.

5   I say 'makes use of the idea' rather than 'expresses the belief', because the specification of real sins leads on to some comic sins, and because a Greek poet is quite willing to adopt any view of the afterlife of which a reasonable man could say 'Well, you never know, there might be something in it'. If the poet is also a comedian in search of material which can be utilized for humorous purposes, even this limitation may not apply. When Trygaios returns from the sky his slave asks him (*Peace* 832f.) 'Isn't it true then, what they say, that whenever anyone dies we turn into stars up in the air? and Trygaios (for the purpose of a series of jokes) assures him that it is true. How many people really thought this, we do not know.

XVII

Contemporaries and Predecessors

THE EVIDENCE

It was in 486 B.C. that the Athenians first made financial and administrative provision for the regular inclusion of comedy in the City Dionysia, and in or shortly after 445 they made similar provision for the Lenaia. It may be that humorous dramatic performances were a 'fringe' activity of the Dionysiac festivals for a long time, perhaps even for centuries, before this official recognition, but historians in the fourth and third centuries B.C. were not in a position to know anything about that; so far as official records were concerned, Attic comedy began in 486. From that date down to the last plays of Aristophanes is exactly a century. Given the information available to us about the number of plays performed on each occasion (information not quite as complete as we would like), it is possible to calculate that in the course of that century not less than six hundred comedies received their first performance, and the number may have been rather nearer seven hundred. We know the names of some fifty of the dramatists whose careers were contained, or at least begun, during that time, and the titles of about half the total number of plays. In some cases the title is all that we do know, but from the remainder more than four thousand words, phrases, lines or passages are cited by writers of the Hellenistic and Roman periods. This material has been augmented in modern times by the recovery of some fragments of ancient copies.

The lost dramatists best represented in the surviving citations and fragments are Kratinos, Eupolis, Pherekrates and Plato (no relation, so far as we know, of the eminent philosopher), and the first two of these were generally regarded in later antiquity as the most important representatives, together with Aristophanes himself, of fifth-century comedy;

Horace (*Satires* i 4.1), describing the freedom of speech which comedy exercised in ridiculing men of bad character, begins: *Eupolis atque Cratinus Aristophanesque poetae* ... Aristophanes mentions both of them: Eupolis in *Clouds* 553f., in the biting terms typically used by a Greek of a rival, Kratinos in *Knights* 526ff. as a once popular poet who has now gone to pieces and lost his public, and (many years after his death) in *Frogs* 357 as the embodiment of the spirit of comedy. Such chronological data as can be assembled indicate that Kratinos began his career about the middle of the fifth century and died in 422, while Eupolis began his in 429 and died not long before the end of the Peloponnesian War. An important chronological framework for comedy is provided by some public inscriptions which list the comic poets in the order of the dates at which they first won a first prize (poets who never won a first prize naturally do not appear on these lists); some other dates are filled in by the extant hypotheses to Aristophanes' plays and by late writers whose information was ultimately derived from the official records; but within that imperfect skeleton of dates absolutely or relatively fixed we have to depend for dating on topical allusions in the citations. Only a minority of citations contain such allusions, and their nature is often uninformative; e.g. Eupolis fr. 7,

> except that I once ate sprats in Phaiax's house,

probably alludes to the politician Phaiax, known to have been active *c.* 425–415 (the name is uncommon),[1] but it would plainly be wrong to exclude a date some years earlier than 425 or later than 415. On the other hand, Eupolis fr. 290,

> fairest of all cities that Kleon keeps his eye on ...,

must precede the death of Kleon in 422. Our chief gain from dating citations from lost plays is not the titbits relevant to political history (though they *are* a gain) but at least a partial understanding of the relation between the individual Aristophanes and the genre to which he belongs, and in particular a glimpse of the extent to which originality and innovation were permitted to the comic poets or demanded of them. One very important fact which emerges with increasing clarity from work on the chronology of comedy is that we know very little indeed about the earlier part of its history. On the list of comic poets arranged in order of their first victories at the City Dionysia, the name of Kratinos comes twelfth; of the preceding eleven names, only fourteen *letters* are legible, we do not know from literary sources more than five names with which to plug this large gap, and those five names cover only fourteen titles and eighteen citations. What is even more striking is that when we go into the dating of the plays of Kratinos himself and the poets who on the victor-list come between him and Aristophanes (22nd on the list) we find remarkably few plays which we have any reason to date earlier than 440 and not a great number datable earlier than 430.[1] Since Aristophanes' career began in 427 and his first extant play is datable to 425, it is fair to say that our evidence for the first forty years of Attic comedy is negligible and that not even the sum of our evidence for what preceded Aristophanes' time is comparable in bulk with the evidence for the work of his rivals during his lifetime. It is important to keep this limitation constantly and prominently before our minds not only when we are trying to form an idea of his importance as an individual in the history of literature but also if we are tempted to construct hypotheses about the origins of comedy by extrapolation from his earliest plays.

INDIVIDUAL AND GENRE

If we knew nothing at all about Aristophanes' rivals except what he himself says about them (by name or in general terms), and if *per absurdum* we took him to be speaking as an objective critic, our assessment of them would be on the following lines:

(1) They relied on exaggeratedly obscene costume (*Clouds* 537–539), vulgar dancing (ibid. 540), jokes at poverty, vermin and physical defects (ibid., and *Peace* 740), rude words alluding to faeces (*Frogs* 1–20), and senseless noise and violence in which (*Clouds* 541–543),

> . . . the old man who speaks the lines hits out with his stick at anyone who's there, to cover up the badness of the jokes.

(2) It had been their custom to attack only individuals of minor importance, but Aristophanes in *Knights* tackled an adversary of great political power (*Clouds* 549, *Wasps* 1029–1037, *Peace* 751–760); thereafter other poets, imitating him, attacked Hyperbolos (*Clouds* 551f.), but—

(3) They went on too long doing the same thing, instead of delivering one mighty blow and then going on to different subjects (*Clouds* 551–559).

---

1   The number of plays whose fragments and titles offer no clue to their date is quite large. Much of the evidence is discussed by P. Geissler, *Chronologie der altattischen Komödie* (Berlin, 1925), but we now have more.

(4) They liked to exploit simple-minded traditional comic motifs such as:

(a) the gluttonous Herakles (*Peace* 741), and

(b) slaves who cheat their masters or try to run away, are beaten, bewail their sufferings, and in that condition are the subject of jokes expressed in outworn imagery (*Peace* 742–747).

If we then took Aristophanes' own work into account, we should see that he himself is vulnerable to all the criticisms under headings (1) and (4); consider, for example, the humorous exploitation of Herakles' appetite in *Birds* 1565–1693 and the violence of Philokleon against the slave in *Wasps* 1292–1325, where the slave congratulates tortoises on the carapace that protects them against blows from a stick. As for the criticisms under headings (2) and (3), it may indeed be the case that many poets were unoriginal in their choice of themes; how far they compensated for this by originality of treatment, we are not in a position to say, but we cannot let Aristophanes get away with the implication that he himself disdained to re-use comic material. Two Athenians of his time, Kleisthenes and Kleonymos, are consistently ridiculed in several of his plays, Kleisthenes for his inadequate beard and effeminate appearance (first in *Acharnians* 117–121 and last—after twenty years—in *Frogs* 48–57 and 426—428) and Kleonymos for an occasion on which he discarded his shield (first ridiculed—for this offence—in *Knights* 1372, last in *Birds* 1474–1477, over a ten-year period). Jokes of this kind are sometimes dragged in artificially, and one has the impression that whatever may have been the real character of the person ridiculed he acquired an independent *persona*, to which his original misdeed or deficiency was no longer relevant, within the comic tradition. The tragic actor Hegelokhos once committed a disastrous error of pronunciation when in playing Euripides' *Orestes* he said *galên horô*, 'I see a weasel' instead of *galên' horô*, 'I see calm weather'. Aristophanes makes fun of this in *Frogs* 302–304:

> XANTHIAS: It's all right! Everything has turned out well, and we can say, like Hegelokhos, 'The storm abates; I see a weasel come'.[2]

The scholion on *Orestes* 279, remarking '*many* of the comic poets made fun of this', cites Sannyrion fr. 8:

2 The joke has a special point in this scene, since the sighting of a weasel was an omen; cf. E. K. Borthwick, 'Seeing Weasels: the Superstitious Background of the Empusa Scene in the *Frogs*', *Classical Quarterly* N.S. xviii (1968), 200–206.

What shall I turn into,[3] and through what crack shall I get in? I must think. Ah, suppose I turned into a weasel? No, that's no good; Hegelokhos would give me away, Hegelokhos the tragic actor; he'd roar out, 'The storm abates; I see a weasel come'.

We do not know whether Sannyrion's *Danae*, from which this citation is taken, was performed before or after *Frogs*, and accordingly we do not know whether it is Aristophanes or Sannyrion who is using a stale joke; but one of them is, and both of them name Hegelokhos to make sure that we understand at whom the joke is directed and cannot take it simply as humorous in its own right.[4] Similar doubts, which can hardly ever be resolved, arise in the case of many humorous images or concocted words which are attested both from Aristophanes and from one or more of his contemporaries.

Just as Aristophanes decried the work of other poets, they too decried his. Kratinos, in a passage (fr. 307) cited by an ancient commentator on Plato, wrote:

'And who are you? some discriminating member of the audience may[5] ask, some subtle quibbler, an idea-chaser, a *euripidaristophanizer*.

The context may have been similar to that of *Peace* 43–45:

So by now some young man in the audience, with a good opinion of himself as a critic, will be saying, 'What's this all about? What's the beetle for?'

The creation of a compound word to denote an 'idea-chaser' whose tastes run to Euripides in tragedy and Aristophanes in comedy is strong testimony in support of Aristophanes' own claim to technical originality, and a sharp rebuff to those who may have taken it for granted that his literary taste was indiscriminately reactionary. How far Aristophanes' humour is actually more intellectual than that of his contemporaries, the available evidence does not allow us to decide; we can only observe that they too satirized contemporary developments in philosophy, science, music and poetry; in Pherekrates' *Khiron*, for

3 The speaker must be Zeus contemplating the seduction of Danae.
4 Strattis fr. 60 handles the same joke better; a character who says 'I see calm weather' is taken by someone else to have said 'I see a weasel', and (unless the citation from Strattis is truncated) no reference is made to Hegelokhos.
5 There is a small textual and linguistic difficulty here, but it does not affect the point.

example (fr. 145), personified Music complains (with sly sexual ambiguities) about the musical innovations of certain poets, and in the same author's *Krapataloi* it is demonstrable (fr. 94) that the ghost of Aiskhylos was a character, as in *Frogs*. Yet a few differences between Kratinos and Aristophanes do seem to emerge,[6] and may point to a difference of taste between two successive generations: extant citations from Kratinos contain a quite disproportionate number of proverbs and proverbial expressions, either 'straight' or given a humorous twist, and when Kratinos parodies or otherwise exploits serious poetry he seems (unlike Aristophanes' generation) to take his material from epic and archaic poetry rather than from tragedy. It may also be remarked (though here the ground is less firm) that the total corpus of citations from lost comic poets provides fewer instances of the humorous treatment of religious procedures than their frequency in Aristophanes would have led us to expect. It is conceivable that Aristophanes was somewhat ahead of the average man in scepticism and irreverence.

We sometimes recognize among the citations certain combinations of form and content which, by analogy with Aristophanes, suggest that they come from parabases or structured contests.[7] For example, Telekleides fr. 1, a citation of fifteen lines from a play called *Amphiktyones*, begins:

> Now I will describe (*léksō toínyn*) the life which in the beginning I provided for mortal men. . . . ,

and this reminds us of the opening words of Right in the first contest of *Clouds* (963):

> Now I will describe (*léksō toínyn*) the nature of education in the old days . . .

The theme of the passage from *Amphiktyones* has something in common with the argument of Poverty in *Wealth*, and all three passages share the same metre. Similarly, in the *Flatterers* of Eupolis, which defeated *Peace* in 421, the chorus of flatterers (or 'parasites') addresses the audience in these terms:

> Now, what way of life flatterers have we'll tell you. Just listen, because we're elegant men in every way. First of all, there's a boy

---

6 I am indebted to Mr. Allan M. Wilson for proving this to me.
7 Cf. M. Whittaker, 'The Comic Fragments in their Relation to the Structure of Old Attic Comedy', *Classical Quarterly* xxix (1935), 181–191.

in attendance—someone else's for the most part, but a little bit my own. . . .

This resembles the epirrhema of the parabasis of *Wasps*, where the chorus says (1071ff.):

Spectators, if anyone among you, having seen my appearance,[8] wonders at my wasp-waist, I'll soon explain the idea of our sting. . . .

Unfortunately, similarities of this kind do not tell us whether any one lost play possessed a complete contest, or complete parabasis, of the form familiar to us from Aristophanes. We can observe that the metrical forms used in the Aristophanic parabasis—trochaic tetrameters for the epirrhema, anapaestic tetramenters or (in *Clouds*) eupolideans for the 'anapaests'—are not a rigid convention, for the passage of Eupolis just quoted uses an attractive metre not found in Aristophanes, a type of tetrameter composed of an acatalectic iambo-choriambic dimeter followed by the catalectic form of the same dimeter. Occasionally there may be evidence that what appears, in the light of Aristophanes' extant work alone, to be an innovation has in fact a precedent. *Lysistrata* has a pair of choruses, old men and old women, in opposition to one another; it has recently been discovered that Eupolis's *Marikas*, ten years earlier than *Lysistrata*, had opposing choruses representing rich and poor.[9] We are even told by a late writer that the *Odyssês* of Kratinos 'has no choral songs or parabasis'. It is hard to believe that it really had no choral songs, and it may reasonably be suspected that a misunderstanding, resulting perhaps from an exaggeration, underlies our information; *Odyssês* certainly had a chorus, for we find it singing (Kratinos fr. 144):

> Quiet, now, everyone, quiet!
> And you'll soon learn what we have to say.
> Our fatherland is Ithake,
> and we sail with the hero Odysseus.

This sounds rather like a chorus introducing itself on or soon after its entry, and something similar happens in a fragment of Kratinos's *Gods of Wealth*:[10]

8 Literally, 'nature'; *phýsis* often refers to external appearance.
9 Fragments of an ancient commentary on *Marikas* are now published in *Oxyrhynchus Papyri* xxxv (1968), no. 2741, pp. 55ff.
10 *Ploutoi*, literally 'Wealths'; Greek personified abstractions which were normally singular (e.g. Eros) could sometimes be treated as plural, like the Graces, Seasons, Muses, etc.

And why we said [. . .
You will now learn.
We are of the Titan race
and we were called Gods of Wealth when [. . .

This play was performed probably a few years earlier than the beginning of Aristophanes' career. It might be the case that it was traditional practice for the chorus to explain itself to the audience on its entry, and that Aristophanes' livelier and more dramatic entries were an innovation, but it is also possible that Aristophanes' entries resume an older tradition from which Kratinos departed.

No amount of citations and fragments can give us much idea of the overall design of any one play, nor can we easily judge a joke to be good or bad, neat or clumsy, when we do not know its dramatic context or by what kind of character it was uttered. The only fifth-century comedy, apart from the extant eleven of Aristophanes, of which we know the plot is the oddly-named *Dionȳsaléksandros* of Kratinos, thanks to a fairly detailed hypothesis preserved in a papyrus fragment. This play presented a burlesque version of the legend of the judgment of Paris (*Aléksandros*), who gave the prize for beauty to Aphrodite in preference to Athena and Hera. Aphrodite rewarded him by causing Helen, the wife of Menelaos, to run off with him; hence the Trojan War. In Kratinos's play it was Dionysos who (disguising himself as Paris, one presumes) judged the goddesses and so carried off Helen to Troy, where the real Paris married her and handed Dionysos over to the offended Greeks. All this happened after the parabasis, in which the chorus (of satyrs) addressed the audience 'about the poets'[11] (as commonly in an Aristophanic parabasis); what happened before the parabasis cannot be reconstructed, because of the fragmentary nature of the papyrus, except that Dionysos learned about the dispute between the goddesses. One interesting aspect of this play is its presentation of the god Dionysos in the role of a cheat and buffoon who comes to grief, rather like the Dionysos of *Frogs* a quarter of a century later, to which we may add the *Taksíarkhoi* of Eupolis, in which Dionysos was portrayed as unhappily compelled to live the hard life of a soldier under the distinguished Athenian commander Phormion.[12] A second interesting aspect is that according to the hypothesis Kratinos used the myth

11   The text is corrupt at this point, but 'about the poets' is the probable interpretation.
12   The name of Dionysos is prominent among the titles of the earliest known comedies, and this may well mean that he was a figure of fun from the beginning.

of Paris, with the considerable distortion involving Dionysos, as a means of criticizing Perikles for bringing the Peloponnesian War on Athens. We should not be too hasty in believing that, since both ancient and modern commentators have a certain tendency to import political allegory into comic themes which are not necessarily intended in a political sense, but we cannot reject it out of hand. The plot, whether or not it had political undertones, is of a type not represented at all among the extant plays of Aristophanes but common in both the fifth and the early fourth centuries, if the titles and citations are any guide. Hermippos's *Birth of Athena*, for example, was undoubtedly a burlesque version of the myth of Athena's birth from the head of Zeus, and we hear of comedies called (e.g.) *Birth of Aphrodite*, *Agamemnon* and *Theseus*. Among the lost plays of Aristophanes no less than six have titles which indicate mythological burlesque, and this interpretation of the titles is supported in some cases by citations, as when the words

There, now, I give you Phaidra to wife

are cited (fr. 453) from a play called *Polyidos*; Polyidos was associated in legend with Minos, and Phaidra, Theseus's wife, was daughter of Minos. It is regrettable that no play of this popular and long-lived genre was included among the Aristophanic plays which the interests and tastes of the late Roman Empire unconsciously selected for survival to posterity.

ORIGINS OF COMEDY

From what has been said so far it will be clear that extrapolation back to the early fifth century from the structure and content of *Acharnians* and *Knights* is not likely to tell us much about the preliterary origins of comedy. At the same time, it is difficult to leave the subject alone, because in tragedy we can get so near to the beginnings of things (Aiskhylos's *Persians* is hardly more than half a century later than the very birth of serious drama in Europe), and the Greeks themselves thought of the 'invention' of comedy and tragedy alike as falling within historical times. It is, however, possible that a distinction should be drawn between serious and humorous drama. If we treat the birth of drama as the moment at which a performer, instead of narrating 'And then Odysseus said, "Woe is me!"', dresses himself up as a means of conveying to his audience, 'I am, as it were, Odysseus' and says 'Woe is me!' without any introductory narrative element, it may be that comedy is not merely older than tragedy but older by hundreds, perhaps by thousands, of years.[13] What the Greeks regarded as the beginning of Attic comedy will then be simply the year in which the names of people who composed humorous drama for performance at the City Dionysia began to be included in the records of the festival, in consequence of which it became customary for those poets to put into circulation written copies of what they had composed. Before that date comedy will have been, as Aristotle put it, 'improvised'; which does not mean (nor, I think, did Aristotle intend it to mean) that any-one appeared before an audience without having given a thought to what he was going to do and say and sing, but simply that there was no written text attributable to an individual.

Aristotle regarded comedy as originating with a differentiation be-tween 'leader' and chorus in phallic songs. This was not an unreason-able hypothesis on his part, since phallic songs (like comedy) were part of the festivals of Dionysos, the word kōmōidíā, 'comedy', means 'singing in a kōmos', i.e. in a noisy, happy, drunken procession (such as formed part of Dionysiac festivals), and most Greeks would have answered the question 'What is . . . ?', asked with reference to any genre of perfor-mance, in terms of the gods at whose festivals that genre formed a part. The evidence, however, for phallic processions in various parts of the Greek world, processions in which the audience and individuals in it were subjected to mockery, does not add much of importance, since it is of comparatively late date, and it should never be assumed that what is sub-literary has preserved from pre-literary times its original character and form free of sophisticated influences. One element in Aristophanes which does seem to be old and to have no discernible connection with phallic songs is the animal-disguise of the chorus. There is good evidence that Magnes, one of the earliest Attic comic poets, wrote plays entitled *Birds*, *Frogs* and *Fig-flies*, and vases which antedate the introduction of comedy to the City Dionysia show men dressed as birds or horses (with riders) dancing to the accompaniment of a piper. Here at least is a traditional ingredient, perhaps of great antiquity, which lasted all through the fifth century. We cannot, of course, assume that the per-formances depicted on the vases were integrated with humorous dia-logue in the manner familiar to us from extant comedy.

13 Compared with the length of time for which *Homo sapiens* has had the capacity to sing and dance dramatically, the world of the Greeks is only yester-day's world. Attempts to reconstruct the preliterate stage of Greek culture on the assumption that it was the dawn of human history should be treated with caution.

In Aristotle's time there existed a theory which gave priority in comedy to the Doric-speaking Greeks and regarded the Athenians as taking up what the Dorians had invented. It is true that there existed at Syracuse in the early fifth century a tradition of literary comedy of which Epikharmos (known to us only through citations and fragments) is the chief representative, but the chronological evidence, such as it is, suggests that he was not the predecessor of the earliest Attic comic poets, but their contemporary. The scale of his comedies is uncertain, but the substantial number of plural titles (e.g. *Revellers, Bacchanals*) points to the use of some sort of chorus, although none of the extant citations contains lyric metres or suggests choral songs in any other way. He seems to have favoured burlesque treatment of mythological themes (e.g. the boxing-match between Polydeukes and Amykos), and there is hardly anything we know about him which lacks echoes and analogies in Attic comedy; this may be because humorous motifs and established attitudes to the humorous aspects of traditional stories were universally diffused in folklore and funny stories and equally available as foundation-blocks for comedy at Syracuse and at Athens.[14]

Free from chronological uncertainty, but highly controversial in interpretation, is a Corinthian vase of the early sixth century on which we see naked male figures moving large jars and, on the other side of the vessel, more naked male figures imprisoned in stocks and fed(?) by a woman; a piper and a masked dancer adjoin the former scene. Three of the figures have names, and two of them have abnormally large genitals; are they slaves or satyrs (using 'satyrs' in a wide sense, to denote any gross and earthy supernatural beings), and is the painter representing the events of a story known (or at least intelligible) to his customer, or is he representing men *acting* a story? If this latter alternative is the right interpretation, the vase gives us direct evidence of comic drama at Corinth a hundred years before the inclusion of comedy in the City Dionysia at Athens; but the weighing of all the factors relevant to a decision between the alternative interpretations produces only a tilt, not a decisive fall, on the side of the dramatic interpretation.[15]

14 It must be emphasized that ridicule of gods is not a product of fifth-century 'enlightenment'. The story of Ares and Aphrodite in *Odyssey* viii 266–366 and the story of the wounding of Aphrodite by Diomedes in *Iliad* v 297–430 treat Aphrodite rather as comedy treats Dionysos.

15 L. Breitholz, *Die dorische Farce im griechischen Mutterland* (Göteborg, 1960), argues very strongly against the dramatic interpretation, and equally strongly against any other evidence which would tend to take the origins of comedy away from Athens and into the Doric-speaking areas; but the evidence is not quite so easily disposed of.

XVIII

Posterity

MIDDLE AND NEW COMEDY

To an educated inhabitant of the Roman Empire, looking back at the history of Greek comedy, it appeared that there had been two outstanding poets who served each as the nucleus of a distinct genre: Aristophanes was the nucleus of 'Old Comedy', Menander of 'New Comedy'. An essay by Plutarch, comparing the two much to the disadvantage of the former, attributes to each of them characteristics which belonged at least as much to period and genre as to individual genius.

Menander put on his first play in 320, a little over a century after the first play of Aristophanes, and died in 293 or 292. Until recent times our acquaintance with his work was partial and indirect. He was the most powerful influence on Latin comedy, particularly on Terence, and through this medium it was possible to go a certain distance in reconstructing his theatrical technique, but we had nothing in Greek except the usual multitude of brief citations; a high proportion of these were moralizing sentiments, which showed that he had a knack of casting an attractive thought into an effortless line of verse, but they told us nothing about the structure and content of his plays, and not even very much about the manner in which moralizing was accommodated to action. The situation was changed in 1907 by the publication of fragments of a papyrus codex which gave us half a play (*Epitrepontes*), very substantial pieces of two more (*Perikeiromene* and *Samia*), and something to go on with of a further two. The next landmark in the recovery of Menander was the publication in 1958 of an almost completely preserved play (*Dyskolos*, performed in 316). Ten years later large parts of *Aspis* ('the Shield') and *Samia* came to light; the former showed that some unidentified fragments known since 1913 belonged in fact to *Aspis*, and the latter could be combined with the 1907 fragments of *Samia*. Smaller pieces of many other plays have come to light at various times during the last sixty years, and the process of identifying and combining fragments continues.[1]

To go straight from the reading of Aristophanes to the reading of Menander is a remarkable experience. In Aristophanes we have grown accustomed to the wholesale exploitation of magic, folklore and the supernatural, to an insouciant disregard for causal sequence, and to the theatrical representation of eminent living contemporaries, personified abstractions, and entities conjured out of linguistic imagery. All this has now gone. Supernatural beings in Menander appear only in order to speak prologues and explain to the audience the situation from which the action of the play springs; sometimes they do this right at the beginning, in the manner of a Euripidean prologue, sometimes, like the slave in *Peace*, after our interest has been aroused by the first scene, but in either case they have the stage to themselves and do not encounter human characters on an equal footing. The human characters are fictitious, bearing names that seem to be drawn from a limited stock, and essentially naturalistic, when due allowance has been made for the heightening of emotional reactions and compression of deliberative processes required by the concentration of complicated events into a short play. The degree of individualization realized in a genre which by its nature tempts the dramatist into the economy of stock types is remarkable. The ambience of each character in Menander is some part or aspect of the world of the Greek bourgeoisie of his time, and the situation at any given moment is a situation which could exist in real life; in the reactions of the characters to it any of us in the audience can recognize, for good or ill, elements of himself. These qualities prompted in the critic Aristophanes of Byzantion the exclamation:

Menander and Life! Which of you imitated the other?

It is only in the totality of situations which make up a play that unreality manifests itself, and this unreality is not a violation of physical causality but simply statistical improbability. Menander's plots tend to

---

1 For a summary of the present knowledge and interpretation of Menander see W. G. Arnott, 'Young Lovers and Confidence Tricksters: the Rebirth of Menander', *The University of Leeds Review* xiii (1970), 1–18; and for more detail on various aspects of his work, see the papers and discussions in *Entretiens de la Fondation Hardt* xvi (1970). Menander's *Dyskolos* has been edited with a full introduction and commentary by E. W. Handley (London, 1965), and translated by Philip Vellacott under the title *The Bad-Tempered Man* (London 1960).

hinge on coincidence, above all on the timely identification of people abandoned or kidnapped in infancy; here, as so often in New Comedy, one discerns the influence exercised on comedy by the recognition- and intrigue-themes of Euripidean tragedy. Fortune, whose mutability and unpredictability were the subject of so much moralizing in the fourth century, leads the virtuous, the generous and the kindly into great perils but in the end her subtle computation of the crossing of paths in place and time rewards them richly. By contrast with (say) *Wasps*, a New Comedy plot tidies everything up and discourages us from asking, as we leave the theatre, 'and what happened *then*?'

The composition of fresh plays in this genre continued into the second century B.C., and when, as happened increasingly, 'old' plays were put on at the dramatic festivals they were not drawn from Old Comedy, in the technical sense of the term, but from Menander and his contem- poraries of the period 320–250. It is doubtful, in fact, whether Aristo- phanes and the other poets of Old Comedy received the honour of performance at any time after their own deaths. Latin comedy drew on New Comedy, and for that reason it was New Comedy, not Old, which influenced European drama in the sixteenth and seventeenth centuries.

In *Women in Assembly* and *Wealth* we have already observed some of the tendencies which were to culminate in New Comedy, in particular the separation of the chorus from the action and its reduction to a series of intermezzi which were not treated as part of the text of the play. But even *Wealth*, with its hungry Hermes, its presentation of abstract con- cepts as speaking persons, and its translation into concrete terms of the old saying 'Wealth is blind', is a long way from the spirit of Menander, and a great deal must have happened to comedy in the course of the two generations which separate *Wealth* from *Dyskolos*. The evidence available to anyone who might wish to trace the steps by which these changes were effected is of the same character as the evidence for the fifth-century poets other than Aristophanes: sixty poets' names, seven hundred titles of plays, well over a thousand citations. Some of the citations, particularly those given by Athenaios, a learned writer of the early third century A.D. with a wide range of antiquarian interests, run to twenty or thirty verses or more, but they do not tell us anything about the structure or plots of the plays from which they are taken. They do, however, disprove one misleading statement transmitted from late antiquity to the Middle Ages, to the effect that ridicule of politicians and other eminent people ceased early in the fourth century. Ridicule of this kind actually puts in a sporadic appearance until a surprisingly late date; we learn, for example, from Polybios (xii 13) that an otherwise obscure comic poet Arkhedikos accused Demokhares of oral sexuality, and the political career of Demokhares is known to have fallen within the limits 325–275 B.C.

Just as poets of Old Comedy could write 'forward-looking' plays, such as the *Odyssês* of Kratinos (p. 216) and the *Aiolosíkɔn* of Aristophanes (p. 195), so a poet in the fourth century could write a 'backward-looking' play, and we should imagine the elimination of fantasy and vilification and the imposition of decorum and naturalism as a very jerky and untidy process. For this reason it has been possible ever since ancient times to argue about the utility of the term 'Middle Comedy' to denote a category of comedy distinct from 'Old' or 'New', except in so far as one might wish to use the term in a strictly chronological sense. If we are confronted nowadays with an extensive papyrus fragment of a comedy of unknown authorship, we cannot assign it to Middle Comedy with any great confidence unless it combines at least one feature characteristic of Old Comedy with at least one characteristic of New.[2]

STUDY AND ENJOYMENT

The seventh and eighth centuries A.D. constitute the only serious interruption to the reading of Aristophanes between the author's own time and ours. Certain attitudes towards him can be traced as continuous strands from the Byzantine scholars of the ninth century to modern editors, commentators, readers and spectators. The most important attitude, in terms of duration and ubiquity, is that which treats him as a means by which the student may attain knowledge of the Attic dialect as written in the classical period and knowledge of Athenian institutions and personalities. The foundations of this approach to him were laid inevitably in the Hellenistic period by the consciousness that the great period of Attic drama and the period during which Athens exercised the greatest power over the rest of the Greek world were one and the same. The tendency to treat classical Attic as a linguistic norm and later Greek as degenerate or perverted gathered strength in the early Roman Empire and reached its zenith in the second century A.D., when many

2 A qualified exception might be made in favour of a long speech about cooking and eating sumptuous meals. Athenaios's own interest in this subject is no doubt the reason why so many of the passages which he cites from fourth-century comedy deal with it, and it does not follow that *all* these comedies were about food; but, given the wide range of his sources, it does look as if there was more about food then than earlier or later.

Greeks indulged in cultural nostalgia to such a point as to believe that it was in some way better to use the vocabulary and morphology of half a millennium earlier than to realize the literary potentiality of the language which they actually spoke. Their effort to project themselves into the past linguistically was not matched by a comparable effort to see the world through the eyes of classical Athens; 'Atticism' at its worst was rather like a superstition that one's brain will work better if it is encased in an antique hairstyle and hat.

When the Byzantines rediscovered the pleasure of reading classical Greek literature, they did not in the first instance think of its language as canonical nor could they, as Christians, regard the pagan culture of Aristophanes' time as a golden age. But before long we find Byzantine historians providing abundant evidence that they believed the language of Thucydides to be the right language in which to write history. Learning and skill in ancient Greek become ends in themselves; that is to say, no one is quite able to explain convincingly to what end they are means, but everyone who possesses them, having by virtue of that possession become a member of a cultural élite, is quite sure of their value. Scholars betray, by the undertone of emotion in which they correct linguistic error, their zeal for the protection of their own status.[3]

Of course, when a literature which is idealized in this way happens to be a great literature in its own right, and when both those who wrote it and those for whom they wrote it were interesting people from whom we have much to learn, it is not always easy to disentangle good reasons from bad in advocating the study of it. If Aristophanes and other Attic authors had not been worth reading for their own sakes, the Byzantines would not have taken them up with such enthusiasm and accorded them so high a cultural rating, but the persistence with which Aristophanes (even, here and there, to this day) has been treated primarily as a means of acquiring competence in a particular form of Greek is a striking example of the difficulty people have in evaluating means and ends in relation to each other. It is perfectly true that the study of Aristophanes provides a good way into the study of the fifth and fourth centuries B.C. as a whole, because he occupies a position which is chronologically and culturally central, his range of language and style is uniquely wide, and anyone who takes the trouble to find out what all his allusions mean will end by knowing a great deal about Greek life; that is true, and there is no reason why we should pretend otherwise;

3 On Classical studies at Byzantium see N. G. Wilson, 'The Church and Classical Studies at Byzantium', *Antike und Abendland* xvi (1970), 68–77.

but the end to which the study of Aristophanes is a means is the enjoyment of Aristophanes, and the utility of this study as a starting-point for the more efficient study and more quickly attained enjoyment of other authors is, however great, incidental.

Erasmus believed that learners of Greek should begin with the study of works which were in themselves attractive and interesting, and to this end he put Lucian first among prose authors and Aristophanes first among poets. There is no doubt which play of Aristophanes Erasmus, or any sixteenth-century scholar, would have set before the beginner. At least as early as the tenth century *Wealth* came at the head of the surviving plays, and it remained the most widely read throughout the Byzantine period. The scholars of the Renaissance in Western Europe did not dissent from the valuation implied by the Byzantine ordering of the plays and by the existence of so many manuscripts in which *Wealth* stood alone. This play, to modern taste the least attractive and interesting, was edited, translated and performed more often than any other (*Clouds* was its runner-up, just as *Clouds* comes immediately after *Wealth* in Byzantine manuscripts), and it retained its dominant position well into the eighteenth century. For this there were several reasons apart from passive acceptance of the Byzantine canon: *Wealth* is less wildly unlike Latin comedy than the earlier plays, it is much less closely tied to the personalities and conditions of Athens at the time of writing, it portrays the reward of virtue and the punishment of vice, and it contains nothing likely to promote sexuality.

The belief that literature inculcates virtue and castigates vice by portraying bad people as repulsive, ridiculous and in the end unhappy and unsuccessful is a belief which has been widely held in all ages; which is not surprising, since literature can observably have this effect. In how many different ways the effect works, and how important it is compared with the other effects of literature, are large and complicated questions. Unfortunately, not much attention has been paid to these questions, since people who attach great importance to the moral influence of literature tend to persuade themselves that the issue is simple, while those who are aware that the issue is not simple tend to deny that literature has any direct moral influence. At any rate, the moral influence of Aristophanes' *Wealth* appeared to very many people for more than a millennium to be obvious, direct and good.[4] *Clouds* was a

4 On the influence of *Wealth* see G. Hertel, *Die Allegorie von Reichtum und Armut: ein aristophanisches Motiv und seine Abwandlungen in der abendländischen Literatur* (Nürnberg, 1969).

harder problem, since Socrates has been treated, ever since the second century A.D., as a kind of honorary Christian; Ioannes Tzetzes in the twelfth century seasons his very detailed commentary on *Clouds* with occasional expressions of anger and disgust at the poet on whom he has spent so much labour, but a more general tendency, up to the present time, has been to admire Socrates and Aristophanes in parallel without allowing the irreconcilability of their attitudes to occupy one's attention too often or for too long. *Frogs* and *Knights* were more easily interpreted as didactic, *Frogs* because the contest between Aiskhylos and Euripides could be regarded as a victory of stern antique virtues over decadence, *Knights* because of its hostility to licentious demagogues, and both because the terms in which Aristophanes expresses criticism are manly, outspoken and violent. These were characteristics which at many times and places have been admired in Christian sermons, and it is interesting to observe that Aristophanes' reputation as a fearless moralist was almost enhanced by his lack of judiciousness and discrimination. Our own century has persuaded itself that it can learn other lessons from Aristophanes: he has been treated as a feminist, as a pacifist and as a liberator from sexual guilt. He would have been surprised, I think, at being cast in the first or second of these two roles, and he would have had some reservations about the third. For us, the equality of men and women in politics, administration and other kinds of work is a genuine practical issue; for Aristophanes and his contemporaries it was not, any more than equality between men and birds. For us, too, the abolition of war and even the sacrifice of freedom for the sake of peace can be treated as practical possibilities; Aristophanes and his contemporaries did not like fighting a war unless the consequences of fighting appeared preferable to the consequences of not fighting, and on any given occasion there was room for disagreement about probable alternative consequences, but they did not consider a man justified in rating his own life or the lives of his wife and children higher than the political independence of his own city-state.[5] As for sexual liberty, Aristophanes may well be thought to show a better understanding of sex and a juster assessment of its relation to the general pattern of our lives than is to be found in the doctrines— ostensibly profound, but in fact superficial—of Platonists and Christians.

5 In 338 B.C., when there was an imminent threat of a Macedonian attack on Athens, a certain Autolykos sent his wife and children away to safety; for this he was prosecuted and punished (Lykourgos, *Prosecution of Leokrates* 53).

To that extent we can learn something from him; but although the defects in the sexual morality of pagan Greek society were, at least in part,[6] different from those in Christian morality, they were neither smaller nor fewer, and they are no more worthy of uncritical imitation than any other defects.

The moral utility of reading the works of a dead author—and whether he died this morning or two thousand years ago makes no essential difference—lies, I suggest, not in the possibility of doing what he appears to recommend and refraining from what he appears to forbid, but in two other directions. First, by adding his experience to ours we can look through his eyes at elements of human life which are common to his culture and ours, and can thus criticize and adjust our assumptions and attitudes, as we can also by understanding and absorbing the experience of contemporary individuals whose lives and environments differ from our own. Secondly, in so far as art is an aspect of our nature, on a par with exercise, religion, sex and work, enjoying literature is better than not enjoying it, and the effort to re-live the intellectual and aesthetic process through which an ancient dramatist gave a play its final form and content has some claim to be considered a self-rewarding activity. The effect of these two considerations has become increasingly conspicuous in the editing and expounding of Aristophanes. A modern commentator is expected, no less than his seventeenth-century counterpart, to explain what the text 'means' at the linguistic level and to identify the people and things mentioned in it, but he is also expected to help the reader to understand what it was like to be a Greek or a slave and to see the world from the vantage-point of Athens in the late fifth century B.C. For example, when in *Wasps* 500–502 Bdelykleon's slave makes a joking reference to his visit to a prostitute 'in the middle of the day' and to the 'jockey' position which he asked her to adopt, a commentator ought to raise and, if the evidence permits, try to answer the questions: Did a slave have enough spending-money of his own to visit a prostitute, or is the slave in this scene being used for a certain dramatic function in which his status as a slave has to be disregarded? And was the 'jockey' position, in which the total bodily contact is small, particularly favoured during the heat of the day? An equally important demand on a commentator is that he

6 Just as what most people mean by 'Christian virtues' are in fact pre-Christian virtues, so much that is nowadays *debited* to Christianity was deeply entrenched in the characteristic social structures and values of the ancient eastern Mediterranean.

should never for a minute forget that the text which he is explaining was composed for performance; in his imagination he must see and hear the whole work from the first line to the last, as if he were producing it and an actor might at any moment turn to him for instructions on stance, movement, gesture or tone of voice. For example, in *Peace* 378f. Trygaios, having arrived at the home of the gods on his giant beetle, offers Hermes some meat; how has he been carrying it? In a hand-held bag, or in a sack slung on a stick over his shoulder (in which case he has had only one hand free for the beetle's reins, if the beetle has reins), or in a pannier on the beetle? And what happens to the bag or sack? And what does Hermes do with the meat when he has taken it? Some readers will be inclined to regard questions of this kind as trivial to the point of absurdity, and it is of course true that we cannot *use* discrete items of information about the pocket-money of slaves or the way in which Trygaios carried his luggage in the sense in which we can use a Platonic insight into the nature of mathematics or a Thucydidean observation on the inherent weakness of oligarchies. But if we wish to make the experience of antiquity available to us, we must concern ourselves with the question of what was important to the people (including the fictitious characters) whom we study, discarding only what is both trivial to us and trivial to them. The slave's choice between alternative positions of sexual intercourse is hardly less important to him than a poet's choice between alternative forms of the choriambic dimeter for the last verse of a stanza; and it is of the highest importance for the actor playing Trygaios that by the time he rises in the air on his beetle he should have the meat with him and know where it is.

We cannot recover the experience of any past culture unless we know the meaning of its utterances, and when these utterances have at any stage been transmitted by manual copying, the question 'What did he actually say?' is prior to 'What does it mean?' The priority, however, cannot be chronological, since consideration of the prima facie alternative meanings of any given passage is relevant to a decision on the correctness of the transmitted text; philology, textual criticism, metrical analysis, literary criticism and the history of literary form must interact continuously with each other and with political, social and cultural history, if Greek literature is to be recovered and understood. The translation and interpretation of a passage of Greek can never be definitive; it can only be the best we can do so far, subject to reconsideration in the light of new evidence.

TRANSLATION

Certain problems are common to all attempts to translate literature from one language into another: the associations of words and phrases, conventional attitudes, allusions to persons and events. The problems are naturally larger when the literature from which the translation is being made is remote in time from our own and the product of a culture unlike our own. Even then, the translation of Aristophanic comedy presents much harder and much more numerous problems than the translation of Greek oratory, philosophy, historiography or even tragedy; it covers all registers from quotation of serious poetry to obscene slang, it is full of topical allusions (sometimes very swift and brief), it uses puns and verbal echoes. Unlike tragedy, it requires us to envisage a great deal of movement and action and gesture and to imagine a varied and quickly-changing pattern of emotional tones; and all this without any continuous transmission of original stage-directions (cf. p. 10). What is perhaps most important to the translator and pro-ducer, the audience of tragedy tolerates a certain degree of obscurity and mystification, but an audience which has been told that Aristoph-anes is funny and therefore expects to be amused is less tolerant.

Let us look at the translator's problem in *Acharnians* 142–144, where Theoros, returned from a visit to Sitalkes, the king of the Odomantian Thracians, is reporting to the assembly:

> And he was prodigiously pro-Athenian, and your true lover, so that he actually wrote on the walls, 'Handsome Athenians!' (*literally*, '(*the*) *Athenians* (*are*) *handsome*').

The idea that if A loves B he should write compliments to B on walls needs no explanation; nor does the humour of representing a king who is in the diplomatic sense 'a lover of Athens' (with *philathḗnaios*, 'fond of the Athenians', cf. our 'francophile', etc.) in terms of one individual in love with another. But a modern reader may want to know whether writing 'handsome . . . !' on walls is familiar, so that the humorous transference will be natural and easy, or unfamiliar, so that the joke is contorted and artificial. He needs to be told, directly or indirectly, that the phenomenon was indeed a familiar one (cf. *Wasps* 97f.), and that the admiration so expressed was nearly always homosexual. It is not easy to tell him this except in footnotes, and the reader of a translation should not be presumed to have an unlimited appetite for footnotes. One alternative is to substitute for the actual meaning of the Greek words something which would be the nearest equivalent in our own culture; hence C. F. Russo (1953) suggests 'viva gli Ateniesi!', which is, after all, the kind of thing people write on walls; but it does not have the erotic associations of the Greek. Keeping to the genre of graffiti, Patric Dickinson (1970) translates 'the Athenians are beautiful', which has the advantage of saying exactly what the Greek says but the disadvantage that the currently fashionable graffito '. . . is beautiful' is rarely erotic (and the same could be said of a more recent arrival, '. . . OK'). The true modern equivalent of writing up '. . . is handsome' would be cutting a picture of the admired person out of a magazine and pinning it up in one's own room; thus a translator might consider representing the king of the Odomantians as putting a pin-up of Athena over his bed.

So much of the distinctive colouring of Aristophanes' language is necessarily lost in translation, and so many verbal allusions recognizable to the Athenians remain unrecognized by any but a learned modern reader, that translators nowadays sometimes compensate by making their English colourful or allusive in passages where the Greek is plain. Consider, for example, *Wasps* 979–985 in the translation by Douglass Parker (1962). Bdelykleon, pleading for the dog which is standing trial, has brought on its puppies to beg for mercy. I print a close translation first, then Mr. Parker's.

(1) PHILOKLEON: Get down, get down, get down, get down!
BDELYKLEON: I'll get down. (*Mistrustfully*) That 'get down' has deceived a good many. All the same, I'll get down.
PHILOKLEON: (*Wiping his eyes*) Damn! It's not a good thing to drink soup! I've gone and drowned my own judgment in tears just because I was full of bean-soup.
BDELYKLEON: (*In consternation*) Why, isn't he getting off, then?
PHILOKLEON: Hard to tell.

(2) PHILOKLEON
Stop! I can't stand it! Step down! STEP DOWN!
PHOBOKLEON
I shall
step down, though I know that Jurors' Trap, that Quasi-Legal Fiction. You let the defendant think he's won by shouting 'Step Down!' and down he steps, breaks off his defense—whereupon you convict him. Nevertheless, I shall step down . . .

PHILOKLEON

Recovering his spleen at the last moment.

> ... STRAIGHT
>
>   TO
>
>   *HELL!*

Disgustedly throwing down his soup-bowl.

>   This eating—
> It's no good, that's all. Just now I melted every grain
> of Sense I own in tears—and why? Because
> I was full of hot soup, that's why!

PHOBOKLEON

>   You mean he's *convicted?*

PHILOKLEON

> It's difficult to tell at this point. The votes aren't in.

The very great expansion 'though I know ... you convict him' explains 'has deceived a good many', and '... at this point. The votes aren't in' also explains why Philokleon says 'Hard to tell'. Making 'straight to hell!' follow on from Philokleon's 'step down!' correctly represents the fact that he recovers himself and repents of his momentary weakening, but exaggerates his recovery in such a way as to introduce a point which Aristophanes almost certainly did not intend; Philokleon's exclamation, *es kórakas*, literally 'to ravens', is often used in angrily telling a person to go away, but it can also be a simple indication of annoyance, as in *Wasps* 852.

Consider now some passages from the opening scene of *Women at the Thesmophoria*, translated by Dudley Fitts (1959); the close translations are numbered (1) throughout, Mr. Fitts' translations (2):

(1) 141–145. OLD MAN: (*To Agathon, who is effeminately dressed*) And
              you yourself, boy—are you a man? Then where's your
              cock? Where's your cloak? Where are your Lakonian
              boots? Or are you a woman? In that case, where are
              your tits? What do you say? Why don't you say anything? Well, do you want me to answer the question
              from that song (*i.e. the one which the Old Man and
              Euripides heard Agathon rehearse*), since you won't tell me
              yourself?

(2)   What are you, you recumbent paradox? A man?
              Show me; or, if that makes you blush,
              where are your Spartan boots, your cavalry cloak?

Or are you a woman? If so, where are your breasts?
No answer. Bashful. If I want to find out,
I suppose I'll have to read your *Collected Poems*.

(1) 189f.   EURIPIDES: I'll tell you (*i.e., why I can't go in disguise*
            myself). In the first place, I'm known; and secondly, I'm
            grey-haired and have a long beard.

(2)   I'll tell you. First of all, they know me;
            secondly—well, I'm not so young as I was,
            silver threads among the gold, you know, and this
            beard is fairly long.

(1) 231f.   EURIPIDES: (*Having shaved off the old man's beard*). What
            are you going 'Mm! Mm!' for? Everything's done
            fine.

            OLD MAN: Oh, my God, I'll be soldiering bare! (*A
            pun on the technical term for a light-armed soldier, looked
            down on by the heavy infantryman.*)

(2)   EURIPIDES: What do you mean, 'woof'?
            —There! That's a handsome job, if I *do* say so!
            MNESILOCHOS:
            Who said a soldier's bearded like the pard?

These extracts will have given some idea of the ways in which a modern
translation of Aristophanic dialogue differs from the original, and I
hope they have also given some idea of why it differs. It is always easy
to pick holes in other people's translations, and nothing like so easy to
produce a translation which will make an audience laugh when it is
performed; the modern American translations do make audiences
laugh.

Lyrics pose more problems than dialogue, not only because it is a
pity to lose, but extremely hard to reproduce, the rhythms of the
original, but also because of their more concentrated imagery. A good
example is provided by the ode of the parabasis of *Frogs* (674–685),
which says literally:

Muse, embark on sacred choruses and come to delight of my song
to see the much throng of hosts, where ten thousand
accomplishments are seated
fonder of honour than Kleophon,
on whose both-ways-talking lips
formidable roars

Thracian swallow
on to barbarian leaf sitting,
and warbles lamentable nightingale's tune, how will perish
even if they become equal.

To understand what this song meant to Aristophanes and his audience, a reader needs to appreciate the following facts. (1) The appeal to a Muse is a conceptual convention, in effect combining an announcement 'Now we will sing' with an explicit acceptance of the traditional and ritual aspects of singing at festivals. (2) 'Sacred' does not have the same contrast with 'secular' or 'temporal' as in English, but can be applied to any procedure welcome to the gods, whether solemn or lively. (3) *Lāoí*, 'hosts', a word taken from epic and serious lyric poetry, serves simultaneously as a jocular compliment to the audience and as a heightening of the contrast between the audience and Kleophon. (4) 'Where ten thousand ... honour' comes within the category of conventional compliments to the audience (always praised for their wits and taste, just as they are always denigrated for dishonesty, imprudence and lechery), but is expressed in unusual terms; *sophíai*, 'accomplishments', denotes all kinds of excellence in artistic and professional skills (cf. p. 187), and *philótīmos*, literally 'fond of honour', is used both of persons who aim at eliciting admiration and also (e.g. Eur., *Iph. Aul.* 341, cf. Demosthenes xix 40) of what deserves it. (5) With '... than Kleophon' we come to what may properly be called the real subject of the song, a combined vilification of Kleophon and a wish (expressed as a confident prediction) that Athens will soon rid herself of him. The corresponding antode (706–717) performs a similar exercise on a certain Kleigenes; and if we wonder whether this kind of polemic is unusual in the ode and antode of a parabasis, we discover that it is not when we look back to the ode and antode of *Peace* (774–818), which are polemic against minor tragic poets. (6) The allegation that Kleophon cannot speak proper Greek, because he is of barbarian origin, is a political commonplace (cf. p. 97). (7) This point is doubly made by 'Thracian' and by 'swallow', because the Greeks compared languages other than Greek to the conversational twittering of swallows (cf. p. 6). (7) The combination of 'roars' (or 'rumbles') with 'swallow' is humorous in so far as the verb leads us to expect something different, and *deinón*, cognate with verbs meaning 'fear', can denote not only what is formidable because it is majestic or brilliant but also what is outrageous or intolerable. (8) *amphílalos*, 'both-ways-talking', occurs only in this passage, and through its associations with other words suggests (i) dispute and contention (*amphi-*), (ii) mere talk (*-lal-*) as opposed to coherent and rational speech, (iii) equal readiness to talk in two different ways, in this case Greek and another language. (9) The idea that the swallow sits *on* Kleophon's lips and thus metaphorically 'on a barbarian leaf', as a real bird sits on a twig, is evidently less remarkable an image in Greek than in English, for Eupolis (fr. 94.5) praised the oratory of Perikles by saying that 'persuasion sat on his lips'. (10) The Greeks thought of the nightingale not as singing happily, but as always mourning (cf. p. 148). (11) The fact that swallows do not sing like nightingales does not matter, since it is normal practice for a chain of images in Aristophanes to alter course. (12) *Epíklautos*, 'lamentable', is, like *amphílalos*, a word unique to this passage in extant Greek, but on the analogy of similar words it suggests that the bird's utterance is due to be lamented over, and it thus by implication predicts the fall of Kleophon. (13) Since 'will perish' has a third person termination, it does not differentiate between 'he', Kleophon, and 'it', the swallow. (14) Since *ísai*, 'equal', is feminine plural, a feminine noun is understood as subject, and this must be *psêphoi*, 'votes'; the reference is to the normal practice by which equal votes for condemnation and acquittal in a court with an even-numbered jury was interpreted as acquittal,[7] and there is a comic extravagance in suggesting that normal practice will not hold for anyone as objectionable as Kleophon.

It will be apparent that only a minority of these points can be brought out in translation, and that a reader who is familiar with all the considerations listed above, either before he reads the song or in consequence of reading a commentary on it, is in a much better position to hear it with the ears of the original audience than someone who insists on maintaining his distance from an alien culture. When we turn to the translations, we may be surprised at the extent to which they import trains of ideas absent from the original, or even in conflict with it, and omit what we might reasonably have supposed to be essential to the original. For example, John Hookham Frere (1840) expands *sophíai* but fails to make Aristophanes say that Kleophon, by comparison with the audience, lacks *sophíai*:

---

7 Normally an odd number of jurors was empanelled; but the Areopagus, a court which tried cases of deliberate homicide and certain types of sacrilege or impiety, was composed of ex-archons, and was therefore as likely to be even-numbered as odd-numbered at any given time.

> ... the assembled commons,
> Congregated as they sit,
> An enormous mass of wit,
> —Full of genius, taste and fire,
> Jealous pride, and critic ire,—
> Cleophon among the rest ...

He apparently misunderstands the last two verses of the original, and he sacrifices entirely the 'sting in the tail' so characteristic of Aristophanes:

> But we fear the cheerful strain
> Will be turned to grief and pain;
> He must sing a dirge perforce
> When his trial takes its course;
> We shall hear him moan and wail,
> Like the plaintive nightingale.

Benjamin Bickley Rogers (1902) uses a clever but thumping rhyme-scheme, and strikes a discordant note when he makes the swallow 'rejoice ... to her spirit's content':

> ... From that perch of exotic descent,
> Rejoicing her sorrow to vent,
> She pours to her spirit's content, a nightingale's woful lament,
> That e'en though the voting be equal, his ruin will soon be the sequel.

David Barrett (1964) brings out the reason why Aristophanes regards the audience as 'ten thousand *sophíai*':

> ... ten thousand men of sense,
> A very enlightened audience,
> Who expect a lot of a dancing choir ...

and also one aspect of 'Thracian swallow':

> A rather enigmatic swallow
> Whose words, though difficult to follow,
> Should not defy interpretation
> When once translated from the Thracian.

But he diverts us in the wrong direction when he prefaces those four lines with:

> ... CLEOPHON—for he has heard
> The warning of a fateful bird,

as if the Thracian swallow were a bird of omen and its utterance
oracular ('enigmatic', 'interpretation', 'warning', 'fateful'). Patric
Dickinson (1970) imports another idea, equally discordant with the
original, when he says:

> ... and spluttering out hollow
> Imitations of nightingale-odes,

as if a contrast between swallow and nightingale symbolized the contrast between barbarian solecisms and pure Attic. None of these
English translators has paid any attention to the effect created by the
word-order 'formidable roars Thracian swallow'. The humour of it is
admittedly simple-minded; but even simple-mindedness is touched
with sublimity when it expresses itself in a mere four words disposed
in two pairs of contrasted ('double-short' vs. 'single-short') rhythm:

$$— \; \cup \; \cup \; — \; \cup \; \cup — \; | \quad — \; \cup \; — \; \cup \; — \; —$$
deinòn epibrémetai | *Thrāikíā khelīdṓn.*

The rhythms of the original are captured in the translation of Ludwig
Seeger (1848, revised by Peter Rau, 1968):

> ... dem auf seinem
> Argen, geschwätzigen Mund fremdartig zwitschert und schnarrt
> Eine Thrakerschwalbe. ...

Yet even here *fremdartig* is a shade too particular for *deinón*, and the
order *zwitschert und schnarrt* obliterates the intention underlying
Aristophanes' own order.

IMITATION

The possibility of substituting new jokes for old, or modern topicalities
for Athenian, inevitably leads to a certain blurring of the distinction
between translation and adaptation. Some amateur productions of
Aristophanes in schools and universities replace so much of the original
with new material that they would more fairly be described as 'after
Aristophanes' or 'based on an idea of Aristophanes'; for instance,
the contest between Right and Wrong in *Clouds* may be entirely discarded in favour of a satire on arguments for and against the 'permissive
society', or the new characters who appear in the second half of *Birds*
may be replaced by their nearest modern equivalents (as types or as
named individuals) and the dialogue reshaped accordingly. This kind
of adaptation is not a purely modern phenomenon; as early as 1578

Pierre Le Loyer published a play, *Néphélococcugie*, which adheres closely to the sequence of events of *Birds*, and intermittently to Aristophanes' actual words, but replaces Peisetairos and Euelpides with two gentlemen of Toulouse, the hoopoe with Jean Cocu, and jokes about politics and litigation with much lengthier humorous moralizing about adultery and the faithlessness of women. In the nineteenth century the dramatic form and style of Aristophanes were occasionally used for political satire with serious intent (most often, but not always, in the politics of localities or professions), and they are used to this day to divert audiences in which the author can safely assume a fairly high degree of cultural homogeneity and some recollection, however vague, of Aristophanic comedy.

Modern popular entertainment on a scale far below that of drama, in the normally accepted sense of the word, contains much that is akin to Aristophanic fantasy, especially in its highly selective treatment of reality, indifference to causal sequence, rupture of dramatic illusion, and discontinuity of characterization; but these phenomena are common to popular entertainment in most cultures at most periods, and can hardly be regarded as showing specifically Aristophanic influence. How far it is possible deliberately to imitate Aristophanes in writing a comedy for the general public, either in the theatre or in the cinema, is a difficult question. A chorus and a lot of rude words will hardly suffice, and neither is even necessary if the Aristophanic spirit can be captured on a less superficial plane. Two works in our own time which have, in my opinion, captured that spirit are Peter Ustinov's play *The Love of Four Colonels* (1951) and Jacques Feyder's film *La Kermesse héroïque* (1935). Ustinov's play is founded on a contemporary political situation, the quadripartite administration of Berlin; it employs a supernatural mechanism, a 'good fairy', to sidestep normal cause and effect; and it incorporates a series of literary parodies accurate enough to amuse those who are familiar with the styles parodied but also extravagant enough to amuse those who are not. The blending of these elements and the symmetrical structure imparted to the blend would certainly have appealed to Aristophanes. Feyder's film portrays an occasion on which a town in the Low Countries, in the early seventeenth century, is faced with the disagreeable prospect of a Spanish army staying the night. The town council being torn between helpless panic and a desire to close the gates and put up a heroic resistance, the burgomaster's wife organizes the women of the town, pretends to the Spaniards that her husband has just died, and sees to the entertainment of the army in such style that rape is unnecessary and drunkenness does not issue in resentful violence. The townswomen will keep the good-looking Spaniards in a secret and cherished corner of their memory for a long time to come. Now, what gives this film its Aristophanic character is not simply the seizure of initiative by the women, nor even their uncomplicated sexuality, but the fact that the perils which the town council so vividly imagines, the spearing of babies on pikes, the roasting alive of old men, are, at that time and place, part of the real world with which people have to come to terms; which does not prevent them from enjoying themselves and maintaining their preferred style of life in the intervals between perils.

We must, however, draw an important distinction between *The Love of Four Colonels*, which adopts standpoints accepted at the time of composition, and *La Kermesse héroïque*, which sets out to re-create (very selectively) an ambience three centuries older than the film; it would hardly have been possible in 1935 to set the same story in Manchuria and invest it with the same humour. Aristophanes' contemporaries would have understood many fundamental aspects of seventeenth-century life in the Netherlands[8] more easily than they would have understood our own propensity to reflect contemporary suffering in art. The audience of *Acharnians* had seen more than one third of the entire population of their city-state die of a hideous disease; that information we have from Thucydides, not from any mention or hint in comedy. The audience of *Lysistrata* and *Women at the Thesmophoria* had heard the news, on an autumn day only a year and a half earlier, that the whole naval strength of Athens had been wiped out at Syracuse, and they knew that their enemies and their rebellious subject-allies were looking forward to finishing them off; but if we had no historical information on the Sicilian expedition, how could we tell from those two plays that the danger had been of such magnitude? In 404, when Athens was starved into surrender—and the degree of starvation needed to yield that result was formidable—Thebes and Corinth advocated the extermination of Athens as a city-state. Sparta did not accept this proposal. Nine years later we find Athens enthusiastically allying herself with

---

8 In this connection the Aristophanic affinities of the paintings of Jan Steen should be mentioned; in particular, his fondness for portraying rustic feasts, complete with drunken vomiting. *Het Sneyden van de Kei* (in the Boysman Museum at Rotterdam), in which some country people laugh delightedly at the agony of a man undergoing an operation, seems to me rather less civilised than anything in Aristophanes, to whom pain is only funny if it is somehow or other deserved.

Thebes and Corinth in a new war against Sparta. The interstate politics of the Greek world can be regarded, from one point of view, as a depressing record of follies. They are at the same time a record of inextinguishable resilience, a quality which comes most easily to people who, like the Greeks, reject self-pity and are impatient with excuses. Aristophanes' contemporaries would not have accepted from him the plea that recollection of past disaster and the prospect of future disaster prevented him from achieving the same technical standards as he would have achieved if there had been no disasters to remember and none in prospect. They would have been more inclined to think that the existence of bad times is a very strong reason for making good times better. What are art and literature for (a Greek would have asked) if not to *compensate* for the inadequacies of life? It is necessarily difficult for us to recapture Greek attitudes, because we have the advantage of twenty-three more centuries of experience, and, knowing better what is in principle preventable and what is not, we take the consequences of our own mistakes harder. Aristophanes would have thought our own culture obsessed, even to the point of demoralization, with pity, fear and guilt; we may think his culture complacent, ruthless, narrow and rigid in its loyalties. It is too late for him to learn anything from us. Whether we can learn anything from him depends on our capacity for genuine, intelligent self-criticism; and whether it turns out to be worth learning, on our ability to create and maintain new syntheses.

Select Bibliography

This bibliography includes the principal editions and commentaries, some modern translations, standard works, and a few recent articles and monographs. References already given in footnotes are not repeated here.

Abbreviations: comm(entary), ed(ition), f(oot)n(otes), intr(oduction), tr(anslation).

A. General

CANTARELLA, R., intr., ed., Italian tr., fn. (Milan, 1949–1964).

COULON, V., intr., ed., fn., VAN DAELE, H., French tr. (Paris, 1923–1930).

HALL, F. W. and GELDART, W. M., ed. (Oxford, vol. i [ed. 2] 1906, vol. ii 1907).

ROGERS, B. B., intr., ed., English tr., comm. (London, 1902–1915).

———, intr., ed., English tr. (London, 1924).

VAN LEEUWEN, J., Latin intr., ed., Latin comm. (Leyden, 1896–1909).

BARRETT, D., English tr. of *Wasps, Women at the Thesmophoria* ('*The Poet and the Women*') and *Frogs* (Harmondsworth, 1964).

DICKINSON, P., English tr. (Oxford, 1970).

FITTS, D., English tr. of *Lysistrata, Frogs, Birds* and *Women at the Thesmophoria* ('*Ladies' Day*') (New York, 1962).

SEEGER, L., revised by H.-J. Newiger and P. Rau, German tr. (Munich, 1968).

WILLEMS, A., French tr., fn. (Paris and Brussels, 1919).

ARNOTT, P. D., *Greek Scenic Conventions in the Fifth Century B.C.* (Oxford, 1962).

BIEBER, M. *History of the Greek and Roman Theater* (Princeton, ed. 2 1961).

BOUDREAUX, P., *Le Texte d'Aristophane et ses commentateurs* (Paris, 1919).

COUAT, A., *Aristophane et l'ancienne comédie attique* (Paris, 1892).

CROISET, M., *Aristophanes and the Political Parties at Athens*, translated by J. Loeb (London, 1909).

DALE, A. M., *Collected Papers* (Cambridge, 1969), especially Chapters 3, 8–9, 11, 14–15, 19–25.

DOVER, K. J., 'Greek Comedy', *Fifty Years (and Twelve) of Classical Scholarship* (Oxford, 1968), 123–158.

EHRENBERG, V., *The People of Aristophanes* (Oxford, ed. 2 1951).

FRAENKEL, E., *Beobachtungen zu Aristophanes* (Rome, 1962).

GELZER, T., *Der epirrhematische Agon bei Aristophanes* (Munich, 1960).

GOMME, A. W., *More Essays in Greek History and Literature* (Oxford, 1962), Chapter v, 'Aristophanes and Politics'.

GRENE, D., 'The Comic Technique of Aristophanes', *Hermathena* l (1937), 87–125.

HÄNDEL, P., *Formen und Darstellungsweisen in der aristophanischen Komödie* (Heidelberg, 1963).

JERNIGAN, C. C., *Incongruity in Aristophanes* (Menasha, Wis., 1939).

KASSIES, W., *Aristophanes' Traditionalisme* (Amsterdam, 1963).

KOCH, K. D., *Kritische Idee und komisches Thema: Untersuchungen zur Dramaturgie und zum Ethos der aristophanischen Komödie* (Bremen, 1965).

LESKY, A., *History of Greek Literature*, translated by J. Willis and C. J. de Heer (London, 1966).

LEVER, K., *The Art of Greek Comedy* (London, 1956).

LORD, L. E., *Aristophanes: his Plays and his Influence* (London, 1925).

MAZON, P., *Essai sur la composition des comédies d' Aristophane* (Paris, 1904).

MURRAY, G., *Aristophanes* (Oxford, 1933).

NEWIGER, H.-J., *Metapher und Allegorie: Studien zu Aristophanes* (Munich, 1957).

NORWOOD, G., *Greek Comedy* (London, 1931).

PICKARD-CAMBRIDGE, A., *Dithyramb, Tragedy and Comedy*, ed. 2, revised by T. B. L. Webster (Oxford, 1962).

——, *The Dramatic Festivals of Athens*, ed. 2, revised by John Gould and D. M. Lewis (Oxford, 1968).

——, *The Theatre of Dionysus at Athens* (Oxford, 1946).

RAU, P., *Paratragodia: Untersuchung einer komischen Form des Aristophanes* (Munich, 1967).

RUSSO, C. F., *Aristofane: autore di teatro* (Florence, 1962).

SCHMID, W., *Geschichte der griechischen Literatur*, Part I, Vol. IV (Munich, 1946).

SEEL, O., *Aristophanes oder Versuch über die Komödie* (Stuttgart, 1960).

SIFAKIS, G. M., *Parabasis and Animal Choruses* (London, 1971).

STEIGER, H., 'Die Groteske und Burleske bei Aristophanes' *Philologus* lxxxix (1934), 161–184, 275–285, 416–432.

SÜSS, W., *Aristophanes und die Nachwelt* (*Leipzig*, 1911).

——, 'Scheinbare und wirkliche Inkongruenzen in den Dramen des Aristophanes', *Rheinisches Museum* xcvii (1954), 115–159, 229–254, 289–316.

TAILLARDAT, J., *Les Images d' Aristophane: études de langue et de style* (Paris, revised ed. 1965).

VAN LEEUWEN, J., *Prolegomena ad Aristophanem* (Leyden, 1908).

WEBSTER, T. B. L., *Greek Theatre Production* (London, 1956).

——, *Studies in Later Greek Comedy* (Manchester, 1953).

WEBSTER, T. B. L., *Studies in Menander* (Manchester, ed. 2 1960).
——, *The Greek Chorus* (London, 1970).
WHITMAN, C. H., *Aristophanes and the Comic Hero* (Cambridge, Mass., 1964).

B. Individual Plays

Acharnians

FORREST, W. G. G. 'Aristophanes' *Acharnians*', *Phoenix* (Toronto) xvii (1963), 1–12.
MERRY, W. W., intr., ed., comm. (Oxford, ed. 5 1901).
PARKER, D., English tr. (Ann Arbor, 1961).
RENNIE, W. intr., ed., comm. (London, 1909).
STARKIE, W. J. M., intr., ed., English tr., comm. (London, 1909).

Birds

ARROWSMITH, W., English tr. (Ann Arbor, 1962).
KOCK, Th., intr., ed., comm., revised by O. Schröder (Berlin, 1927).
MERRY, W. W., intr., ed., comm. (Oxford, ed. 3 1896).

Clouds

ARROWSMITH, W., English tr. (Ann Arbor, 1962).
DOVER, K. J., intr., ed., comm. (Oxford, 1968; with abridged intr. and comm., 1970).
MERRY, W. W., intr., ed., comm. (Oxford, ed. 2 1889).
STARKIE, W. J. M., intr., ed., English tr., comm. (London, 1911).

Frogs

LATTIMORE, R., English tr. (Ann Arbor, 1962).
LITTLEFIELD, D. J., (ed.) *Twentieth Century Interpretations of the Frogs* (Englewood Cliffs, N.J., 1968).
MERRY, W. W., intr., ed., comm. (Oxford, ed. 5 1901).
MURRAY, G. English tr. (London, 1908).
RADERMACHER, L., intr., ed., comm., with additional notes by W. Kraus (Vienna, 1954).
STANFORD, W. B., intr., ed., comm. (London, ed. 2 1963).
TUCKER, T. G., intr., ed., comm. (London, 1906).
RUSSO, C. F., *Storia delle Rane di Aristofane* (Padova, 1961).
——, 'The revision of Aristophanes' *Frogs*', *Greece and Rome* xiii (1966), 1–13.
SICKING, C. M. J. *Aristophanes' Ranae: een hoofdstuk uit de geschiedenis der griekse poetica* (Assen, 1962).

Knights

LANDFESTER, M., *Die Ritter des Aristophanes* (Amsterdam, 1967).
MERRY, W. W., intr., ed., comm. (Oxford, ed. 2 1895).

NEIL, R. A., intr., ed., comm. (Cambridge, 1901).
POHLENZ, M., 'Aristophanes' Ritter', *Nachrichten der Akademie der Wissenschaften in Göttingen*, Phil.-hist. 1952, no. 5.

Lysistrata
PARKER, D., English tr. (Ann Arbor, 1964).
VON WILAMOWITZ-MÖLLENDORFF, U., intr., ed., comm. (Berlin, 1927).
DE WIT-TAK, T. M., *Lysistrata: Vrede, Vrouw en Obsceniteit bij Aristophanes* (Groningen, 1967).

Peace
MERRY, W. W., intr., ed., comm. (Oxford, 1900).
NEWIGER, H.-J., 'Retraktationen zu Aristophanes' Frieden', *Rheinisches Museum* cviii (1965), 229–254.
PLATNAUER, M., intr., ed., comm. (Oxford, 1964).
SHARPLEY, H., intr., ed., comm. (Edinburgh and London, 1905).

Wasps
MacDOWELL, D., intr., ed., comm. (Oxford, 1970).
MERRY, W. W., intr., ed., comm. (Oxford, 1893).
PARKER, D., English tr. (Ann Arbor, 1962).
STARKIE, W. J., intr., ed., comm. (London, 1897).

Wealth (Plutus)
HOLZINGER, K., comm. (Vienna and Leipzig, 1940).

Women in Assembly (Ecclesiazusae)
FRAENKEL, E., 'Dramaturgical Problems in the *Ecclesiazusae*', *Greek Poetry and Life: Essays Presented to Gilbert Murray on his Seventieth Birthday* (Oxford, 1936), 257–276.
PARKER, D., English tr. ('*The Congresswomen*') (Ann Arbor, 1967).
USSHER, R. G., 'The Staging of the *Ecclesiazusae*', *Hermes* xcvii (1969), 22–37.

Indexes

Passages of Aristophanes

General Index